Countryside Planning Policies
for the 1990s

Countryside Planning Policies for the 1990s

by

Andrew W. Gilg MA(Edin)
Senior Lecturer in Geography
University of Exeter
UK

C·A·B International

C·A·B International   Tel: Wallingford (0491) 32111
Wallingford   Telex: 847964 (COMAGG G)
Oxon OX10 8DE   Telecom Gold/Dialcom: 84: CAU001
UK   Fax: (0491) 33508

A catalogue entry for this book is available from the British Library

ISBN 0 85198 744 3

Typeset by Alden Multimedia Ltd.
Printed and bound in the UK by Redwood Press Ltd., Melksham

Contents

Preface and Acknowledgements

When I was asked to write this, my first solo book on rural issues for six years, I thought it would be an easy task. I imagined a quick trawl through my *Countryside Planning Yearbooks* and the drafts of its successor *Progress in Rural Policy and Planning*. How wrong I was.

Such has been the explosion of policy proposals since the watershed election of Mrs Thatcher in May 1979 that during the summer of 1989 I was able to find over 1200 references. During the time that this book has been researched and references read, i.e. January 1990 to March 1991, this total grew to over 1500 references. Out of this total over 1200 references have been read, notes made on 1100 and around 600 have found their way into this book.

Two central themes in the book are first the degree to which the radical policies set in train by Mrs Thatcher in May 1979 will continue or be reversed in the 1990s, and second, how far the underlying forces restructuring agriculture and thus the entire countryside will set an agenda which will only allow politicians to be reactive rather than proactive. A key theme running through the books is whether the 1990s will see the creation of a 'Really Radical Rural Britain' or not.

In attempting to answer this question the book takes an encyclopaedic type approach based on letting each policy proposal speak for itself. If the book reads at times like a list, this is because it is meant to read like a list. Commentary on each proposal is kept to a minimum, and analysis is left to the reader. In my rational scientific days I would have written this book very differently. I would have assembled what facts I could, constructed summary tables and created a false order, e.g. a list of all the surplus land forecasts, and then taken an average. But this type of so-called meta-analysis is to some extent ridiculous since each study uses different assumptions, time periods and areal units. Instead, I have assembled material in a loose, some might say undigested or postmodern way, but to suggest such a structure is to miss the point. The message of the book is the message of each reference.

A good deal of background knowledge is assumed. However, for fairly new readers each chapter begins with a short resume of the key issues, and for new readers Chapter 3 provides a resume of the main policy changes of the 1980s.

The book is mainly intended, therefore, for those interested in the countryside and its future in a wide variety of disciplines, since it provides an aide-mémoire for all planners, researchers, advisers, and decision makers at all levels and in all types of organization. It is not, however, a policy-making manual presenting each policy in turn for description and evaluation. Instead it adopts an approach based on the policies proposed by different groups and organizations. In this sense it takes a loose political economy approach by identifying the political stance or profession of each proposee. It does not, however, take on board the full strictures of the so-called political economy approach of my friends on the left of British politics. The only author whose political stance remains unacknowledged is of course the author.

This is justifiable because this is not a polemic. As I have discovered to my cost there are already too many of these. Nonetheless I do present a brief manifesto in Chapter 11, since the temptation was too great. Otherwise I hope I have presented what my less liberal colleagues say is impossible, a detached and impartial view from the centre.

From this viewpoint the key issue in the development of rural planning thought must be the restructuring of the countryside as a consequence of political action taken to reduce surplus agricultural production, and underlying forces restructing the world and thus the rural economy.

In more detail Peter Hall, the famous academic geographer, has used published data to argue that profound changes are shaping the geography of contemporary Britain with major consequences for land-use policies. These changes include the slowdown in population growth to near zero-level albeit coupled with a marked shift in its distribution; the shift of land out of agriculture; the shift away from heavy industry into high-technology manufacturing and services; and the demand by wholesalers and retailers for large units with generous car access.

According to Hall these forces have been powerful enough to overcome policies of urban containment and are causing both people and jobs to decentralize as people begin to realize that many kinds of economic and social activity can be carried out more efficiently and pleasantly in the countryside rather than in towns. There is, therefore, a need for an urgent review of countryside policies which according to Hillman (1986), a fellow at the Policy Studies Institute, should embrace; the breadth of perceptions of the role that the countryside plays in our culture; the uses to which rural land could be put, and their justification; how the viability of the rural economy can be sustained with the minimum of State intervention; the adequacy of current mechanisms for the control of rural activity; and the role and influence of various non-Governmental agencies. In addition, according to members of the Centre for Agricultural Strategy at the University of Reading (Craig *et al.*, 1986), a whole host of questions need to be answered; for example, what is the countryside for? what should it look like? who should have access? what does conservation mean? and so on. There are no simple answers to these questions but it is the purpose of this book to provide some of the answers provided by various authors and groups and to evaluate them as far as this is possible.

This is no easy task since the last few years, as Harvey and Wilson (1990) have shown, have witnessed an explosive growth in the membership of 'green' groups as shown below:

	Members Feb 1990	**Change** $+/-\%$	**Income** £m
CLA (Country Landowners Association)	48,189	+5	3
CPRE (Council for the Protection of Rural England)	45,000	+28	1
FoE (Friends of the Earth)	180,000	+461	2.9
GreenPeace	339,000	+156	3
NFU (National Farmers Union)	102,390	−4	11.4
National Trust	1,864,951	+12	54.8
Ramblers Association	75,577	+11	1
RSPB (Royal Society for the Protection of Birds)	680,000	+3	13

A notable feature of the pattern is the sheer size and spending power of the newer non-farming groups, most notably the RSPB. In the 1990s conservation groups can outgun the traditional farming groups of the NFU and CLA both in numbers of members and income, and increasingly too in political clout. The general public, too, is increasingly anti-farming in its opinions. For example, *Farmers Weekly* on 15 February 1991 reported that a MORI poll of 2023 people found that over half the sample believed that farmers have harmed the environment, with agrochemical and river pollution, topping the list of concerns.

Forty years of assumptions which have influenced public policy are thus now coming to an end, and so we need to decide according to Newby (1988) just what is the balance we wish to see between agriculture, forestry, conservation, recreation and rural economic development. What we conspicuously lack at the moment is a strategy to guide policy makers and the rural inhabitants themselves over the balance to be struck between these competing claims. It was the original purpose of this book to fill this gap by outlining the issues, discussing in depth the choices and proposals on offer and then to offer a scenario for how rural planning policies may develop in the 1990s.

However, space considerations have forced me to concentrate on outlining and discussing the issues, leaving the reader to formulate his or her own policy scenarios. Anyone who does this either relatively easily using this book or more laboriously by examining the mountainous source evidence will need as much inspiration and support as I have had. I would therefore like to thank first, my colleagues at Exeter University, notably Mark Blacksell; Dave Higgens and Terry Bacon; second, my erstwhile colleague Andy Griffiths who helped me when I should have been helping him with his PhD; and third, my family – Joyce my wife for feeding me and allowing me to feed her at weekends, Julie, my daughter for typing up the draft notes, and Alastair for showing me how to use the word processor, except for the comma key. I hope the long cycle rides and lunches on the days when I played hooky in the 'greenhouse summer' of 1990 provided some recompense. Penultimately the 'greenhouse winter' of 1989/90 provided just enough snow – and I'm not telling you where – to set me up for the long days that writing a book entails. Finally, skiing around the Chetseron Restaurant in January 1990 as we had done in January 1984 set up a repeat of not only another book but also a second Scottish Grand Slam in my lifetime, and this time I was there.

And so this book is dedicated to David Sole (an Exeter graduate) and his 15 fellow players, not least Uncle Ben, the flower of Scotland,

Dublin 3 February 1990:	Ireland 9 Scotland 13	*'Did we win?'*
Murrayfield 17 February:	Scotland 21 France 0	*I was there so was Julie*
Cardiff 3 March:	Wales 9 Scotland 13	*I was there so was Alastair*
Murrayfield 17 March:	Scotland 13 England 9	*I was there so was Joyce*

Part One

A Policy and Political Context for the 1990s

1 Policy and Politics

A week is said to be a long time in politics, and so it may seem unwise to write a futuristic book about the politics of a whole decade, especially when it seems that politicians are ever alert to all forms of pressure, but most of all from the electorate as expressed by the media. This hysterical view of politics is the very stuff of political memoirs; for example in August 1990 Lord Young's account of the 1987 election campaign in Britain, written by a leading member of the campaign team and a Cabinet Minister, informed us that only two weeks before the election Mrs Thatcher was ready to concede defeat in private. Yet two weeks later she recorded a massive 100-seat win, after a change in tactics. In contrast, another political cliché – that politics is the art of the possible – asks us to believe that the inertia in the political system is so great that in reality very few changes ever occur, and then only over a relatively long period like a decade. Every now and then, however, truly radical changes occur in two or three years, for example, the 1947–1949 period which saw the creation of the welfare state, and in the countryside, the passage of the 1947 Agriculture Act, the 1947 Town and Country Planning Act and the 1949 National Park Act.

Although both clichés, by definition, are broadly true they are not in fact very helpful views of politics except as lively ways of introducing the topic, and they are moreover a parody of the billions of words written about political theory over the centuries, from Aristotle and Plato in ancient times to Marx and Bagehot in Victorian times and to Keynes and Habermas in this century. The first purpose of this chapter is thus to review the main theories of politics currently in vogue, in order to provide a framework for evaluating the policy proposals presented later in the book. The second aim of this chapter is to examine the transformation of British society and its voting habits, before concluding with a brief review of Thatcherism, and some possible political scenarios for the 1990s.

Political theory

Overview

There are many different theories and explanations for the way in which political power is held and implemented. At the simplest level, a simple dichotomy can be made between Liberal Democrat (Pluralist) and Marxist views. However, Held (1984), after considerable analytical and empirical discussion of the two views, concludes:

> Political order is not achieved through common value
> systems or general respect for the authority of the state, or
> legitimacy, or, by contrast, simple State force: rather it is the
> outcome of a complex web of interdependencies between
> political, economic and social institutions and activities
> which divide power centres and which create multiple
> pressures to comply.

For the future he argues that a state implicated deeply in the creation and reproduction of systematic inequalities of power, wealth, income and opportunities will rarely enjoy sustained legitimation, and thus, only a political order which places the transformation of those inequalities at it's centre will enjoy legitimacy in the long run.

An alternative overview and one not based on the controversial crisis response assumption of Held is provided by Abercrombie and other social science academics (1988) who examine three models of power and politics in Britain. First, there is the *pluralist* model which argues that power is dispersed and fragmented. Because there are a large number of different groups and interests which seek to influence policy, no particular group is able to control the state or influence policy on a large number of different issues. The role of the state is thus to act as a neutral referee. Second, there is the *elitist* model which argues that a number of key institutions whose members come largely from private schools and Oxbridge, dominate British politics by only allowing certain issues to be politically debated. By limiting the agenda they thus largely maintain the status quo of a bureaucratic state. Third, there is the *ruling-class* model which argues that capitalist employers form the most powerful elite of all, and that the only debate is how to run the economy as efficiently as possible and hence maximize the rewards accruing to the capitalist class.

A fourth model is provided by a hybrid of the *pluralist* and *elite* models, the *corporatist* model, under which employers and trade unions form the two largest power blocs.

According to Abercrombie *et al.* (1988) the pluralistic account is largely incorrect, the elite model is undemocratic and maintains exceptional levels of secrecy, while the ruling-class analysis is not altogether correct since financial interests although extremely powerful have not been all powerful.

A similar overview is provided by Cloke (1987), a geographer who, in a penetrating and scathing attack on rural planning, has claimed that it has been very limited in its scope and ineffective in its implementation. He bases these claims on an analysis of the state which can be conceptualized in any one of four ways. First, the *pluralist* concept in which the state acts as an independent arbitrator and everyone has an equal say. Second, the *elitist* concept in which pluralism is continued but some groups are more equal than others. Third, the *managerialist* concept in which professional agents of the state act as gatekeepers to policy making or, in Plato's words, guardians. Fourth, the *structuralist*, political economy or Marxist concept which suggests that class distributions represent the only real forum of societal disaggregation for the analysis of power and political policy making.

Using this fourth concept, but sometimes also the managerialist thesis, Cloke argues that the role of rural planning has changed over the years as the central state has sought to further the requirements of capital. In particular, local government has lost power by: restrictions on its financial freedom; by more stringent monitoring of its activities, and by distributing powers among more agencies thus creating a divide and rule situation. In addition, the shift to privatization has reduced the power of rural planning agencies to control rural policies and services, Cloke therefore concludes that rural planning is a gesture.

As such according to Cloke from the evidence of ten case studies it has made some short-term incremental opportunistic advances by adopting pragmatic measures for isolated issues, but these have been battles not the war, and the fundamental class injustices of rural areas remain unquestioned.

Until rural planning addresses these social justice issues Cloke has concluded that rural planning cannot be radical and:

> Far from being a rational process whereby clearly conceived
> objectives are enacted via channels of implementation,
> planning action constitutes a search for consensus within
> prevailing arenas of power – a search which usually
> precludes any radical or progressive prescriptions. For rural
> planning a dramatic change of attitudes towards rural
> communities and environments is required before this
> situation can be significantly altered. (p. 222)

Cloke and Little (1990) in a further development of this Marxist view of the rural state argue that whereas the pluralist *status quo* misrepresents power, an overlapping view of the state based on aspects of structuralism, elitism and managerialism provides a better theoretical view. From this standpoint they have written a major book on the rural state distilling Cloke's work over the 1980s. This book argues that the engine of change in late capitalist nations is the drive towards enhanced capital accumulation by international corporate capital. The state is thus strongly influenced by this engine, but is not a mere puppet. For example, where pressure groups can show that their proposals will benefit certain members of the ruling political party or help the party to be re-elected, these proposals may well be enacted as long as they do not conflict too much with the process of capital accumulation. A fine example was provided in March 1991 with the decision to scrap the poll tax after it had been seen to be electorally disastrous.

From this overview it is clear that there are three main views of the political process: the official neoclassical pluralist view; the elitist/ instrumental/managerialist view; and the Marxist/political economy/ structuralist view. These are now considered in turn.

Three main views of the political process

Official neo-classical pluralist views

The official view of British politics is provided by the Central Office of Information (1984) which notes, because there is no written constitution, that Parliament is in theory virtually free to legislate as it pleases, but in practice, works within the constraints of common law, historical precedence, and the broad limits of acceptability set by public support.

This view is not, however, fully supported in a classic text, *Mackintosh's The Government and Politics of Britain* (Richards, 1988). This text argues that the view of a pluralist society in which no party or group is wholly dominant is in fact grossly exaggerated. Instead it is argued that governments have views and are in a powerful position to put them into effect. The advent of Mrs Thatcher enhanced this power. This is because Mrs Thatcher had a firm majority, believed that she was elected to govern with a capital G, and that her Government alone could take a broad balanced view of the public interest whereas pressure groups have biased, partisan and self-interested attitudes. In another neoclassical analysis Gilg (1985a) pointed out that there are four key features of the current system. First, the unrepresentative nature of the party that wins an election, but is not elected by a majority of the people. For example, no post-war government has ever gained more than 40.3% of the electorate's vote, and then ironically it did not win the election (Labour in 1950). Second, the bipartisan adversarial and at times gladiatorial nature of the system with Labour and Conservative governments reversing each other's decisions in the preceding government, and thus confronting each other rather than consulting each other in the formulation of policy. Third, the top-down and complex nature of the system (Fig. 1.1), and fourth, the inertia of the system with, *de facto*, only 2 or 3 years to pass major legislation in each 4–5 year parliamentary cycle, and only one major piece of legislation allowed for any one department in each annual session of Parliament.

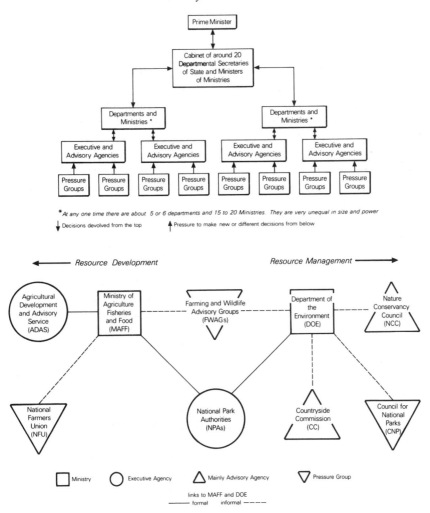

Fig. 1.1. Hierarchical structure of government in the UK. Top, overall model. Bottom, examples of the complex links between the three main tiers.

Smith (1976), a political scientist, concurs that the political system acts within the sphere of the possible and largely accepts the real world, its institutions and laws as they are. In this sense, really radical policies are impossible without a revolution or by a slow process of transition via incrementalism by which time axiomatically, they no longer become radical but part of the transformed *status quo*. This view of an evolutionary incremental state leads on to the next major viewpoint.

Elitist/instrumentalist/managerialist views

Bruce-Gardyne and Lawson (1976), two Conservative MPs, one of whom rose to become a long-standing Chancellor of the Exchequer in the 1980s, have examined decision making from the inside. They conclude that real power lies with the Civil Service and the self-perpetuating oligarchy, educated at Oxbridge and working either at the Treasury or the Civil Service Department. No successful Minister or Department has taken these men on. In contrast pressure groups need to lobby them and other key civil servants hard if they are to get their case over, but not too aggressively since as Sir Derek Barber after 10 years of chairing the Countryside Commission has observed in the March 1991 issue of *Countryside Commission News* those who park their tanks at Westminster achieve nothing. MPs and the public are dismissed by Bruce-Gardyne and Lawson as having only a negative impact because their only power is the chance every now and then to vote their immediate if not their ultimate masters out. The real power of the Prime Minister is also limited and as far as it exists comes through the power of patronage, and the power of a Cabinet Minister is too transitory to have much effect. This view is upheld by Miliband (1982), a political scientist who argues that if democracy is defined in terms of: (i) popular participation in the determination of policy; and (ii) popular control over the conduct of affairs, then the British system is far from democratic, instead, the political system has been used to prevent rather than facilitate populist democracy. This has been achieved by a powerful elite of capitalists, leading politicians, top civil servants, managers of state enterprises, judges, professionals and communicators, who, by and large, are a homogeneous male group derived from middle class backgrounds and a few universities (Oxbridge, London and Edinburgh). Together they control the means of production, the means of persuasion and the means of coercion. Collectively the 'Establishment' according to Miliband have used their powers to contain pressure for change and have managed class conflict to conserve a state of limited democracy.

Marxist/political economy views

These views relate to the notion of class struggle and capital accumulation first formally proposed by Marx in the 19th century. In the present century many scholars have attempted to reinterpret Marx in the light of modern economies. Some but not all are Marxists, but most of them have hijacked the 19th century name for economics (political economy) as a badge of courage for their views. For example, Giddens (1984), a sociologist, links sociology with geography, history and other disciplines via the theory of structuration to advance the view that capitalist states exhibit three traits.

1. Political power is prohibited from organizing production according to its own criteria. In other words, large sectors of the economy are coordinated not by government but by the private sector.

2. Political power depends indirectly on the mechanisms of taxation and is thus dependent on the private sector and the rate of economic growth within this sector which the government cannot indirectly control.
3. Since the state depends on a process of economic growth which is beyond its power to organize, every occupant of state power has a vested interest in promoting those conditions most conducive to economic growth.

Therefore, underlying economic and social forces limit the freedom of any political party or the state to influence events. The difficulty with this 'political economy' approach, however, is that it assumes that capitalism is only supported by capitalist enterprises and not by the populace as a whole. The overwhelming evidence from around the world is that people support free enterprise in a mixed economy. The real challenge for planning in a pluralist society is thus one of giving people a democratic say. On this test the UK fails miserably, offering only the pathetic first past the post system and then only once every five years.

Other views

In a review of the political process, with special reference to local government Gyford *et al.* (1989), three political scientists, explain politics not in terms of groups but in terms of the changing fortunes of particular individuals or groups, namely the politics of personality and locality. They also examine the so-called dualistic theory of the state under which there is a basic distinction between the 'politics of production' (private sector profitability) and the 'politics of consumption' (provision of social consumption, e.g. housing, education). National government concerns itself with both issues but local government confines itself to consumption.

Finally, Barnes (1988) rejects explanations of society based on logical positivist, economic, Marxist, religious and structural viewpoints and instead reasserts the realist view of human beings as active agents linked together through shared knowledge and mutual susceptability. Power is thus defined as the capacity for action allowed by society and the possession of power is defined as the amount of discretion allowed by society to use this capacity by any one person or group.

Nature of decision making

Whichever view of political theory is taken, the question of whether decisions are taken incrementally or not still remains. In reviews of this question based on actual decision making Collins *et al.* (1990) and Baldock *et al.* (1990), two different teams of social scientists and environmentalists have argued that the incremental case rests on the view that: (i) policy makers are faced with blocks of inertia e.g. long-term commitments; (ii) policies can only be gradually altered in a democracy; (iii) relatively fixed policy making structures; and (iv) general uncertainty about the future. There is thus a strong temptation to act incrementally rather than rationally.

In the alternative rational model priorities would be listed and evaluated, alternative ways of achieving the objectives would be posed, and the programmes which best reconcile the costs and benefits involved would be identified. In the incremental model in contrast the process is acknowledged to be constrained by cognitive capacity, time and information, a reluctance to widen the process to others outside the magic circle of influence, and thus a propensity for the process to be fragmented rather than integrated. There is, of course, a hybrid model, the quasi-rational model which stands anywhere in the continuum between the incremental and rational models.

As has already been seen in the dualistic model, decision making can take place at the local as well as at the national level, with inherent conflicts of interest between the national and local levels, and also within the local level. In a review of the crisis in central–local state relations during the Thatcher era, Duncan and Goodwin (1988), two geographers, have shown that in a franchise democracy like Britain, local states are necessary for the adequate management of society, but the need for local states to raise finance and be electorally accountable has caused problems for the reforms put in place by Mrs Thatcher. With the abolition of local government, a political non-starter, Duncan and Goodwin have also shown how the growth of non-elected subnational agencies has been one way of reducing the power of elected local states, though it does also pose the option of transferring these subnational agencies to non-electorial local states.

Nonetheless policies, including radical policies, may also emanate from below, and Cloke and Little (1987a) have shown from a study of the preparation, review and implementation of the Gloucestershire Structure Plan, how a County Council can produce quite radical and innovative proposals for resource dispersal in declining rural areas. However, these proposals were virtually eliminated by the Secretary of State following the Examination in Public, and although the County Council attempted to persuade other agencies and district councils to implement the spirit of the deleted innovatory policies, Cloke and Little conclude that most of these attempts were blocked in favour of a search for low-cost policy responses which relied increasingly on the resources of the private and voluntary sectors.

Furthermore, Cloke and Little (1988) also conclude that none of the agencies involved with planning in Gloucestershire had any specifically rural policies, over and above general policies for their whole area. At the local level, therefore, rural policy may be more apparent than real.

However, this may change since Cloke and Thrift (1987) have argued that the growing conflict between locals and newcomers in rural areas is in reality a class struggle and, using the concepts of the Austro-Marxist Karl Renner, they highlight the role of the new 'service class' of professionals and managers. They then speculate in Marxist terms that the 'service class' is now in a class struggle with the traditional seat of power in rural areas, land-owners, for political hegemony over the local state, and in particular, for control over the environment of agriculture and the number of houses that may be built.

Cloke and Little (1987b) also note that the increasing gentrification of rural areas is leading to a rejection of radical policies based on providing social housing and public transport requested by the diminishing number of lower class residents. Ironically the increasing number of elderly people who are moving to the countryside and represent a significant proportion of the gentrified population may in years to come, as their incomes and ability to look after themselves decline, become a new group of disadvantaged people seeking radical policies.

Environmental politics

To some extent the gentrification of rural areas and British society as a whole has focused attention on a new branch of political thought, environmental politics, based on environmental ideologies. O'Riordan (1981), a geographer, has produced a fourfold classification of environmental ideologies as shown in Tables 1.1 and 1.2. Within these broad views, however, there are also deep political issues. For example, within the ecocentric camp there is a fundamen-tal split between a reformist wing and an elitist wing. O'Riordan (1977) has used Hardin's well-known lifeboat metaphor to illustrate this division. In the metaphor, a number of lifeboats and their passengers represent the popula-tion of the developed world while struggling swimmers in the ocean represent the peoples of the developing world. It is impossible to take everyone on board and so the critical questions become, should anyone be allowed on board and if so whom, and at what cost to the quality of life on board. Elitists would allow nobody on board, moderate reformists would fill the lifeboat to capacity, while deep reformists would pitch everyone into the sea, the ulti-mate Malthusian nightmare.

Owens (1986), a geographer, has examined the environmental policy statements of the main political parties and concluded that environmental consciousness has been raised to a new threshold. There is, however, a striking similarity in the rhetoric employed by each party largely because they try to accommodate environmental issues without confronting any fun-damental contradiction between the issues and the free market economy they all espouse. This leads to a certain blandness in the policies. Another similar trend is the adoption of a broadly technocentrist view of environmental conflict, which is seen as resolvable within the dominant ideology of growth. Similarly, Lowe and Morrison (1984), academics expert on pressure group

Table 1.1. O'Riordan's environmental ideologies (1981 version).

ECOCENTRISM

A   *Deep environmentalists*   B   *Self reliance soft technologists*

1.   Lack of faith in modern large-scale technology and its associated demands on elitist expertise, central state authority and inherently antidemocratic institutions.

2.   Implication that materialism for its own sake is strong and that economic growth can be geared to providing for the basic needs for those below subsistence levels.

3.   Intrinsic importance of nature for the humanity of man.

4.   Ecology and (other natural) laws dictate human morality.

5.   Biorights – the right of endangered species or unique landscapes to remain unmolested.

3.   Emphasis on smallness of scale and hence community identity in settlement, work and leisure.

4.   Integration of concepts of work and leisure through a process of personal and communal improvement.

5.   Importance of participation in community affairs and of guarantees of the rights of minority interests. Participation seen both as a continuing educational and political function.

TECHNOCENTRISM

C   *Accommodators*

1.   Belief that economic growth resource exploitation can continue assuming:
(a)   suitable economic adjustments to taxes, fees etc.
(b)   improvements in the legal rights to a minimum level of environmental quality.
(c)   compensation arrangements satisfactory to those who experience adverse environmental and/or social effects.

2.   Acceptance of new project appraisal techniques and decision review arrangements to allow for wider discussion or genuine research for consensus among representative groups of interested parties.

3.   Provision of effective environmental management agencies at national and local levels.

D   *Cornucopians*

1.   Believe that man can always find a way out of any difficulties either politically, scientifically or technologically.

2.   Acceptance that pro-growth goals define the rationality or project appraisal and of policy formulation.

3.   Optimistic about the ability of man to improve the lot of the world's people.

4.   Faith that scientific and technological expertise provides the basic foundation for advice on matters pertaining to economic growth, public health and safety.

5.   Belief that any impediments can be overcome given a will, ingenuity and sufficient resources arising out of wealth.

Source: O'Riordan (1981).

Table 1.2. O'Riordan's environmental ideologies (1985 version) and their relationship to interest groups and political parties.

Ecocentrism		Technocentrism	
Gaianism	Communalism	Accommodation	Optmism
Belief in the rights of nature and of the essential co-evolution of humans and natural phenomena.	Belief in the cooperative capabilities of societies to be collectively self-reliant using 'appropriate' science and technology.	Faith in the adaptability of institutions and mechanisms of assessment and decision making to accommodate environmental demands	Faith in the application of science, market forces and managerial ingenuity.

Redistribution of power towards a decentralized, federal, political economy based on the interlinkage of environmental and social justice.

Maintenance of the *status quo* in existing structures of government power.

Not-in-my-back-yard private interest groups.

Public interest environmental groups

Green groups and alternative subcultures

Labour Party and Liberal Democrats

Green Party

Conservative Party

Source: O'Riordan (1985).

politics, have found that most environmental protests are not a complaint against the capitalist system but about its performance. Only the more radical groups advance values subversive to the capitalistic logic of society and one of its underpinnings, science, as a method of obscuring value conflicts.

Turning to individuals rather than groups Lowe and Rudwig (1986), an expert on pressure groups and a sociologist, have concluded that people do not have a set of environmental values which are universally applicable by age, sex or class. Instead environmental ideas and actions are responses on the part of people with particular aspirations and perceptions about their lives and surroundings. These aspirations and perceptions interact with changing environmental circumstances leading to the major weakness of the environmental movement, its lack of cohesiveness and its tendency to react to events. As yet Lowe and Rudwig do not see the emergence of a post-industrial or post-materialist value change.

In contrast two sociologists, Cotgrove and Duff (1981), have identified a growth in support for environmental issues which is not merely a result of greater affluence, but also a move towards service jobs and a new kind of liberal middle class family. These changes are perpetuating and extending a post-materialistic way of life, which, according to Cotgrove and Duff (1980), does not reflect the traditional left–right polarization of politics, but instead an increase in direct action or membership of pressure groups, and a fall off in support for traditional parties. In spite of these trends there is no effective environmental political party in Britain.

Planning and political theory

In the absence of practical environmental politics consideration is now given to some of the theories that have been advanced to relate land use planning to politics. Using a number of case studies and theorectical analysis Sillince (1986) has produced a book which provides a theory of planning, as it is, rather than as it might be. His main conclusion is that the presentation of plans is stage managed to make policies seem self-evidently justified and to hide questionable assumptions. The main method used is utilitarianism, namely seeking the alternative policy which satisfies the largest number of people while discomforting the smallest number. This is most useful to powerful groups since they command the values by which the satisfaction of the largest number is judged. It is least good for minority groups and individuals. Sillince concludes that planning is in fact a political activity but that the use of rational utilitarianism masks the real social and environmental issues which have direct ethical relevance to us all.

Similarly, Blowers (1980), from the position of an academic and a councillor, has concluded that planning is a dependent activity, subservient to the needs of the state, and therefore its potential for independent action is severely limited. Furthermore, the pressures of existing resources, pressure from all sorts of groups, and existing laws and statutes further constrain the amount of freedom. Within these constraints, power is unequally exercised by a few officials and politicians who are happy to see it for what it is, a passive, reactive and dependent service, and have no desire to make it a dynamic agent for social change for that would require a level of political commitment threatening to the state. Indeed, planning is part of the state's defence, by helping to relieve pressures, protect resources, and reconcile competing interests.

More critically, Ambrose (1987), an academic in urban studies, has argued that the 'Liberal democratic' and 'pluralist' interpretations of the state are too naive and uncritical. Instead he favours the: 'work of Miliband, Poulantzas and others who advocate that the state can only be properly understood in the context of capitalist laws of motion' and that the main imperative driving land-use change is the drive for further capital accumulation. In his view of the state, planning's job is to legitimize the process of capital accumulation, but at the same time it must offer some sort of welfare to the general mass of people.

Finally, Paris (1982), an academic planner, in a conclusion to a set of readings on planning theory from a Marxist perspective has argued that capitalism is entering a period when limits to growth imposed by natural resources and the contradictions in capitalism itself will lead to economic decline. He sees the choice for society as one between authoritarian capitalism or socialism, as social democracy collapses under social tensions. Planning as part of the state will thus evolve depending on the outcomes of the struggles between social classes and within and between political parties as capitalism reorganizes itself.

Elsewhere in the readings Kranghaar and Gardels (pp. 281–305), two American academics and consultants, argue that planners will have to offer their services in one or other of three not necessarily mutually exclusive roles.

1. Planners as managers of decline.
2. Planners as technicians of development, as in 1960s regional planning.
3. Planners as facilitators of change, as in 1980s 'positive planning'.

In conclusion no one view of political theory seems to account for all the permutations of real life. The Marxist view is flawed by its everlasting forecasts of crises which never seem to occur, and by the failure of corrupted Marxism in Eastern Europe. In contrast, pluralism is flawed by the undemocratic nature of Britain's Government and its obsessive secrecy. The problem lies not with the theories but the underlying indifference and apathy of British society. It is to this topic that attention is now turned.

Transformation of British society

Cooke (1987), an academic planner, has argued that the 1980s saw a transition from one spatial paradigm, the egalitarian spread of wealth in the post-war years, to another, the post-modern one, in which many of the familiar cultural, social and spatial features of the past were jettisoned. Not least among these was the commitment to full employment and progressive income distribution policies, with the effect of a marked social and spatial polarization between north and south not seen since Victorian times. The south prospered because of its continued possession of global sources of financial power, the seat of government with all its powerful decision making powers and the largest numbers of the socially dynamic service and technical classes.

Within rural areas traditional patterns of rural life based on a community where people frequently met each other in lots of different ways, where people had close knit social networks, where most people worked on the land, where status was ascribed by family origin and it was difficult to change your status by achievement, where social conflicts were kept at arm's length because people were bound to meet, and where social inequalities were allowed to continue because they were said to be 'traditional', are said to have disappeared (Abercrombie *et al.*, 1988). In their place during the post-war years a series of changes have transformed these patterns, namely, the growth of owner-occupancy, the ownership of land by financial institutions, the industrialization and mechanization of farming, and the appearance of 'newcomers' in the rural community.

In an Open University text (Cochrane and Anderson, 1989) a team of political experts have asked whether the 1980s also marked a significant change in British politics to accompany the wider changes outlined above. No clear conclusion is reached but one theme does emerge, namely that a crisis in British politics occurred in the 1970s largely due to consumption running ahead of production.

Reactions to the crisis in the 1980s were manifested by the decline of class-based voting to a pattern based more one issues and ideologies as first the centre parties and then the green parties emerged as major third forces.

The rise of the so-called new politics has also been charted by Abercrombie *et al.* (1988) who note three trends.

1. The erosion of consensus politics which required a stable two-party system, broad agreement over policies for running a mixed economy/welfare state, and a politically passive population.
2. The introduction of a new ideology of self-help under Thatcherism.
3. The growth of new social movements which encouraged unconventional political action issues around which had little to do with traditional class politics.

Taking these trends together produces the new politics shown in Table 1.3.

One of the main features of the new politics is the rise of green issues and Young (1987), a political scientist, in a social attitude survey of 1500 people has revealed a gradual greening of the electorate with 40% of people being very concerned about the countryside. This greening is most marked in the 35–54 year age group, but it is still passive and the political base for the Green Party remains very small.

The British voting system does not of course encourage the multiplication of parties or multivariate contradictory views across the two main parties. Cox, Lowe and Winter (1986), two sociologists and a chemist turned academic countryside expert, have noted how this represents a major problem for the greening of British politics since the policy community for rural conservation is large but, diverse and pluralistic, whereas the agricultural community is small, tight knit and corporatist. When the need for agricultural growth was accepted by most policy makers, the agricultural community was in a powerful position, but in the 1980s as agricultural fundamentalism began to fall away the unity of policy crumbled into smaller parts and the

Table 1.3. 'Old' and 'new' politics.

		'Old' politics	'New' politics
Issues and values		Economic growth and management; social security; material distribution	Preservation of peace and the environment; establishment of equal human rights
		Security: equal opportunity; personal consumption and material improvement	Opposition to centralized, bureaucratic or state control. In search of personal autonomy and democratic self-management
The organization of action	Internal organization	Formal organization and large representative associations (e.g. parties, pressure groups)	Informal, spontaneous, egalitarian, impermanent groups of campaigners
	Channels of interest	Interest-group bargaining; competitive party politics	Protest based on demands, formulated in negative terms about single issues, using unconventional tactics
Social bases of participants		Classes and occupational groups acting in their own group interests, especially with respect to material rewards	Certain socio-economic groups (especially the 'new middle class') acting not in own interests but on behalf of other ascriptive collectivities (e.g. women, youth, humankind)
Axis of politics		Class interest	Moral concern

Source: Abercrombie *et al.* (1988).

Table 1.4. Class and voting in Great Britain 1983.

Class	Percentage voting			
	Conservative	Labour	Alliance	Other
Petit Bourgeoisie	71	12	17	0
Salariat	54	14	31	1
Routine non-manual	46	25	27	2
Foremen and technicians	48	26	25	1
Working class	30	49	20	1

Source: Johnston *et al.* (1988, p. 49).

diverse policy community in favour of conservation was able to enter the policy community at a number of places and began to have influence, but still only as pressure groups rather than political parties.

Voting habits of British society

In a general election only 70% of the electorate vote and a government can be elected, like Mrs Thatcher's, for three terms with only just over 30% of the potential votes. The key feature of the system is thus one of engineering enough people to vote for you once every four or five years, no matter what happens to one's political popularity in between elections. For example, Mishler *et al.* (1989), 'American political scientists concluded from an analysis of quarterly public opinion poll data between 1964 and 1988 that the balance of public support between the major parties continues to be highly unstable inbetween elections and subject to large and precipitous fluctuations in response to relatively small economic changes and ordinary political events. More intriguingly they suggest that the landslide Conservative wins in 1983 and 1987 were due more to good timing and luck than to any fundamental long-term dynamic change in British politics, which they believe remains committed to centreground consensus politics.

With regard to actual elections Johnston *et al.* (1988), in a major analysis of the elections of 1979, 1983 and 1987, have shown how voting in Britain is basically correlated with Conservative support in the affluent rural south, and Labour support in the industrial north. However, as Table 1.4 shows, voting is no longer completely conducted along class lines, especially for the centre party, the former Alliance.

For the future the only way in which the Conservative Party can lose power is either for the old Alliance (now the Liberal Democrats) to collapse or to form an electoral pact with Labour, since the Alliance has been the major challenger to the Conservatives in most Conservative seats in the 1979, 1983 and 1987 general elections. Many of these are in rural areas where

Labour support is very unlikely to grow given the nature of rural society today (Johnston, 1987).

Without an electoral pact, however, analysis shows that only about 20–30 seats are now truly marginal, unless as Johnston *et al.* discuss, the Labour Party broadens its appeal and moves dramatically and radically into the centreground, and in the process abandons: (i) socialism in favour of social democracy; and (ii) ideology in favour of pragmatic eclecticism. Johnston *et al.* (1988) conclude that if the Conservatives can maintain prosperity among the growing ranks of the middle classes they will remain in power and Labour could become the 'class party' of a shrinking deprived north.

To some extent this is confirmed by Heath (1991) who from an analysis of the 1964–1987 period finds that Labour's natural level of support may have fallen by eight points between 1964 and 1987. To some extent the five-point swing that relates to the electorate's judgement about each party's competence at an election can compensate for this but if it were to work against Labour it would leave them 13 points adrift of their 1964 position. More encouragingly for Labour the study finds that class politics remained strong with the percentage of home-owning working class people voting Tory only rising from 35% in 1964 to 37% in 1987.

From an analysis of voting and change in the structure of British population since 1959 Crewe (1988), a political scientist, has concluded that Labour faces two further immense problems. First, the number of marginal seats has fallen from 157 in 1959 to 88 in 1987, and second, the contraction of the traditional working class has diminished Labour's natural vote without new social bases of significance emerging in its place.

Indeed an increasing number of commentators now argue that both parties represent only a fraction of the electorate. For example, Rose and McAllister (1990), two political scientists, have used factor analysis to identify the values of voters, and cluster analysis to group voters using data from the 1987 British election survey. They concluded from their analysis, part of which is shown in Table 1.5, that as the old divisions of right and left crumble, the formidable task facing Britain's politicians is how to win the support of groups with disparate and even conflicting values. They might also have added that their analysis called into question the existence of both two-party or even three-party politics, and the impossibility of accommodating these pluralist views in a first past the post system. The data indeed provide strong evidence both for coalition government and a proportional representation system of democracy backed up by referenda on major policy decisions.

At the time of writing (April 1991) this once again seemed to be a possibility with a win by the Liberal Democrats in one of the safest Tory seats having just been achieved in Lancashire leading to speculation about a hung parliament. In such an event one of the key conditions for the Liberal Democrats to enter a coalition would be the introduction of proportional representation. The Liberal Democrats may, however, be squeezed in the

Table 1.5. Political values and party support 1987.

Group size[a]		Con	Lab	Alliance
	Anti-Labour values			
7	Victorian right	6	0	0
17	Social market	14	0	2
11	Conserve environment	8	1	3
8	Strong defence	5	1	2
	Cross bench values			
8	Anti-nuclear centrists	3	2	3
11	England alone	3	4	3
	Anti-Conservative values			
18	Muck and brass welfare	3	9	6
15	Soft left	1	10	4
5	Hard left	0	5	0
	Totals	43	32	23

Source: Rose and McAllister (1990).
[a] Percentage of electorate.

centre. First, by the rapid re-entry to the centreground by the Labour Party after their third defeat in 1987, and second, by a clear retreat from the right by the Tories after the defeat of Mrs Thatcher in November 1990, ironically after she had received 52% of MPs votes.

Thatcherism

Much of the debate about the Thatcher effect has been over its lasting impact on attitudes and whether there could ever be a return to socialism based on central planning responding to crises in capitalism. During the 1980s this seemed unlikely with a worldwide rejection of socialism in Reagan's America, Thatcher's Britain and most significantly of all the collapse of communism at the end of the 1980s. Views concerning the wisdom of the move to the right and its longevity are, however, varied, and starting from the most enthusiastic and working through to the most critical they can be outlined as follows.

In a eulogistic review of the first ten years of Thatcherism the Conservative Party, (1989) itself has argued that the Thatcher revolution was most of all about 'common sense'. The revolution itself took three forms. First, a quiet but real *political* revolution redrawing the political map in favour of freedom and free enterprise, second, an *economic* revolution based on the free market, and third a *social* revolution in terms of creating a property- and share-owning democracy via council house sales and privatizations. Historically, the document sees the period as a very radical one in which a new fourth policy option was added to the Party's arsenal. Traditionally only three options as follows had been available to a party of the Right. Option one is to resist change, option two is to make concessions when expedient, and option three is to judiciously appropriate the programmes of the opposition. In the 1980s, option four was instead chosen, a creative line of policy in order to outflank the opposition and force it back on the defensive. The politics of the 1980s were also revolutionary in that the Labour Party, after being soundly beaten in the elections of 1983 and 1987 had no other alternative but to abandon socialism and return to pragmatic social democracy. In this sense the Thatcher period not only moved the goalposts, but the pitch as well, in a major shift to the right in British politics. However, in early 1991, the climbdown over the poll tax and other sacred Thatcher totems, e.g. the uprating of child benefit, indicated that the Tory Party was returning to the three option strategy, especially, options two and three.

In spite of this move back towards the centre Kavanagh (1988) a political scientist in a review of the Thatcher years concludes that their legacy will be a movement of British politics to the right, and that any future Labour government will start much further back than in 1979 in terms of instruments to steer society and the economy.

In a counter view Crewe and Searing (1988), political scientists from both sides of the Atlantic, have examined the rise of Thatcherism and concluded that her new right values were not as radical as they seemed, since, especially in the areas of law and order and morality they had always appealed to a large sector of middle Britain. The shift to the right was therefore more apparent than real, and on matters of public services especially the health service the electorate continues to attach great importance. In light then of a divided and weak opposition and via an appeal to gain votes over moral issues, Crewe and Searing argue that Mrs Thatcher was able to maintain electoral success in spite of radical policies which moved away from the centre of British politics.

In a further development of this view Young (1989), in a major biography of Mrs Thatcher, has concluded that her radical views which apparently held so much sway in the 1980s and particularly in the third term from 1987 onwards, had not however led to a change of views in the electorate, with most people rejecting the values of the new Right in favour of consensus socialism. He concludes that she may well have been a one off, first because of the lack of a credible opposition in the 1980s, and second, because no obvious successor emerged to challenge such a vigorous and forthright leader.

Indeed on her demise the Conservative Party was left with a choice of John Major, Douglas Hurd and Michael Heseltine, each very different.

Returning in more detail to Thatcherism's effects on two issues, the environment and rural planning, O'Riordan (1988) has dubbed the period an 'elected dictatorship' under which a so-called 'Enterprise Culture' used privatization, self-regulation, cost-recovery by hived-off agencies, and green capitalism as the main agents of environmental policy.

Blowers (1987), an academic planner, in a wider review of environmental policy under Thatcher, has divided the characteristics and functions of her environmental policies into three headings as shown in Table 1.6. The policy response has been different in each of three areas. In the 'Development' area there has been a triumph of the free-market ideology with deregulation of planning controls and the promotion of private development (option four). In the 'Conservation' area, however, the politics of pragmatism has had to be followed (option two) and this has pleased no one set of the groups involved. In the third area, of 'Ecology', the policy has been one of the politics of survival in the face of growing international pressure to reduce pollution (option three).

In conclusion, Blowers argues that:

> major changes in the environment occur less because of
> ephemeral ideology impulses than incrementally, in response
> to long-term structural changes, economic booms and
> recession, and shifts in values, Environmental policy, unlike
> most other areas of policy, requires enduring commitments
> which transcend the shifting sands of political doctrine.
> There is evidence, even under the pronounced radicalism of
> the Thatcher government, that long-term conservation has
> not been entirely surrendered to immediate economic
> priorities (p. 292).

Turning to rural planning Potter and Adams (1989), in their review of the Thatcher decade 1979–1989, pick out four key themes. First, the replacement of countryside planning with countryside management. Second, the opportunity provided by the retreat of agriculture to develop the revolutionary notion that habitats can be restored and re-created as well as maintained and protected. Third, the clash between the conservation branch of the Tory Party based in the shires, and the development lobby based in the cities, and fourth the dichotomy between the political need to be seen to espouse green politics and the ideological stance committed to the neoliberal interplay of market forces.

In rural but socio-economic review of the 'new Right' policies espoused by Mrs Thatcher, Bell and Cloke (1989) argue that the effects have been social rather than locational and that any impact on rural areas has been accidental rather than intended, notably, in two key areas of 'Thatcherism': the user pays principle and deregulation of services both of which have been particularly relevant to rural transport. Even here, these policies have had most impact on the rural poor, rather than on the entire rural population.

Table 1.6. The characteristics of environmental policy under the Thatcher Government.

| Functions | Characteristic | | | | | |
	Policy determinants	Policy emphasis	Time-scale	Spatial impact	Political interests	Policy outcomes
Development	Demand for development from public and private sectors	Promote market forces through deregulation	Immediate pay-off	Localized	Private developers especially big companies	Urban dispersal within limited inner city regeneration
Conservation	Impact of agriculture, minerals and other development	Achieve conservation through compensation to farmers	Long-term need to preserve amenity, and conserve resources	Limited to areas of high amenity	Reconcile farming and other rural interests	Protection of best environments; voluntary agreements elsewhere
Ecological	Impact of polluting activities	Discretion applied by pragmatic regulation	Conflict between economic benefits and long-term environmental impact	Widespread and transboundary	Environmental pressure groups and alliances and international community	Shift towards tighter control in interest of health and survival

Source: Blowers (1987).

However, the impact so far has been small and the attempt to dismantle old collectivist structures, and to build a new relationship between the state and the private sector, is likened by Bell and Cloke to the test drive of a revolutionary new car which is still in the early stages of development. Bearing these cautionary words in mind this chapter can now be concluded with a brief review of the possible political changes that the 1990s might bring.

The 1990s

Proceeding from the most optimistic to the most pessimistic forecasts (loosely using O'Riordan's environmental ideologies shown in Tables 1.1 and 1.2) we can begin with the work of two influential futurologists, Naisbitt and Aburdene (1990) whose book *Megatrends* sold 8 million copies. In a follow-up entitled *Megatrends 2000* they forecast that the 1990s will be a period of unprecedented prosperity as we move from trade among countries to a single global economy. In addition biotechnology will free us from the limits to growth. This process will be paralleled by a rise in individualism and the rejection of collectivism, and thus a basic shift from corporatism to privatization. In housing and work this will lead to more house ownership and to an increase in home working where the Henley Forecasting Centre has forecast that 7 million UK employees could do all or part of their work at home given the appropriate telecommunications technology.

In a similar vein Lefcoe (1987), a lawyer, has traced the development of work and noted how the great divide between work and play, controlled by the clock, was the dominant feature of the industrial revolution. Now modern technology gives more and more people control of their workspace and the ability for them to enter and leave at will is highly significant. Lefcoe concludes that in the agrarian age man toiled against nature. In the industrial era he pitted himself against machines. In the age of the information society he plays a game between people, and that game can now be played anywhere, at anytime.

Hall (1989), the Anglo-American planning guru, is another one who believes in a new golden age, and quoting from Keynes he notes:

> Thus for the first time since his creation man will be faced
> with his real, his permanent problem – how to use his
> freedom from pressing economic cares, how to occupy the
> leisure, which science and compound interest have won for
> him to live wisely and agreeably and well (Keynes, 1930
> p. 328).

Hall argues that the first manifestation of this leisured age, which Keynes forecast for the year 2030, is a concern for green issues, so for the future, the advent of the leisured age will see the rise of green planning in the UK, but according to Hall, academic planners have failed to tackle these issues. Instead they have retreated 'to a quite extraordinary philosophical position', which argues that planning is an attempt to stave off terminal crisis in the capitalist system. In disbelief Hall notes that they have decided to observe this process in spite of all evidence to the contrary, and failed to observe that it is socialism which is in terminal crisis not capitalism, as evidenced by the collapse of East European communism in the autumn of 1989.

Although Hall's diagnosis is as ever, lucid and persuasive, he fails to deliver a prescription. Instead he points out two issues which need to be tackled.

1. A way of resolving conflicts between various countryside groups must be found which involves new and better decision criteria; and
2. A way of dealing with negative externalities in order to find methods for meeting the burden that development imposes on the local community.

In another review of the 1990s, *Town and Country Planning*, the monthly magazine of the Town and Country Planning Association (the conscience and soul of planning throughout the century) published 17 articles on 'Planning for the Environmental Decade' in its January 1990 edition (Hardy *et al.*, 1990). The five main themes for the 1990s were thought to be: sustainability; livability (quality of life); responsibility (planning for all social classes); popularity (planning based on populist participation); and visibility (a high profile for planning).

The last three of these themes have also been taken up elsewhere. For example, a greater use of: (i) voluntary groups (Rogers, 1987); (ii) select committees of the Houses of Parliament (Marsh, 1988); (iii) the Courts (Hays, 1984); and (iv) the public inquiry system (Barker, 1984) have all been advocated as means of reversing the growing secrecy, centralization, and authoritarian nature of British government in the 1980s.

Turning to party politics Barlow (1988) has considered two scenarios for the 1990s. The first is one which an ultra-Right Conservative Party abandons support for farming and moves to a substantially deregulated planning system. Under this scenario farm land prices fall, thus releasing much land for leisure use in the north and Scotland, and for development in the southeast leading to the development of dozens of private new towns and villages. The second scenario is regarded by Barlow as the more likely, and portrays a cut in state support for agriculture, an extension of supralocal land use planning and public/private development partnership. This will occur whichever party is in power for Barlow sees a growing consensus between the two parties on pragmatic approaches to the countryside by cutting back on agriculture and allowing more development as imbalances in wealth between groups and regions within the country grow.

Continuing leftwards and ecologically a number of writers have tried to revise Marxism, notably Gramsci who has stressed the active 'voluntarist' side of Marxist theory, in contrast to the fatalistic reliance on objective economic forces and immutable 'scientific' laws, followed, for example, by an enlightened elite who governed as in the case of Lenin not for the wishes of the proletariat but on their behalf while they awaited enlightenment (Femia, 1981). In contrast Gramsci argues that since the dominant ideas in capitalist society arise from the experience and exclusive needs of the bourgeois class, and that since a consensus over these values and beliefs is the major source of cohesion in society, the only way to subvert capitalism in favour of socialism is by a long march through bourgeois society changing individual attitudes one by one. Unfortunately for Gramsci who spent most of his working life in an Italian prison in the 1930s, the 1990s has already witnessed the subversion of an admittedly corrupt communism throughout Eastern Europe and the Soviet Union by the very process he advocated, but in reverse. I know, for I was there in Czechoslovakia in November 1989 when day by day more and more people had the confidence to reject hegemony for the uncertain future of a liberal democracy.

It is largely because socialism in the form of Marxism has now been so discredited as a political force that we can safely ignore it as a political factor in Britain in the 1990s. However, as a philosophical, intellectually interesting and academic concern, Marxism and the continued debates over critical theory and structuralism by luminaries such as Giddens, Habermas and Foucault (White, 1988) will continue to be interesting for those concerned with theory and diagnosis rather than prognosis and action in the real world.

However, there still may be a way forward for Marxism, via ecology. For example, Frankel (1987) a political sociologist, has concluded from a Marxist analysis of the policies of Labour, Socialist and Communist Parties that they have become bankrupt in the face of an emerging post-industrial society. From an analysis of non-Marxist, radical and alternative theories (mainly eco-pacifist and green movements) and the work of Bahro, Gorz, Jones and Toffler he concludes that a major if not totally revolutionary shift of thought is needed if these policies are to free themselves from their pragmatic prisons. He, therefore, advocates that these parties should seek the goal of a 'concrete utopia' based on eco-socialist, semi-autarkic (self-sufficiency) principles, geared to existing, but surmountable problems.

In a similar view Ryle (1988) an active member of the Green Party calls for a restructured coalition of the Left in which eco-socialism comes to power through adopting proportional representation.

In conclusion, it would appear solely from the weight of historical evidence that the British semi-democratic system will continue to evolve pragmatically and incrementally, for this is the British way. It also reflects the lack of any institutions which look at the British political system in any systematic way. In their absence the speed of reform is akin to that of some of the more cautious glaciers (Barker, 1984). Nonetheless, the impact of full entry to the EC in 1992, and any unforeseen consequences of the Gulf War could yet see revolutionary rather than evolutionary change. Attention will return to these topics in Chapter Eleven but in the meantime it is now time to turn the policy options and techniques open to politicians of whichever party is in power in the 1990s.

2 Policy Options, Issues and Approaches in Rural Planning

The options available for rural planning depend on three factors: the aims of the system; the available legislation; and the range of technical measures available. Taking these in turn Gilg (1978a, 1985b) (Tables 2.1 and 2.2) has demonstrated that the only really common aim is the protection of the environment. It is, therefore, difficult to provide a set of options applicable to all areas of rural planning. Another problem relates to the limited powers available from existing legislation and its slow rate of evolution for as shown in Chapter 1, there is limited scope for introducing new legislation since only one major Act can be passed in any one area in any one year. This limits change to the powers provided under existing legislation via Statutory Instruments and to non-statutory advice under Circulars, Notes, and political speeches.

General policy options

Under existing legislation rural planners have five main planning option areas.

1. Public ownership or management of land.
2. Regulatory controls, mainly negative, e.g. planning permission.
3. Taxation and fiscal controls, mainly negative but can be positive by default, e.g. lead-free petrol.
4. Financial incentives, mainly positive, e.g. forestry grants and management agreements.
5. Exhortation, mainly voluntary methods via the provision of advice, but backed up by the threat of future controls, e.g. straw burning.

Table 2.1. Four different sets of aims for rural planning.

Orwin's 4 Aims
1   To develop employment opportunities in the countryside
2   To improve living conditions
3   To ameliorate the handicap of small population size for socio-economic life
4   To preserve the amenities of the countryside and the beauty of the rural scene.

Thorn's 4 Aims
1   To reconcile the competition for land between agriculture, housing development, industry and recreation
2   To preserve the beauty and character of the countryside
3   To redistribute the population into viable villages both economically and socially
4   To give people a greater say in the future of the countryside.

Wibberley's 5 Aims
1   The role of the countryside is to produce food
2   The role of the countryside is to act as a reservoir of land for urban development, and to provide resources for urban life, such as timber, minerals and water
3   The role of the countryside is to provide a location for outdoor recreation
4   The role of the countryside is to be a haven for wildlife and plants
5   The role of the countryside is to be a place of peace and solitude, to be like it was when one was young, or to be like it was when one first arrived

Royal Town Planning Institute's (RTPI) 3 Aims
1   To conserve and prevent waste and pollution of our natural and environmental resources
2   To increase production of food, fuel and timber
3   To provide opportunities for the physical, intellectual and emotional enrichment of people
Our essentially urban culture does not always lead to spontaneous action to achieve this purpose and hence some conscious planning and management of the countryside is necessary.

Elsewhere Blunden *et al.* (1985) in an Open University textbook have identified five similar policy option areas: (i) incentives via grants; (ii) incentives via tax concessions, price control and import restrictions; (iii) guidance via plans, demonstrations and experiments; (iv) controls via land-use designations, development control, notifications, tree preservation orders and land acquisition; and (v) agreements.

In more detail Hill *et al.* (1989), agricultural economists at Wye College, in a joint project for MAFF and DOE were asked to assess the current systems of support for rural areas, identify gaps and explore the options for alternative integrated systems based on existing procedures. In their analysis they identified no less than 178 subprogrammes involving either intervention in the market and in the consumption process, or the provision

Table 2.2. Correlation between various aims and roles for rural planning and the countryside.

Aims	Orwin	Thorn	Wibberley	RTPI
1 Protecting the environment/ecology/beauty	+	+	+	+
2 Providing food			+	
3 Reservoir of land for other uses			+	
4 Contributing to economic growth and stability				+
5 Providing employment/income support	+			
6 Social factors/living conditions	+			
7 Ameliorate handicap of small size	+			
8 Recreational/aesthetic considerations			+	+
9 Reconcile conflict		+		+
10 Provide more democracy		+		
11 Redistribute population		+		

of infrastructure or social goods like education. Specifically eight types of programme were identified.

1. Cash payments to producers, e.g. management agreements, Hill Livestock Compensatory Allowances, and farm capital grants.
2. Taxation concessions, e.g. non-rating of farm land at a cost of £450 million a year.
3. Market manipulation, e.g. manipulating farm gate prices by import taxation and commodity price support.
4. Direct cash payments to households, e.g. pre-pension payments to farmers.
5. Non-cash transfers, e.g. provision of advice, subsidy on rural bus services.
6. Payments for the production of public goods, e.g. amenity tree planting schemes which may increase tourism.
7. Payments to improve marketing, e.g. Food from Britain.
8. Cross-subsidizing services, e.g. the cost of posting a letter is the same all over the UK.

In total, the cost of these subprogrammes was calculated at £2301 million for 1987/8. Agriculture is the main beneficiary with market regulation consuming 70% of the total and farmers absorbing 92% of the total albeit after filtering through merchants and other middlemen.

In terms of the efficiency of the system Hill *et al.* point out that it is not set up in a way which enables either, its overall performance, or most of its parts to be assessed. There is, therefore, an obvious need to change it. Before this is done, however, they pose a number of key questions.

1. Is there any need to be concerned over the welfare of residents in rural areas?

2. If so what aspects and which groups deserve support? and if so at what level should the support be pitched?
3. Are the problems spatially differentiated?
4. What are the justifications and priorities for protecting the natural environment?
5. How much weight should the natural environment be given *vis-à-vis* other areas of support?
6. Similarly how to weight other areas, e.g. recreation.
7. Do the policies for welfare, recreation, protection and food supply conflict or interact?
8. Having identified priorities what is the best way of achieving them?
9. Do we support rural areas via agriculture or other ways and what are the multipliers of different policy inputs?
10. What are the preferred ways of developing rural economies, via increasing efficiency, via investment, or via more direct means?

After such an exhaustive analysis of the support systems and the questions they raise for the evaluation of policy Hill and his team come up with some rather mundane policy proposals, although the first proposal shown below could be revolutionary if carried out in a radical and positive way. Most of the proposals, however, relate to the need for further research and only three policy proposals are made as follows.

1. A policy review group should be established at a high level in Government to determine the overall set of objectives for rural areas, the allocation of resources by objective, and the reallocation of functional responsibility between the agencies concerned.
2. More integration should be encouraged at the local level by perhaps the introduction of area-based development plans.
3. Consideration should be given to re-organizing existing systems at the margin notably conservation and rural enterprise.

Most usefully, however, Hill *et al.* provide a hierarchy of functional objectives for rural areas as shown in Fig. 2.1.

In an alternative view of the spectrum of public community powers over private land Selman (1988a), an environmental scientist, has divided them into five main approaches.

1. Education of landholders by provision of advice and information.
2. Financial incentives and grants, e.g. taxes and grants.
3. Restraints on undesirable uses, e.g. planning consents, licences, quotas.
4. Removal of property rights by free market purchase.
5. Removal of property rights by compulsory purchase.

Selman argues that although these options provide a battery of imperfect measures they do at the same time display an unrealized potential for a radical new approach to planning. This would involve operating the system

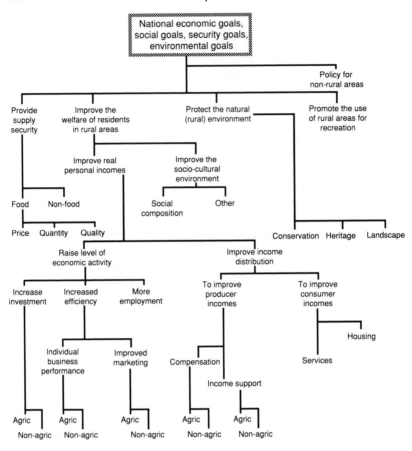

Fig. 2.1. A hierarchy of functional objectives for rural areas. In converting this hierarchy to a working form the terms improve, promote, raise, increase etc. will need to be expressed in a testable form. Source: Hill *et al.* (1989).

in a new integrated way under which planners would play the role of the squire in former days and manage the rural estate in a benevolent and long-term way based on stewardship and sustainable resource development. Selman concludes that we are on the verge of a new landscape, in which radical new patterns could emerge. If planners are to shape this landscape they must regain a feeling for the broader estate and give expression to this through clearly articulated policies and designs. The scope is there, according to Selman, for immediate and active participation in an imaginative restructuring of the countryside.

McDonald (1989) has also stressed the need for integration by pointing out that there are at least nine subfields within rural land use planning which produce an extra complexity due to the variety of professionals involved.

Nonetheless each subfield has two main tasks. First the choice of land use for each parcel of land, and second, the management strategy to achieve that land use. This could be done, and is done by the private sector but McDonald argues that rural policy is needed to oversee private land management because in spite of the claims of the resurrected free market school, the free market does not take sufficiently into account social costs and benefits. Unfortunately according to McDonald most existing models of planning: the rational approach pioneered by Geddes; the normative approach based on standard goals; the conflict resolution approach; and the allocative style are also unsatisfactory, first, because they imply a knowledge of the real world that is illusory, and second, because they assume a consensus in society about its goals that may not exist. McDonald, therefore, advocates a style of planning based on bargaining between all the different groups involved. In such a process the plan would take the form of an introductory discussion statement in order to get the process rolling, in common with the 'Plans Directeurs' process in Switzerland (Gresch and Smith, 1985).

In addition to general policy options, there are also a number of options available to specific policy areas, for example, agriculture, land use planning and rural welfare, and also a number of possible techniques, for example, economic analyses. These are now considered in turn.

Agricultural policy options

Bowler (1979), a geographer, has divided agricultural planning into two tiers, first, goal setting as shown in Fig. 2.2, and second, policy measures to achieve these goals as shown in Table 2.3.

Most of these measures deal with agriculture itself and the last column of Table 2.3 on environmental quality only contains two items. To some extent this gap is filled by Bonnieux and Rainelli (1988), civil servants in the French Ministry of Agriculture, who have provided a review of the policy options available to control environmental change in farming as shown in Table 2.4. From this review they conclude that where environmental change is irreversible regulation is the best policy. In contrast where the impacts are reversible they argue that economic incentives, especially in the form of prices, are socially efficient. Finally, they conclude that the polluter-pays principle if implemented in farming against the wishes of the farm lobby will not be as expensive as the lobby claims, using the evidence of similar claims made by manufacturing industry two or three decades ago which were subsequently found to be exaggerated.

In a more mundane review of the options available for cutting CAP surpluses Blunden *et al.* (1985) list: price restraint; quotas; co-responsibility levies; setaside; reducing agricultural inputs; and changing people's attitudes. They do not, however, advocate the 'New Zealand' solution where farm

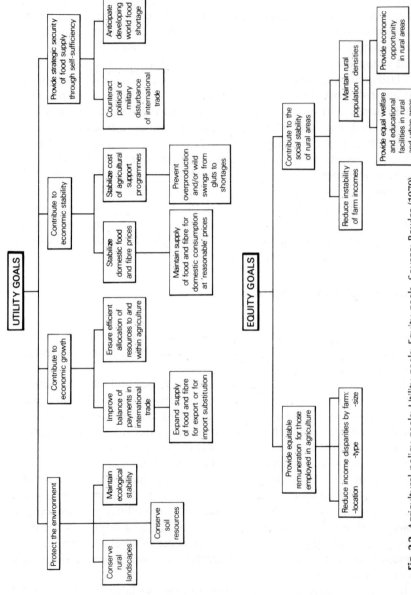

Fig. 2.2. Agricultural policy goals: Utility goals: Equity goals. Source: Bowler (1979).

Table 2.3. Types of agricultural policy measures.

Measures designed to influence

The growth and development of agriculture	The terms and levels of compensation of production	The economic structure of agriculture	The environmental quality of rural areas
Subsidies on the cost of inputs (fertilizers, machinery, buildings) drainage, ploughing	Demand management Advertising Produce grading schemes Multiple pricing	Financial assistance for land consolidation schemes	Pollution control measures Land zoning ordinances
Preferential taxes	Supply management Land retirement Import quotas Tariff protection and import levies	Farm amalgamation grants	
Preferential credit interest rates	Marketing quotas Production quotas Buffer stock schemes	Land reform schemes	
Financial assistance to cooperatives or syndicates for the joint purchase of inputs	Target/threshold prices with intervention (support) buying Export subsidies Bilateral/multilateral commodity agreements	Retirement and discontinuation pensions/ grants	
Financial assistance to agricultural educational extension and research establishments	Direct payments Deficiency payments Fixed rate subsidies/ production grants Direct income support payments	Retraining schemes	
		Financial assistance to cooperatives for production or marketing	
		Inheritance laws (land taxation)	
		Farm wage determination	

Source: Bowler (1979).

Table 2.4. A taxonomy of policy instruments available for linking agriculture with environmental protection.

Type of instruments	Suitability regarding		Feasibility	
	Efficiency (performance)	Farm income distribution	Farmers' view	Governments' view
1. Economic instruments				
(a) Market incentives				
Taxation of environmental damage	Theoretically these incentives achieve social welfare	–	– –	+ +
Subsidy + per unit of reduction of effluents + cover for costs of damage–control equipment		+	+ +	+ +
Tradeable permits (rights, licences)			– –	–
Refundable deposits			– –	– –
Specification of property rights		?	+	+
(b) Public investments				
Damage prevention and waste treatment facilities	+			+ +
Extension and reduction services			+	+ +
Research				
2. Enforcement instruments (including monitoring and police)				
General regulation	These incentives perform differently according to individual cases	–	+	+
Specific regulation			–	– –
Standards + of effluents			–	– –
+ of technology			–	– –

Source: Bonnieux and Rainelli (1988).

income supports and subsidies have been almost totally removed provoking a dramatic decline in land prices and farm incomes (Robinson, 1990). The extent to which other governments will 'bite the bullet' of scaling down farm price supports is one of the most intriguing questions for rural development over the next two or three decades.

Approaches to land use planning

The main debate in land use planning is not about the major instruments, namely plan making and development control, for they are largely fixed and agreed to be generally satisfactory (Smart and Wright, 1983). This is not to say that there is no debate about the details of plan making and development control, and these are in fact discussed in Chapter 8. Similarly there is a debate about how much land should be released for housing, and this too is discussed in Chapter 8. At issue in this chapter, where general principles are outlined, are the possible approaches to formulating, and setting out policy goals, rather than the means of implementing policies which are examined later in the book.

There are three broad approaches to formulating and setting out policy goals. First, the rational/linear/systems approach; second, the normative/ goal setting/conflict resolution/managing change approach; and third, the decision-centred approach.

The rational/linear systems approach

Jeffers (1988), a statistician, has argued that there are two weak links in current uses of this approach. The first is a failure to generate a sufficiently wide range of alternative solutions, partly due to over reliance on the adversarial process in our institutional procedures. Second, there is a lack of a rigorous examination of the likely consequences of adopting each of the possible options. Accordingly Jeffers suggests the use of a four-stage process: The Question; The Alternatives; The Consequences; The Decision, possibly using expert systems as an aid. In addition four guiding principles should be followed. First, we should not adopt policies which foreclose on future options. Second, the options considered should maintain essential ecological processes. Third, preserving genetic diversity should be a primary aim of any alternative use of agricultural land. Fourth, any alternative use of agricultural land should utilize species and ecosystems sustainably.

Friend and Hickling (1987), two consultants specializing in operational research, have developed an alternative method of making planning choices from those advocated by either the Geddes linear school or the systems view of planning. Under these methods flow management norms are set out as follows:

- aim for *linearity*   – Tackle one thing at a time
- aim for *objectivity*   – Avoid personal or sectional bias
- aim for *certainty*   – Establish the full facts of the situation
- aim for *comprehensiveness* – Don't do things by halves

But Friend and Hickling then advocate that the mode of producing strategic planning decisions should be achieved by group interaction with meetings hammering out choices from first principles and not discussing the options provided by technical experts.

The normative/goal setting/conflict resolution/managing change approach

This pragmatic view of planning is espoused by Cherry (1982), an academic geographer/planner and one time president of the RTPI, who in a traditional liberal democratic view of planning claims that planning is a cultural activity derived as a response to the undesirable effects of industrialization and urbanization. It is an activity about choices and it establishes goals which ultimately must win political approval. It is itself apolitical but it operates in a political framework.

For the future Cherry would like to see a gradual change to planning as a technical job framed by social awareness and guided by ideas and ideals which positively contribute to human happiness, with primary respect for the individual. Within this enabling philosophy its targets should be: improved housing; employment generation; wise management of transport; the provision of leisure; stewardship of natural resources; the furthering of participatory democracy; and the decentralization of government to the lowest appropriate levels.

Bruton and Nicholson (1987a,b) also take a limited if pragmatic view of planning from the experience of a major study of local planning. They argue that the role of planning has altered to one of managing change where the process is all important.

The decision-centred approach

This approach developed by Friend and Hickling (1987) rejects not only the Geddesian approach of survey followed by plan, but also the view of planning as problem solving. Instead, as advocated by Faludi (1987), it takes a pragmatic view of planning as decision taking in a wider context and in particular notes that planning is not a 'superior' form of decision taking, but is one of many taking place alongside, and in competition with, those taken by national and local governments, by free enterprise groups and organizations and by State and other corporations. Faludi concludes by advocating an environmental planning system which orders public environmental measures into coherent schemes for the management and improvement of the public estate, presumably land. The crisis of current planning is that so often plans are failing to be implemented or are achieving only small portions of their aims.

Cloke (1987) has focused attention on this implementation gap and Cloke and Little (1986a) from a survey of rural planners have argued that the main reasons for this are that planners have insufficient powers and inadequate financial resources. Faced with this problem they have two solutions. First, to accept the *status quo*, or second, to seek ways of doing things that will benefit the rural community by working behind the scenes or by employing informal non-statutory plans. In the same survey Cloke and Little (1986b) found that planners were increasingly cynical about the formal processes of planning and were replacing them with a system of planning by opportunism. In many cases this relied on the voluntary sector method of 'making do' especially in the area of social and other services (Cloke and Little, 1987c).

Another problem with planning policies is the lack of appraisal they undergo after they are put into operation. Sorenson and Auster (1989), two geographers/planners, observe that planning policies are fairly infrequently evaluated. This is a pity since if planning failures were analysed, policy makers could then eliminate the sources of failure and produce more effective plans. However, Sorenson and Auster caution that planning will always have to grapple with two immense problems: uncertainty about the future and the impossibility of understanding the very complex present, a burden placed on planners by Geddes' holistic approach. For the future Wathern *et al.* (1987), environmental academics and local authority staff, have argued that a system of policy appraisal would represent a significant advance in environmental management, since it would provide an opportunity to anticipate and hopefully ameliorate the adverse environmental effects of a policy at an early stage of its formation.

Approaches to rural welfare

A continuum of approaches to rural welfare based on political ideology and class interest has been provided in a book by Lowe *et al.* (1986) as shown in Table 2.5. Empirically, this is supported by interviews with around 120 households in two Wiltshire villages which found the lower classes to be in favour of more houses, but the higher classes against more housing. Continuing with current *laissez-faire* approaches would therefore lead to an affluent upper class society in rural areas. More radical options to prevent this would include in ascending order: (i) the use of self-help schemes; (ii) shifting corporate planning mechanisms so that they favoured the well

Table 2.5. Approaches to rural welfare.

Model of society	Ideal approach to welfare	Political ideology	Political prescription	Class interest
		Economic liberal (laissez-faire)	Non-interventionist state. Provide only basic physical infrastructure and access to markets in labour and capital. Restrictive eligibility to social security. Deregulation e.g. 1985 Transport Bill.	*Petit-bourgeois*
	Residual			
		Paternalist (Tory)	Defence of rural *status quo ante*. Power nexus and hegemony established within the 'deferential dialectic'. Protectionist support of traditional rural working class e.g. 1980 Housing Act.	Traditional landed capital
Consensus				
	Institutional	Social democratic	Protect the needs of minority groups and interests, by use of statutory instruments e.g. Wages Boards. Land-use planning machinery used to defend environmental and property rights and advocate functional hierarchy of service provision. Emphasis on equity, territorial justice and means of access to information. Selectivism in welfare policy.	Upper service

		Lower service
	Egalitarian reformist	Advance further the 'strategy of equality' to alter social distributions. Emphasis on antipoverty, social security and labour market programmes. Reduce dependence of working class on ascription and market-based disadvantage. Key role of universalist State welfare.	
Conflict	Structural		
	State socialist	State assumes total control of agricultural and related production. Redistribution via a command economy. Re-emergence of clear spatial division between agricultural and urban-industrial production. Elimination of social divisions of welfare.	Working

Source: Lowe *et al.* (1986).

being of rural communities; and (iii) most radically, by accepting that most current policies do not recognize the underlying causes of deprivation, introduce a radical policy of personal subsidy and wealth redistribution in favour of the lower classes.

The use of economic analyses

There are two main themes in the use of economic analysis, first, as a direct policy option, and second, as a way of putting cash values on various options as an aid to decision making. In the first case a series of reports by Pearce *et al.* (1989) in the late 1980s have floated the idea of using taxes and other fiscal instruments as the main instrument of environmental policy. In a critique of these Pearce reports for the British Association of Nature Conservationists, Bowers (1990), an economist, has criticized their over-reliance on market-based solutions. First, Bowers points out that sustainable world development involves a major redistribution of wealth from rich to poor countries which could not be achieved by the market. Second, sustainable development has to rely on population control, an issue not discussed by Pearce. Third, Bowers notes that many environmental problems are not the consequences of market failure but due to ignorance about the long-term effects of certain operations, e.g. the effects of chlorofluorocarbons (CFCs) on the ozone layer which was due to a lack of basic research, and fourth, Bowers rejects the view that there are acceptable techniques for valuing the environment and argues that they all have serious defects including the much vaunted contingent valuation method. Bowers concludes by rejecting the overemphasis on the price mechanism but recognizes that it has a role to play in a suite of policy mechanisms which should be as eclectic as the real world.

In a less critical view of the Pearce approach the Institute of Fiscal Studies (1990) in their green paper on the 1990 budget conclude, from the Dutch experience with fertilizer taxes, that such taxes are more likely to raise revenue for cleaning up operations rather than to reduce use, unless they are set at very high levels.

Turning to the second case, the use of economic analysis as an aid to decision making, even economists are cautious about this. For example, Bressers and Klok (1988) argue that, although most people would prefer to continue with 'muddling through' pluralist democracy instead of moving to a technocracy, economic theory can nonetheless provide politicians with a more rational way of making environmental decisions. If this is to be achieved, Nijkamp and Soetman (1988) argue that conventional tools of economic analysis have to be replaced by methods which can integrate the two systems of environment and economics into a measure of welfare.

There is, however, a considerable degree of doubt among economists as to whether they have acceptable methods to achieve this or not. For example, Young and Allen (1986), two agricultural economists, in a review of three methods: the travel cost (Clawson) method; the hedonic pricing (market goods produced) approach; and contingent valuation (willingness to pay) have concluded that only contingent valuation provides an estimate of the wider value of the countryside other than its recreational value. They do, however, caution that unless the valuation is remarkably well designed it is likely to produce biased estimates. They conclude, therefore, that such methods are only justifiable if the expected deviations of the estimated valuations are more acceptable than complete ignorance. This is confirmed by Willis (1989), an academic planner, who from a study of the value to be put on conserving three Sites of Special Scientific Interest (SSSIs) using contingent valuation, concludes that its reliability is questionable. The use of such methods thus depends on the level of risk or uncertainty in the numbers that political decision makers are willing to take.

Finally, in another review of economic methods of evaluation Willis *et al.* (1987) concluded that most of the methods based on ordinal or ranking measures pose a variety of problems. They, therefore, argue that rational choices in land use ultimately depend on cardinal or fundamental measures of the alternatives to be compared.

Turner (1988a,b) an economic geographer goes further and queries whether economics is able to offer decision makers foolproof policy options. For example many traditional methods treat the environment as a free good and man merely as a profit maximizer. However, although some progress has been made in the valuation of environmental goods and services, economists have yet to incorporate successfully the notion of the environment as an amalgam of assets requiring careful management, and their assumptions about human nature are at best only a partial reflexion of a complex reality.

Accordingly, Sagoff (1988) an American philosopher has argued that economic methods of measuring environmental decisions are as arbitrary as any other, for example, using alphabetical order. The solution then is to recognize that utopian capitalism is dead and with it the concepts of welfare and resource economics. There is thus a need to replace spurious rationality with policies based on moral, aesthetic and other unquantifiable variables. It is to these deep and worldwide issues of how we should view our planet and its planning that attention will be turned to in Chapter 4. But before this Part One will conclude with a short review of policy changes in the 1980s, for those unfamiliar with this period.

3

The 1980s:
a Radical Decade?

Although this chapter mainly considers the legislative changes of the 1980s as a background to the possible policies of the 1990s, it does also consider the last two or three years of the 1970s. There are two reasons for this. First, 1979 marked the major turning point in British politics when Mrs Thatcher was elected. Second, almost all the material in this chapter has been culled from the author's series of Countryside Yearbooks – which review change since 1978/1979 – namely: *The Countryside Planning Yearbooks*, Volumes One to Seven, 1980–1986; *The International Yearbook of Rural Planning*, Volumes One to Two, 1987 and 1988, and the new annual journal *Progress in Rural Policy and Planning*, Volume One which was published by Belhaven Press in 1991. Collectively these update the author's basic text on *Countryside Planning* published in 1978. New readers in countryside planning policy are therefore directed to these volumes for further background reading in addition to the brief review of the 1980s provided here. Alternatively newcomers to the field may like to read the series of excellent reviews provided by Blunden and Curry (1988), Blunden *et al.* (1985), Blunden and Turner (1985) and Rogers *et al.* (1985). Afficionados of the rural planning scene are, however, advised to proceed to Chapter 4 since they will be familiar with most of the material in this chapter. It should also be noted that neither this chapter nor its sections are mutually exclusive; for example, reviews of the 1980s are also provided in each chapter. Finally, although reference is made in the text to Circulars, Statutory Instruments (S.I.), Command or House of Commons (H.C.)/Lords (H.L.) Papers etc. which refer to the changes of the 1980s, these are not listed in the references at the end of the book. These can be followed up in the author's Yearbooks if necessary.

International changes

There were very few major international agreements over the countryside in the 1980s, but the importance of the European Community (EC) was further strengthened by the agreement to move to a single European market in 1992. In advance of this, the EC continued to be dominated by agriculture. For example, in 1989 the EC budget broke down as follows; CAP Guarantee payments £17,043 million; Regional Development Fund payments £2,498 million; Social Fund payments £1,880 million; and CAP Guidance Fund payments £989 million, giving these four funds the lion's share of the total expenditure of £27,206 million (H.C. 15-xxxvii (88–89)).

However, other European or International agreements did make an impact. For example, agreements on wildlife protection via various conventions (e.g. Ramsar) and directives forced the passage of the Wildlife and Countryside Act 1981 (see the section on Conservation for further details).

The most important agreement, however, was over EC directive 85/337 on Environmental Assessment (EA). The UK Government had resisted the introduction of this directive throughout the 1980s claiming that existing legislation provided for EA procedures via the public inquiry system. The Directive did, however, introduce new methods to the UK. In more detail the Directive sets out two types of development. All Annex/Schedule I developments, e.g. oil refineries, airports, motorways and other major proposals, require an EA. However, Annex/Schedule II projects, e.g. afforestation, land drainage, only need an EA if national or local governments deem it to be necessary. In the case of forestry, only those proposals which involve significant planting in designated areas or which would cause major ecological consequences are expected to need an EA. Similarly, other projects would only need an EA if they passed the basic test of having a 'significant environmental effect', would be of more than local importance, would take place on particularly sensitive or vulnerable locations, or involve unusually complex effects (DOE Circular 15/88 and Statutory Instruments 1199, 1207, 1217, 1218, 1221, 1241, 1249 and 1272/all of 1988).

The low key implementation of EA was reflected in the fact that in the first nine months of the system up to May 1989, only nine statements were requested under Annex/Schedule I and only 33 under Annex/ Schedule II. A few months later the total of Annex/Schedule II projects had reached 82 but only one of these was for agriculture, and none had been requested for drainage or afforestation projects. In 1989 a further dimension was added to environmental control with an EC proposal (COM (89) 303 final) for the creation of a European Environmental Agency to monitor and advise on all manner of environmental issue (H.C. 612 (88-89)).

General UK legislation

There were two main changes in general rural planning powers in the 1980s. First, an attack on planning organizations and second, growing controls over pollution in contradiction to the antiregulatory stance of the Thatcher administration.

In the first case a very early White Paper (Command 7746, 1979) forecast the demise of organizations: The Advisory Council for Agriculture and Horticulture; Regional Economic Planning Councils; The Environment Board; The Inland Waterways Amenity Advisory Council; The Recreation Management Training Committee; The Centre for Environmental Studies; The National Water Council; and The Water Space Amenity Commission. Other bodies changed their status, for example, The Countryside Commission and the Development Commission (for more details see the relevant sections).

The attack on pollution began with the belated implementation of the Control of Pollution Act 1974 between 1984 and 1986 (DOE Circular 17/84), making the very important point that Acts do not always operate immediately. The Act which was largely based on voluntary codes of practice also showed that such an approach is often the precursor to mandatory controls, e.g. straw burning, which after a voluntary code of practice had failed in the late 1980s, is to be banned from the end of 1992. In the case of water pollution by farmers, a 13% rise to 3890 cases in 1987 forced the Government to introduce mandatory controls (H.C. 543 (87-88)) since voluntary exhortation and advice had failed.

Another change over pollution was occasioned by the privatization of the water authorities which separated supply and control although the original proposals had been to keep them together (Command 9734, 1986). In the event the Water Act 1989 gave supply to the new private companies, but retained control in a new public body, the National Rivers Authority, which controls water pollution, water resource management, flood defence, fisheries, and in some cases navigation. In the Government's view this removed the inherent gamekeeper/poacher conflict inherent in the previous system.

However, the Act also introduced the threat whereby the new water company PLCs could sell off and develop surplus land around reservoirs for residential, recreational and other developments. The Act does contain a safeguard that the 110,000 hectares of such land found in National Parks, AONBs and SSSIs may be offered for sale first to conservation groups or be made subject to management agreements if the Secretary of State for the Environment requires it. This still leaves 70,000 hectares of land unprotected. Already by August 1990 several proposals had been made for the development of such land and this will surely be one of the main conflicts of the 1990s unless these sales are further controlled.

The Environment Protection Act 1990 also contained a wide range of pollution control measures to bolster the controls over pesticides introduced earlier in the Food and Environment Protection Act 1985.

The main changes contained in the Act return us, however, to the starting point, the attack on rural planning organizations instituted in 1979. Under the Act the Nature Conservatory Council (NCC) was split into three separate organizations over the first few years of the 1990s.

1. The NCC for Scotland was planned to merge with the Countryside Commission for Scotland to form a new body, Scottish National Heritage in 1992 under the Natural Heritage (Scotland) Bill 1990–1991.

2. The NCC in Wales merged with the Countryside Commission in Wales to form the Countryside Council for Wales in April 1991.

3. A separate NCC for England, 'English Nature', was set up on 1 April 1991 and was planned to remain separate from the Countryside Commission at least for the immediate future.

4. In order to counter criticism of the reduced effectiveness of the NCC as a national and international force, the Act also created a joint Nature Conservancy Committee drawn from the three national councils with an independent chairman.

In addition to these changes, there have been a number of proposals which have not been accepted. For example, despite numerous calls for a White Paper on the countryside, notably from both chairmen of the NCC and the Countryside Commission in 1984, none has been forthcoming, although some 350 bland policy statements were made in the so-called Green White Paper published in the autumn of 1990. In more detail the White Paper contained rehashes of existing policies, and lots of ideas, but few specific plans for real action or radical changes in the direction of policy (Environment, 1990). Nonetheless it did mark a change in emphasis if not of direction.

Agricultural policy

The 1980s were a decade which continued to heap the by-products of production success at the door of policy makers in the form of increasingly complex social, environmental, and economic issues. Unfortunately, their response was often piecemeal, panic stricken or inactive, with the result that at the end of the decade many of the problems of 1980 were still in place. The main change of the decade, however, was the realization that policies for expansion were no longer tenable, although putting this into practice has been very difficult to achieve. Ironically, the only UK white paper on agriculture in the Thatcher period argued that an increase in production was desirable because of the cost and insecurity of foreign supplies (Command 7458, 1979).

The European and international dimension

In 1980 an EC paper on the CAP (H.L. 126–I and -II (80–81)) began the decade by considering the many ways in which farm policies could be moved away from the single goal of production to wider social and environmental goals, with at the same time the aim of meeting four objectives: first, to control production and expenditure; second, to reduce stocks; third, to preserve the European pattern of agriculture; and fourth, to preserve Europe's position as the world's second largest exporter of farm produce. Like all succeeding proposals this document, however, rejected price cuts as the main weapon in favour of co-responsibility levies and aid targeted at specific farms or regions.

These ideas were carried forward in a 1985 European Commission Green Paper on the future of the CAP ((7872) 8480/85) which placed much emphasis on relating support prices to target levels of production via so-called stabilizers with a drop in price if target levels were exceeded. The use of stabilizers was endorsed in 1987 by the Commission ((9662) 8250/87 COM (87) 410) and by the Agriculture Committee of the House of Commons (H.C. 43-iii (86–87)).

In 1986 further strains were placed on the CAP with the accession of Spain and Portugal, and in 1990 by the reunification of Germany. International pressures to reform the CAP were also increased in 1990 with the so-called Uruguay round of GATT calling on all the industrial nations to cut agricultural support severely in order to prevent an industrial trade war.

The UK dimension

While the European Commission was grappling with the intricacies of reforming the CAP and largely failing, the UK Government passed the Agriculture Act 1986. This Act marked a major change away from a unilateral farm policy towards a multipurpose policy with Section 17 imposing on Agriculture Ministers a duty to:

> have regard to and endeavour to achieve a reasonable
> balance between the following considerations: (a) the
> promotion and maintenance of a stable and efficient
> agriculture industry; (b) the economic and social interests of
> rural areas; (c) the conservation and enhancement of natural
> beauty and amenity of the countryside . . . ; and (d) the
> promotion of the enjoyment of the countryside by the
> public.

The Act also included measures to introduce Environmentally Sensitive Areas (ESAs) (see a later section), extended the range of grant aid subject to management agreements, and extended the possibilities of charging for ADAS services. Having considered the general background to policy change in agriculture six detailed aspects of farm policy will now be considered: support prices, grant aid, guidance and socio-structural policies, extensification/ setaside, and environmental programmes.

Support prices

Throughout the 1980s there were four main areas in which support prices were changed. First, in the first half of the decade support prices were raised at a rate generally below the inflation rate and then in the second half of the decade prices were generally frozen giving even greater real cuts in prices. Second, in 1988 a system of stabilizers was introduced. Under this scheme a maximum guaranteed quantity for cereal production in the EC was set at 160 million tonnes between the years 1988/89 and 1991/92. A 3% co-responsibility levy is imposed on all growers who sell grain if this quantity is exceeded, and in subsequent years a 3% cut in support prices is also imposed. However, doubts about the scheme centre on the gap between demand in the EC which totals 135–140 million tonnes and the threshold figure of 160 million tonnes, and also on the similarity of the scheme to its forerunner, guaranteed thresholds, which was thought by many to have failed (H.L. 43-I and -II (87—88)). Third, selling into intervention was made more difficult for farmers by delaying payments, restricting the period for sales, by imposing stricter quality controls, and by paying less than the intervention price. Fourth, specific support schemes for beef and sheep and hill livestock were much reduced in the late 1980s by restricting the schemes to certain animals only and by imposing upper limits for the number of animals which would be supported. In the UK the effects of these changes were cushioned or exacerbated by using the green pound (monetary compensatory amount) mechanism. For example, in 1990 a general price freeze in Europe was translated into a 9% rise in UK prices by a devaluation of the green pound, but from October 1990 this no longer became possible, since the UK joined the Exchange Rate Mechanism which allows only limited movement in currency rates.

Grant aid

The 1980s witnessed two significant changes in grant aid. First, as shown in Table 3.1, there were major cuts in expenditure; taking account of inflation, and second, a gradual shift via the three major schemes away from production centred aid, initially to better management of farmland, and then gradually, towards the direction of direct expenditure on conservation. At the same time grants for drainage and hedgerow removal were taken away. Another change

Table 3.1. Expenditure on agricultural grants in the UK 1979–1990 (£million)

	Awarded from	1979/80	1984/5	1986/7	1989/90
Community schemes					
FHDS	1973 to 1980	73.9	100.8	51.3	12.2
AHDS	1980 to 1985	73.9	100.8	51.3	12.2
AIRS	1985 to 1988	0.0	0.0	9.4	24.9
FCGS	1989 onwards	0.0	0.0	0.0	2.9
Western Isles IDP	1982 to 1987	0.0	4.3	2.4	0.0
ESAs	1986 onwards	0.0	0.0	0.0	9.9
Setaside	1989 onwards	0.0	0.0	0.0	11.6
Total		73.9	105.1	63.1	68.9
UK schemes					
Crofting	1912/49 onwards	3.9	6.4	6.2	7.2
FHGS	1977 to 1980	72.5	96.3	37.8	2.2
AHGS	1980 to 1985	72.5	96.3	37.8	2.2
AIS	1985 to 1988	0.0	0.0	13.7	4.1
FCGS	1989 onwards	0.0	0.0	0.0	10.3
FDGS	1988 onwards	0.0	0.0	0.0	0.5
FWS	1989 onwards	0.0	0.0	0.0	5.0
Total		76.7	102.7	57.7	28.8
Overall total		150.8	207.8	120.8	97.7
At 1988 prices		321	272	138	69

Source: National Audit Office (1990) *Grants to Aid the Structure of Agriculture*, HMSO, London (H.C. 105 (89–90)).
AHDS/FHDS: Agricultural/Farm and Horticulture Development Scheme; AIR/AIS, Agriculture Improvement Regulations/Scheme; FCGS, Farm and Conservation Grant Scheme; IDP, Integrated Development Programme; ESA, Environmentally Sensitive Area; FHGS/AHGS, Farm/Agriculture and Horticulture Grant Scheme; FDGS, Farm Diversification Grant Scheme; FWS, Farm Woodland Scheme.

was the dropping of prior approval in the early 1980s, except in National Parks and SSSIs, thus removing one opening for MAFF officials to advise on environmental matters.

However, since the introduction of the Farm and Conservation Grant Scheme in 1989 conservation has become an aim of grant aid. Under this scheme, funded with £50 million between 1989 and 1992, grants of 50% are available for the installation of facilities for the storage and disposal of slurry and silage effluent in order to reduce water pollution. More positively, new grants at a rate between 35 and 50% were introduced for the range of measures shown in Table 3.2, subject to the acceptance of a farm improvement plan.

Table 3.2. Grants under the Farm and Conservation Grant Scheme (% rate).

	Less favoured areas	Elsewhere
Regeneration of woodland or marshland by fencing	50	40
Repair and reinstatement of traditional buildings	35	35
Heather burning and bracken control	50	40
Hedges, stone walls and shelter belts	50	40
Maintaining drainage, fencing etc. to keep farmland in good condition but without increasing surplus production	25	15
Orchard replanting	35	35

Quotas

Neither price controls or reductions in grant aid have managed to solve the two main problems of the CAP, surpluses and excessive expenditure. In 1984 milk production threatened to bankrupt the CAP in spite of the attempts by various outgoer schemes to encourage farmers to leave the industry. In a panic response in 1984 the Commission imposed quotas on milk production almost overnight, setting Community output at 1981 levels plus 1%, and national output at 1983 levels minus 6%. For the UK this translated into a 9% reduction in 1984/85 on 1983 output. There was a further reduction of 8.5% in 1987 and the scheme was extended in 1988 to 1992. After initial criticism of the scheme (H.C. 274 (84–85)) dairy farmers found that the scheme offered the chance to increase real profits by staying within the industry (McInerney, 1988) or by taking up revised outgoer schemes which offered the average dairy farmer £107,000 over seven years for leaving and staying out of milk production (H.L. 84 (85–86)).

The success of milk quotas in restructuring the dairy industry by providing a stable situation for stayers and reasonably attractive terms for goers, in spite of its *ad hoc* and panic stricken introduction, raises the question whether quotas should be introduced for the other main area of surplus production, cereals. However, these have been resisted in favour not only of changes in support prices and grant aid as outlined above but also changes in guidance as outlined below.

Guidance and socio-structural policies

In 1985 the EC agreed to a new agricultural structures policy (797/85) which until then had been concentrated on the Less Favoured Areas (LFAs) and on retirement schemes. The new policy covered six areas: (i) investment aids to diversify agricultural holdings and provide help for young farmers; (ii) specific measures for mountain and hill farming; (iii) allowing national funds to help set up Environmentally Sensitive Areas (ESAs) (see a later section for more detail); (iv) encouraging forestry on agricultural holdings; (v) vocational training; and (vi) other measures. In 1986 further proposals included a pre-pension scheme, measures to encourage less extensive farming (extensification), greater flexibility for setting Compensatory Allowances, Community Premia for ESAs, and help with training and marketing for diversification into tourism and craft industries.

The main aims of the new structure policy were to help farmers adapt to the new market situation, to achieve a better balance between supply and demand, to support farming, to contribute to the conservation of the environment and the preservation of the countryside. Initial reactions were that the new policy tried to do too much with too few resources and without enough integration (H.L. 242 (85–86)).

In the UK at the same time, the Agricultural Holdings Act 1984 made it easier to set up lifetime tenancies in order to encourage the letting of farm land. More fundamentally, the Farmland and Rural Development Act 1988 provided the necessary legislation for the introduction of both diversification aids and the Farm Woodland Scheme (see the section on forestry policy for details).

Under the diversification schemes (S.I.s 1948, 1949 and 1950/87 and 1125/88) both capital and non-capital grants can be paid to farmers investing in diversification of their business to non-agricultural enterprises. This includes: the processing of farm produce; farm accommodation; recreational activities; and pick-your-own schemes. Grants can be paid for training and market research as well as providing facilities. The Agricultural Training Board Act 1987 also allowed the Agricultural Training Board to add diversification to its training schemes. In the first two full years of the scheme, 1 January 1988 to 31 December 1989 more than 1500 grants were made totalling over £2 million, but the National Audit Office found that many grants had been given either to marginal projects or conversely to schemes that would be profitable even without the grant (H.C. 105 (89–90)). Accordingly, in January 1991 grants for tourism, which were often viable without grant aid and were also found to produce the lowest rate of return at around 10%, compared with 20–30% for other projects, were withdrawn from the scheme.

Other structural changes in the 1980s included an extension of the UKs LFAs by 1.2 million hectares in 1984 to 8 million hectares, and an application in 1989 to extend the areas by a further 95,000 hectares. LFAs were given a further boost in February 1991 with an average increase in payments of 14%. Finally in a move to cut government expenditure on agriculture, from 1986 ADAS was increasingly able to charge for services, except for diversification and conservation advice, and in 1990 the Government announced that the Farm and Countryside Service within ADAS should become a privatized agency if at all possible by April 1992, alongside the Soil Survey which had lost much of its public funding during the 1980s.

The EC review of the socio-structural funds in the mid-1980s also led to the creation of extensification programmes.

Extensification/setaside

One of the main planks of the revised socio-structural policy was the adoption of a setaside policy as employed in the USA since the 1930s. An extensification regulation (1760/87) was passed in 1987 to operate between 1986 and 1992. The aim of the scheme is to cut production by 20% for cereals and beef and sheep.

In the UK the regulation was implemented first of all by a setaside scheme (S.I. 1352/8) under which a farmer has to setaside at least 20% of his arable land for five years in return for the following payments.

| | £ per hectare | |
	Non-LFA land	LFA land
Type of setaside		
Permanent fallow	200 (222)	180 (202)
Rotational fallow	180 (202)	160 (182)
Woodland setaside only	200	180
Woodland with farm woodland scheme	190	150*
Non-agricultural use excluding residential retail or industrial use	150	130

* 100 in severely disadvantaged areas; () new rates for third year 1990–1991.

In seven counties in Eastern England the Countryside Commission set up a Countryside Premium Scheme in 1989 topping up the payments for five environmental options, for example, creating native meadowland (£120 per hectare) or wooded margins (£85 per hectare). By September 1989 123 farmers had taken up the premium scheme covering 3641 hectares, and in 1990 some environmental benefit payments were added to the national scheme.

In the first three years of setaside, 132,000 hectares, a tiny amount compared with the 20% target, was setaside, the vast majority to permanent fallow. Polls for *Farmers Weekly* showed the scheme to be unpopular with more support either for quotas or for a return to the free market. To most commentators the scheme only represented a toe-in-the-water (H.L. 65 (87–88)).

Setaside is an extreme version of the overall extensification scheme. However, proposals to implement extensification in the UK have come after setaside and only in July 1990 were 100 beef and sheep farmers invited to take part in a pilot extensification scheme. Under the scheme, payments of £55 per head for beef and £14 per head for sheep are paid to those farmers reducing sales by between 20 and 70% for five years, and agreeing to maintain environmental factors such as moorland on their farms.

Meanwhile, also in July 1990, the EC proposed broadening the extensification scheme to include measures for cutting the use of fertilizers, pesticides, and insecticides, extending setaside payments from 5 to 20 years, increasing setaside payments by up to £70 per hectare, and adding an organic farming regulation as part of the extensification package.

Environmental programmes

During the debate over the draft socio-structural regulations in the early 1980s much emphasis was placed on the need for them to contain environments as well as socio-economic measures (H.C. 247 (83-84)). At the same time a crisis over the proposed draining and possible ploughing up of the Halvergate marshes in the Norfolk Broads led to the introduction of the Broads Livestock Grant Scheme in 1985. In return for maintaining low input farming, farmers were paid a flat payment of around £120 per hectare. This scheme was used as a model by the UK Government when it successfully proposed that ESAs should be included in the new structures regulation.

Eleven ESAs have been designated in England and Wales and five in Scotland. Typical payments range from £35 to £200 per hectare for agreeing to comply with the management programme set out for each ESA. For example, keeping to low grazing rates, only applying limited amounts of fertilizer, or not cutting key meadows until wild flowers have set their seeds. However, the ESAs so far designated only cover a fraction of those originally proposed by the NCC and Countryside Commission in 1985. Within the existing ESAs the take up has been good with around 110,000 hectares or over 80% of the potential area now covered by agreements.

Another environmental programme relating to agriculture dates back to a 1980 EC Directive (80/778) which limits the amount of nitrate in drinking water to 50 mg/litre. In 1988 the Commission in a draft directive (4136/89 COM (88) 708) proposed the designation of vulnerable zones in which action to reduce nitrates would be taken by curbing intensive agricultural activity. In an attempt to influence the debate the UK has set up an alternative Nitrate Sensitive Areas (NSA) Scheme, since if the EC directive were to be implemented it could mean the loss of between 49 and 73% of all arable land in the drier parts of the UK (H.L. 73 (88–89)). In June 1990 ten NSAs were set up in which nitrogen use has to be limited and arable land converted to unfertilized ungrazed grassland in return for payments ranging from £55 to £380 per hectare. In the first year of the scheme 52% of potential land was put into the scheme. In another nine areas, advice only is given on reducing nitrogen use as a control experiment.

Other environmental programmes relating to the EC or the UK's ALURE (Alternative Land Use and Rural Economy) package notably grants for woodland and forestry are considered below.

Forestry policy

This section is divided into two parts which consider UK forestry policy as it evolved throughout the 1980s and attempts to create an EC forestry policy.

UK forestry policy 1980–1990

The Forestry Act 1981 set in motion a policy to sell off state forests in order to raise cash for the Treasury. However, in 1984 the programme was scaled down, after much criticism (H.C. 233 (84–85)) and its aim was revised to one of rationalizing the Forestry Commission's estate. In 1989, when 140,000 hectares of both forested (72,000 hectare) and bare land had been sold, a new target of a further 100,000 hectares to be sold by the end of the century was set. However, from November 1990 all sales whenever feasible had to be made subject to access agreements with local authorities.

Other changes in the decade included several changes to grant schemes, taxation policy, and to where planting should take place. In 1981 the Basis II Dedication Scheme was closed to new entrants and a new scheme, the Forestry Grant Scheme introduced, with payments as in Table 3.3. In 1985 the payments were increased as shown in parentheses, and a new scheme was designed to maintain and create broadleaved woods. The Broadleaved Woodland Grant Scheme was instituted with the payments, payable by instalment, varying from £1200 per hectare for small woodlands below 1 hectare to £600 per hectare for woodlands above 10 hectares.

Table 3.3. Forestry Grant Scheme 1981.

Area of wood (ha)	£/Hectare	
	Conifers	Broadleaved
0.25–0.9	600(630)	850(890)
1.0–2.9	480(505)	700(735)
3.0–9.9	400(420)	600(630)
10.0 and over	230(240)	450(470)

In 1986 the abolition of Capital Transfer Tax and the introduction of Inheritance Tax meant that lifetime transfers of farmland or forestry are taxed on a sliding scale depending on how long the donor survives. The full rate of tax is paid in the first three years, but then reduces in stages to no tax being paid if the donor survives seven years.

In 1987 in a bid to counter criticism of the Regional Advisory Committee system the Government decided to advertise proposals referred to them, inviting the public to assist them in making their decision.

Three major changes occurred in 1988. First, in the budget tax relief (Schedule B) on commercial woodland was abolished thus ending the tax incentive for rich individuals to plant up land. At the same time a reduction in the top rate of tax from 60% to 40% reduced the attraction of forestry as a long-term tax avoidance measure. Second, the target rate of planting was confirmed at 33,000 hectares a year to be provided mainly by the private sector and almost exclusively in Scotland and Wales. In England approval for forestry would no longer be given in upland areas above 800 feet except in those small areas where it would be environmentally acceptable as in the industrial Pennines. Afforestation of surplus farmland would, however, be acceptable, and in 1989 the threshold for consultation with MAFF over such afforestation was raised to 40 hectares. Third, a new grant scheme, the Woodland Grant Scheme (WGS) replaced both the Forestry Grant Scheme and the Broadleaved Woodland Grant Scheme. The much increased rates of this scheme offset the tax losses of the budget as shown in Table 3.4.

Table 3.4. Woodland Grant Scheme 1988 (£ per hectare).

Area approved for planting or regeneration (ha)	Conifer	Broadleaved
0.25–0.9	1005	1575
1.0–2.9	880(505)	1375(1375)
3.0–9.9	795(420)	1175(1175)
10.0 and over	615(240)	975(975)

Figures in parentheses are for the Farm Woodland Scheme.
Note: In December 1990 the supplements for planting on better land (arable or cultivated grassland) were increased from £200 per hectare to £400 per hectare for conifers and £600 per hectare for broadleaves.

In the first nine months of the scheme applications for new planting were made for 34,000 hectares, well above the target rate, of 33,000 hectares per year for all planting.

Also in 1988 a totally new scheme, the Farm Woodland Scheme limited to 36,000 hectares over three years was set up, with the aim of diverting farmland out of surplus production. Grants under the scheme are extra to the WGS and are intended to bridge the gap between planting and harvesting. For example, 40 years for oak, but only 20 years for conifers and 10 years for coppice, at the rates given in Table 3.5.

Take up of the scheme has been below the target rate, which is perhaps why in July 1990 a further £5 million scheme, the Woodland Management

Table 3.5. Farm Woodland Scheme, 1988 (£ per hectare).

Conversion from	Lowlands	Less Favoured Areas Disadvantaged	Severely disadvantaged
Arable land or improved grassland	190	150	100
Unimproved grassland or rough grazings	—	30	30

Grants Scheme was announced to take effect from April 1992 with the first payments on a retrospective basis to be made in 1993. Payments under the scheme intended to improve management and subject to the approval of a management plan are as in Table 3.6.

Also for the future, the Scottish Development Department has urged the Scottish regions to prepare indicative forestry strategies by dividing their regions into areas where forestry would be preferred, potentially acceptable or sensitive areas where the pressure for new planting should be eased. In England meanwhile the Countryside Commission has proposed the creation of a new Midlands forest covering 150 square miles, between Leicester and Burton upon Trent and twelve Community forests in urban fringe areas, covering 400,000 hectares.

Finally in March 1991 the Government announced that the Forestry Commission would be reorganized internally to take account of its enhanced environmental role in lowland forestry.

Table 3.6. The Woodland Management Grants Scheme, 1990.

Type of grant	Period of eligibility (age of wood in years)	Rate of grant (£/ha per annum)
Standard Management Grant		
Conifer	11–20	10
Broadleaved	11–40	25
Special Management Grant for woods of particular environmental value	11 onwards	35
Support for small woods (less than 10 hectares)		
Standard conifer	11–20	5
Standard broadleaved	11–40	10
Special management grant	11 onwards	10

EC forestry policy

In 1978 the EC proposed a Community forestry policy with three main objectives: (i) a sustainable increase in the economic production of timber; (ii) conservation and improvement of the environment; (iii) public access for recreation. By 1988 (10753 8415/88 COM (88) 255) these had grown to eight objectives including the addition of encouraging the development of rural life.

In 1989 when the policy was finally agreed the main aims of the new forestry policy were to mop up surplus farm land via afforestation, to provide alternative employment by improving existing forests, and to act as an attractive background for recreation. Between 1988 and 1992 £105 million was allocated for afforestation and £293 million for improvements to existing woods. Most of the UK share of this money was diverted to help pay for the Woodland Grant and Farm Woodland Schemes.

Land use planning

For land use planning the *Zeitgeist* of the 1980s were deregulation, simplification and relaxation. However, the rhetoric never really matched the reality and at the end of the decade land use planning in its essential principles looked remarkably like it had done in 1980.

Rhetoric was provided in four white papers. At the outset Command 7634 in 1979 promised to remove a mass of minor central government controls over planning, and this was continued in both Command 9501 (1985) and Command 9794 (1986). These two papers with their tell-tale titles of 'Lifting the Burden' and 'Building Businesses not Barriers' outlined proposals for reducing planning control, simplifying procedures, striving for greater efficiency and speed in decision making, and taking a positive approach. Most of the proposals were urban orientated, however, but in the last of the sequence, Command 512 (1988) 'Releasing Enterprise' the idea of giving permitted development rights for a number of environmentally acceptable uses of open land and existing buildings compatible with rural areas, as an aid to diversifying the rural economy was floated. An idea which was followed up in July 1989 in a consultation paper on 'Efficient Planning' from the DOE.

Although many of the proposals were enacted by the three main planning Acts of the decade most of the changes were relatively minor. In more detail, the only really major Act of the decade, the Local Government Planning and Land Act 1980, removed from county councils virtually all controls over the local plan and development control work of district councils. Other changes were largely procedural in nature and transferred planning functions from one organization to another. Similarly, the Housing and Planning Act 1986 provided legislation for the introduction of Simplified

Planning Zones as the only major change, but otherwise transferred controls, for example, control over opencast coal mining to mineral planning authorities.

The third main act The Town and Country Planning Act 1990 was largely a consolidating Act, bringing together all the changes made since 1971, but removing legislation on Listed Buildings and Conservation Areas to a separate Act.

Apart from legislation, the decade also saw the adoption by the DOE of the Scottish system of planning guidelines with a series of 15 Planning Policy Guidance Notes. The most relevant for rural areas were; (1) General Policy and Principles; (2) Green Belts; (3) Land for Housing; (7) Rural enterprise and development; (12) Local Plans; and (15) Regional planning guidance, structure plans and development plans. A series of notes on minerals planning was also issued.

In 1989 and 1990 a series of consultation papers were published proposing changes in policy. For example, in a proposed revision to Note 3 proposals were made to allow modest releases of land for low-cost housing in villages and also to give permission for the creation of new villages of between 200 and 4000 dwellings, although this latter idea was said to have died a death with the return of Michael Heseltine as Secretary of State for the Environment in November 1990, and the collapse of Consortium Developments in early 1991. Note 3 was followed in November 1989 by a draft replacement for Note 7, retitled 'The Countryside and the Rural Economy' which further emphasized the need to find new uses for old buildings in order to help the rural economy, but still reiterated the traditional role for planning of balancing the needs of development and conservation.

Plan making

With regard to more specific matters the 1980s saw virtually no real changes to plan making. A series of DOE circulars, 23/81, 22/84, and 24/87 updated and modified advice, and in particular reduced the role of structure plans and enhanced the role of local plans . In Scotland a similar attack on strategic planning saw the demise of the statutory regional report in 1982.

Dissatisfaction with over-long and complex structure plans led the Government in 1986 to issue a consultation paper proposing their end. This was followed in 1989 by a White Paper (569) on 'The Future of Development Plans'. This contained the key proposal to replace the two-tier system of plan making with a one-tier district-based system. The counties would retain a strategic role via new statements of county planning policies dealing with key issues but excluding agriculture. The main feature of the new system, however, would be single-tier district wide development plans at the district level. The National Parks would prepare both a county-type statement and an area-wide development plan.

In the absence of any legislation to implement the proposals, the DOE issued a draft revision of the Planning and Policy Guidance Note (15) on plan making in November 1989 asking counties to continue updating structure plans but in a more concise way focusing only on key issues. At the same time the draft note promised greater regional guidance in the form of the new series of regional guidance notes already in existence for metropolitan areas.

In September 1990 structure plans were reprieved but with self-adoption in line with local plans after an Examination in Public, subject to reserve powers of call-in by the DOE. Provisions for these changes were made in the Planning and Compensation Bill 1990/91, which also included provisions for area-wide District and National Park Local Plans. However, all these proposals were thrown into confusion when in March 1991 the Poll Tax debacle threw the whole future of local government into disarray, with the potential for some areas to have county councils only, other areas to have district councils only, and other areas to have both types of council.

Development control

The mood of relaxation also permeated development control throughout the 1980s. At the outset DOE Circular 22/80 asked local authorities to pay a greater regard to time and efficiency and always to grant planning permission unless there are sound and clear cut reasons for refusal. However, these reasons still included the need to protect landscapes and good agricultural land. In 1981 a revision to the General Development Order (GDO) (S.I.s 245 and 246/81) continued the theme by relaxing controls in a minor way, but not in the National Parks, AONBs and conservation areas, and introducing to some extent a two-tier planning system. This was reinforced in 1986 with a special order (S.I. 1176/86) which allowed planners in all the National Parks and some adjoining land to have a limited form of control over the design siting and appearance of farm and forestry roads and buildings elsewhere exempted from control. It did not, however, include power to prevent a construction, only power over its detailed design and siting.

In 1988 a consolidation of the GDO (DOE Circular 22/88) made two main changes for rural areas. First, planners no longer had to consult with MAFF over proposals involving the loss of more than 4 hectares of farmland. This was replaced with a requirement to consult only where proposals for development involve the loss of at least 20 hectares and then only on Grade 1, 2 or 3a land. Second, farm buildings, livestock buildings and associated buildings such as slurry tanks ceased to be permitted development if they are built within 400 metres of buildings occupied by people. A number of other changes were also made, including removing the right of highway authorities to make decisions over developments along classified roads, and removing stone cladding from permitted development in conservation areas. Finally, in 1987 the Use Classes Order was also updated and consolidated.

For rural areas the only change was a general one of making it easier to change from one use to another by collapsing the number of classes.

Other changes in the 1980s included a simplification of the planning inquiry system and more devolution of decision making to inspectors. In a move which could pave the way to privatize development controls, fees for planning applications were imposed in 1981. Initially set at £40 per house they had risen to £76 in 1989, and in July 1990 the Government announced that they would rise by 20% in November 1990 in a bid to increase their contribution from 50% to 100% of the costs of development control.

Another change was provided by the introduction of Simplified Planning Zones in the Housing and Planning Act 1986. In these zones, permission can be granted in advance for a wider range of developments, but DOE Circular 25/87 reminded local planning authorities that they cannot be used in National Parks, green belts, SSSIs or in conservation areas. Any individual in an ordinary rural area can, however, request an authority to declare a zone.

Finally, proposals at the end of the decade included, in May 1989, a consultation paper from the DOE which suggested relaxing planning control over a mass of rural activities related to farm diversification. After a large amount of adverse reaction, the paper on 'permitted uses in the countryside' was withdrawn in October 1989. In Scotland, by contrast, proposals to increase rural planning controls have been accepted, notably over farm buildings greater than $465 \, m^2$ housing pigs or poultry (S.I. 977/88) and over fresh water fish farming in 1990 (S.I. 508/90), with further controls being proposed in August 1990.

Specific planning issues

The most controversial planning issue of the decade concerned land for housing, and the Government twice made proposals for a major relaxation of planning controls only to be defeated by an alliance of its own supporters and other groups. At the beginning of the decade, DOE Circular 9/80 set the tone by calling on local authorities to maintain a five-year supply of housing land in their plans. This advice was continued in Circular 15/84 and expanded to include proposals for limited extensions to villages and provision for new settlements in structure plans. But this was a much watered down version of a previous draft circular.

A second attempt at providing a more relaxed regime was made in 1986 and 1987 when a draft circular proposed removing the need to protect agricultural land from planning advice. However, after much lobbying, mainly from Tories resident in rural areas, the advice in Circular 16/87 on 'Development Involving Agricultural Land' began by arguing that in the light of farm surpluses and the need to diversify the rural economy there was no longer such a need to protect farmland. Nonetheless, the quality of land

and the need to control the rate at which land is developed remained factors for planners to consider, and in a subtle but important change the Circular advised on the need to protect the countryside for its own sake rather than primarily for the productive value of the land.

Thus rural land continued to be protected from development but for wider reasons than before. This was confirmed in 1989, when Circular 18/89 invoked powers under the Local Government, Planning and Land Act 1980 forcing local authorities to compile annual registers of unused or underused land held by local authorities and other public bodies, in a bid to divert land development pressures from rural areas into inner city sites.

Related to the land for housing issue was the future of green belt land, the area of which had grown enormously via the process of structure plan preparation in the 1970s and 1980s. In 1984 after a draft circular had attempted to weaken green belt controls, a new circular 14/84, the first since 1957, reaffirmed a strong commitment to their preservation and a new commitment to their improvement via land management.

However, the green belts, in the absence of major regional policies, only serve to divert development pressures a little bit further afield, and in the 1980s an alliance of builders loosely titled Consortium Developments announced plans to apply for planning permission for a series of 12 small new towns in the south east. At the time of writing, three of these had reached the public inquiry stage and all had been turned down; Tillingham Hill, Essex (1987), Stone Bassett, Oxon (1989) and Foxley Wood, Hants (1989). The pressures still remain, however, and in 1988 SERPLAN was forced to raise its housing forecasts for the 1990s from 460,000 to 560,000–580,000.

Cherry (1988), a past president of the RTPI, has argued that six themes relevant to planning stood out in the 1980s. First, a reversal of the population and economic growth of the post-war decades; second, continued decentralization; third, a continuation of the north – south divide; fourth, the growth of environmentalism; fifth, the retention of a planning system based on state power rather than market forces in direct contradiction of the New Right philosophy of Mrs Thatcher; and sixth, the emergence of new styles of planning where partnerships between planners, the private sector and citizen groups were actively encouraged so that planning became more a facilitator of development and so, as the catch-phrases of the 1980s put it, planning 'made things happen' and 'managed change'.

In conclusion, to some extent the 1980s was a phoney war in which various attempts to allow more development in the countryside were frustrated by an alliance of existing residents and rural campaigners. This alliance replaced the traditional agricultural lobby who gradually shifted their view away from food production to diversification. At the same time there was also a polarization between those who argued for a planning system designed to protect the environment and those who argued for a planning system designed to plan for people, notably the disadvantaged people increasingly being priced out of rural housing by restrictive planning policies. It is to these topics that attention is now turned.

Social and economic policies

In the 1980s there were significant changes in each of the three main socio-economic areas, housing, transport, and employment.

Housing

In the housing field two main issues dominated the decade, council house sales and homes for locals. At the outset the Housing Act 1980 gave tenants the right to buy council homes at a substantial discount. In 'Designated Rural Areas', however, restrictions are imposed restricting subsequent resale to either local people or back to the local authority. Subsequent Acts, for example, the Housing and Building Control Act 1984 extended and enhanced the right to buy provisions for tenants, but critics remained sceptical that the provisions would do anything more than gentrify the countryside and produce an underclass of poorly housed rural people (H.C. 366–I, –II and –III (80–81)).

In a move to shift the remaining rented tenure from the public to the private sector a series of Acts, culminating with the Housing Act 1988 provided powers to make private renting more attractive for landlords, notably by introducing an assured shorthold tenancy for short lets.

The net effect of the changes was to create three rental sectors. A small healthy private sector for the mobile employed, a heavily regulated housing association sector dependent on public subsidy and a residual local authority sector for the worst off.

The second main issue of the 1980s was that of local need for this residual population. Attempts to provide for local need via plan making were effectively scotched by the DOE's refusal in 1981 to accept a locals-only policy in the Lake District Structure Plan, arguing that planning is concerned with land use not the identity or merits of people.

However, in a series of attempts to ameliorate growing hardship the Government issued a number of statements and policy proposals in the late 1980s proposing the use of covenants or conditions on planning permissions for housing locals that would not otherwise be given permission and at the same time would not count against planned housing provisions in approved plans. Other measures in the Local Government Act 1988 (DOE Circular 12/88) allowed 30% subsidies for the building of rented houses for locals only.

Other changes included a rapid expansion of the special rural housing programme funded via the Housing Corporation from 300 houses in 1989/90 to 1500 by 1991/92. The 1989 budget also allowed charitable donations of land for local housing need to be taxed only on the value of the land as disposed and not on its potential value as building land. Finally, the introduction of the Poll Tax radically changed the tax position of short lets and second homes, but its demise in March 1991 opened up all sorts of uncertainties for rural housing.

Transport

Some radical changes to rural transport were made during the 1980s but only in the methods of control and subsidy. The underlying problem of providing transport for a scattered low density population remained as intractable as ever. Controls over public transport were first relaxed in the Transport Act 1980 which abolished the need for licences for express services (intercity) and also provided for the designation of trial areas in which local stage services would also be deregulated. Following a series of White Papers and reports on the issue (Command 9300 and 9561, 1984 and 1985 and H.C. 38-I, –II, and –III (84–85)), the Transport Act 1985 abolished the licensing of all bus services from 1986, and also further deregulated the use of minibuses and taxis. Transitional grants were made available in order to fund rural buses for a few years, and County Councils were given powers to subsidize rural services where no services were provided by the private sector. In spite of much despondancy at the time there has apparently been little change in the provision of rural transport although little work has been done on the subject. In June 1990 the Transport Minister said that since deregulation, bus mileage outside the big cities had increased by some 21% with 83% being run commercially.

Employment

One of the severest attacks on central planning by the Thatcher Government was mounted on employment planning. At the outset the Regional Economic Planning Councils were abolished, swiftly followed by a reduction in the Assisted Areas from 40% to 25% of the country between 1979 and 1982. Ironically, many of the remaining areas in a further change in November 1984 were rural regions in South West England, Wales and Scotland. A further change was the suspension of Industrial Development Certificates in 1981.

In the mid 1980s the remaining regional policies were revised to be more selective and targeted on jobs provision and social factors (Command 9111, 1983). Planning advice was also reshaped in three Circulars (16/84, 1/85, 14/85) urging planners to be as flexible as possible in granting planning permission for employment-generating projects in rural areas.

Finally, in 1988 the automatic right to grant aid in an Assisted Area was removed by the Regional Development Grants (Termination) Act 1988 (Command 278, 1988) and aid targeted on those companies who can show that they genuinely need grant aid.

Conversely, while general aid for employment was being severely restricted in the 1980s, the Development Commission and COSIRA were given a new lease of life. In 1982 they were given greater freedom to carry out their work and in 1984 they were given grant-in-aid body status. Also in 1984 they replaced the Special Investment Areas with Rural Development Areas, albeit convering both a smaller area and population. In 1988 the two bodies were merged to form a stronger Rural Development Commission. Throughout the decade a stream of innovative grant and other schemes came forward from the Commission in a bid to help the restructuring of the rural economy. However, in January 1991, the Government announced that the Commission's workshops were to be sold off to the private sector between 1991 and 1994, thus striking a damaging blow to its capacity to aid rural economies.

To some extent this blow was offset by the 1987 decision of the European Commission to double all three Structural Funds from 7400 million ECU to 13,000 million ECU between 1987 and 1992 ((9805) 8251 (87) COM (87) 376). The main aim of this increased funding was to help not only the less developed (usually rural) regions but also the adjustment of agricultural structures, and also to remind everyone that the EC was more than the CAP (H.L. 82 (87–88)). Unfortunately, most of the aid is related to the Assisted Areas which the Government had much reduced in size earlier in the decade, thus shooting itself in the foot. However, from 1 January 1989, 24% of the UK, much of the Highlands and Lowlands of Scotland, parts of rural Wales and parts of Devon and Cornwall and south west Scotland became eligible for general support and also for specific support under objective 5b of the structural policy, the promotion of the development of rural areas. This support was therefore added to the support already available under the 1982 EC's Integrated Development Programme for the Western Isles.

Finally, in 1989 the Local Government and Housing Act clarified and simplified the powers available to local authorities for promoting the economic development of their areas (Command 433, 1988) largely via grant aid, although the imposition of poll tax capping will severely curtail any excessive spending plans.

Conservation and recreation

Without doubt the most important piece of legislation in the decade was the Wildlife and Countryside Act 1981 which signalled not only the use of the voluntary approach backed up by compensation or acquisition but also a move away from negative protection in island type reserves towards positive management in the wider countryside.

Conservation

Many of the measures in the 1981 Act were included in a Labour Bill of 1978, the Countryside Bill, but when this Bill was lost in 1979 at the general election, the Tories added all the provisions needed to implement EC Directive 79/409 on the conservation of wild birds. More significantly, the Tories changed the thrust of the Bill from control to persuasion. Conservation therefore ceased to be a matter of consensus but became one of party politics.

The crucial sections of the Act (sections 28 to 42) are those which deal with the measures which can be taken if conservation values are threatened by changes in land use, normally occasioned by the offer of a farm grant. In these cases, various authorities can offer farmers compensation via management agreements for not proceeding with the proposals backed up by the threat of compulsory purchase as a last resort (DOE Circular 24/82 and 4/83). Most of these provisions relate to designated areas like National Parks and in particular SSSIs.

Management agreements were also introduced into Scotland, as well as Regional Parks, a Scottish Concept, in the Countryside (Scotland) Act 1981.

Various loopholes in the main Act were closed in 1985 by two Acts, an Amendment and a Service of Notices Act, but the key issue of debate concerned the efficiency and morality of financial management agreements, especially when only 0.4% of the UK is covered by SSSI agreements and 1.0% by ESA agreements. Despite many calls for major revisions to this procedure (H.C. 6–I and –II (84–85)), the Government remained firmly committed to both the voluntary and financial principle (Command 9522, 1985). To some extent their resolve was made easier by the dismantling of farm capital grants throughout the 1980s, as already outlined, and a general slow down in farm activity. However, although 5283 SSSIs had been declared by 30 April 1990 representing a major advance from the 3329 in existence in 1981 claims by the Government that the 1981 Act had been a success still seemed largely hollow in the face of constant evidence from the NCC showing a continued decline in habitat and species.

A much more exciting proposal came at the end of the period with the introduction of a Countryside Stewardship Scheme. Under this Countryside Commission (CCP329) scheme which began in April 1991 land owners, farmers, or anybody controlling land can apply for annual payments, for up to 10 years, to manage their land for conservation purposes. The scheme is targeted at five landscape or habitat types and has an initial budget of £13.3 million, and 80,000 hectares in its three-year pilot period.

Elsewhere, much of the conservation scene spent a fairly quiet decade. The National Parks passed a scrutiny of their economic efficiency in 1984 and gradually acquired more independence notably in plan making from local authorities (Circular 27/85). Their funding increased above inflation and in 1988 they were allowed to top up farm capital grants by up to 80% of the cost if conservation benefits like stone walls were provided. Nonetheless a shortage of funds prompted the Lake District in 1988 to call for a tourist/visitor tax in order to supplement funding and to deter frivolous visits. Finally, the National Parks family acquired a new member in 1988 with the Broads, a new type of National Park responsible for nature conservation, public enjoyment, planning and controls over boating and navigation.

AONBs also acquired new members in the 1980s including Cranbourne Chase, the Howardian Hills and the High Weald. The designation of the 38th, the North Pennines in 1988 made history by being the largest and the first to be subjected to a public inquiry. In Scotland the National Scenic Areas were given more status with greater central control over certain planning applications, for example, those involving the development of more than five dwelling units.

In 1991 the policies for Heritage Coasts were given a boost by a revised statement on their protection by the Countryside Commission (CCP305) which argued that all the coasts should have a management plan by the year 2000, and be recognized by the DOE by being made the subject of a Planning Policy Guidance Note.

At the beginning of the decade the Ancient Monuments and Archaeological Areas Act 1979 and the National Heritage Act 1980 increased powers over the listing and protection of ancient monuments, and set up a National Heritage Fund with powers and money to buy land for the nation including beautiful scenery or land with a high nature conservation value. However, proposals made in 1986 to set up Landscape Conservation Orders in which harmful operations would have had to be submitted to National Park Authorities in key areas, who could have forbade them in return for compensation were dropped in 1988.

Just as the decade had begun with an EC inspired piece of legislation, so it ended in 1988 with an EC proposal (8149/88 COM (88) 381 final) for a directive on Habitat and Species Protection. The key proposal was to create a network of at least 100 protected areas to be known as 'Natura 2000' by the year 2000. Unfortunately this proposal failed to recognize the need to implement existing international agreements before embarking on others and also the growing need to conserve the wider countryside not just specific islands (H.L. 72 (88–89)).

Recreation

The decade saw very few developments in reaction policy. Initially the 1981 Act had downgraded largely ignored local authority powers to provide access to the countryside via footpaths. This encouraged a series of unsuccessful

Table 3.7. Central Government spending on countryside planning, actual and planned 1984–1993 (£ million).

	1984/85 Actual	1988/89 Actual	1992/93 Planned
Agriculture and forestry			
Net UK expenditure on EC schemes including intervention	1282	1050	1340
Net domestic expenditure	542	500	680
Forestry Commission	54	53	90
Total	1905	1632	2140
Environment and employment			
Rural Development Commission	19.8	24.3	26.9
Countryside Commission	12.7	21.1	26.8
Nature Conservancy Council	15.0	39.0	48.6
Broads Authority	0	0	1.1
Groundwork	n.a.	1.5	2.9
Total	47.5	85.9	106.3

Source: Command 1003 and 1008 (1990) *The Government's Expenditure Plans* HMSO London.
Note: In 1989/90 the DOE provided £9.06 million to cover 75% of the cost of National Parks.

private member's Bills in the 1980s calling for improved access to the countryside (H.C, 64 (81–82), H.C. 63 (83–84)). Eventually the Rights of Way Act 1990 clarified and improved the position but only with regard to the ploughing up or other disturbances of public paths by farmers and by giving local authorities the power to take direct action to restore a footpath and then to charge the farmer for the cost of the work.

In conclusion the 1980s promised to be a radical decade for rural planning and in some ways it was, but ultimately the rhetoric was more powerful than the reality, and in spite of calls for an even more radical fourth Thatcher term of office the expenditure plans for the main countryside planning agencies (Table 3.7) for 1992/93 look remarkably the same as they did for 1984/85. Agriculture retains the lion's share, and until there is a radical reform of the CAP, maybe via GATT it is hard to see any fundamental change.

It is far more likely that the soft underbelly of rural planning, all the small sums of money and minor controls, will continue to undergo change while the skeleton and the body go marching on. To see how true and how accepted this view is, the next and major part of this book presents a review of the policy proposals made by dozens of organizations culled by the author from over 1500 documents, articles and books.

Part Two

Policy Proposals by Subject Area

4 Policies for the Environment as a Whole

A growing number of people are coming to believe that only worldwide holistic policies can manage the environmental problems facing any one area. However, according to Brennan's (1988) book *Thinking about Nature*, there are inconsistencies in many of the current moral philosophies based on ecology and whereas Brennan concludes that lives worth living are lived in nature, he fails to provide a set of moral principles or practical guidelines for living such a life. A main task for the green movement in the 1990s must, therefore, be the formulation of a green philosophy, preceded by a thorough analysis of the issues.

Such an attempt to outline the range of issues and arguments for and against development has been provided by an interdisciplinary group of scientists, philosophers and planners (Attfield and Dell, 1989) under seven headings.

1. Economic arguments:
Economic arguments for development include: (i) it will create wealth for individuals and for society; (ii) it is necessary to keep society technically progressive and innovative; (iii) it will create jobs; (iv) it will increase agricultural yields; and (v) it will make the supply of food and raw materials cheaper or more secure.

Economic arguments against development include: (i) it will reduce property values by introducing undesirable land uses; (ii) it results in the overexploitation of common resources which are used up too fast; (iii) it pays no heed to the long-term cost of destroying resources; (iv) it benefits the wealthy at the expense of the poor; and (v) it ignores costs for the people of centuries to come.

2.   Social arguments:

Social arguments in favour of development include: (i) it will provide houses at reasonable prices; (ii) people have a right to develop their own property as they wish; (iii) it will reduce travel time and stress; (iv) it will enhance communication; (v) it will provide for the social needs of the majority; and (vi) environmentalism is an elitist activity whereas development benefits the whole of society.

Social arguments against development include; (i) it will reduce the value of the environment for human happiness; (ii) development tends to cater for the car-borne; (iii) it will destroy local community life; (iv) a sense of community is preserved by keeping settlements separated; and (v) concentration on material progress will destroy traditional human values.

3.   Psychological arguments:

Psychological arguments in favour of development include: (i) it will make work less tedious; (ii) progress is exciting; and (iii) people identify with a major project and take pleasure in its progress.

Psychological arguments against development include: (i) there is pleasure in enjoying the environment as it is; (ii) preserving the heritage is part of our identity; (iii) it will create a nuisance and therefore lead to illness and stress; and (iv) it will destroy the rhythms of nature, day–night and the seasons.

4.   Political arguments:

Political arguments for development include: (i) it is within our rights in a free society; and (ii) it is what the majority wants.

Political arguments against development include: (i) the majority does not want it; and (ii) inadequate procedures were employed.

5.   Biological arguments:

Biological arguments in favour of development include: (i) it promotes the breeding of more productive strains; (ii) technology can benefit wildlife; and (iii) it preserves existing species.

Biological arguments against development include: (i) the right of species other than humans to be considered; (ii) it will threaten the survival of a species/ecosystem or even the biosphere; (iii) piecemeal erosion may lead to wider damage; (iv) it will be cruel; and (v) preservation sometimes provides unforeseen benefits to future societies.

6.   Aesthetic arguments:

Aesthetic arguments in favour of development include: (i) it allows room for changes in taste; (ii) it is an improvement on the old; and (iii) it gives scope for creativity.

Aesthetic arguments against development include: (i) the inspirational value of unspoilt land and beautiful places; and (ii) it will destroy our heritage.

7. International arguments:

International arguments in favour of development include: (i) global productivity must be increased to feed a growing population; and (ii) industrial development is the only way to raise living standards.

International arguments against development include: (i) the need to reduce pollution of international waters; (ii) the need to prevent overgrazing leading to erosion elsewhere; (iii) the need to combat acid rain; (iv) the need to protect the tropical rain forest because of its global impact on climate; and (v) the need to keep atmospheric pollution within manageable proportions.

Various attempts have been made to coordinate these arguments into integrated environmental strategies, for example Dryzek's (1987) advocacy of a radically decentralized state based on practical reason. The rest of this chapter examines some of these attempts at the international and UK levels before examining some of the methods available for implementing the proposals, and then concludes with cautionary comments about the holistic approach.

Proposals for international environmental strategies

In addition to existing international environmental programmes for example the Montreal protocol on CFCs, major proposals for developing more ambitious and all-embracing measures have been made. Perhaps the best known and most authoritiative examples of the genre are the World Conservation Strategy (WCS) and the World Commission on Environment report on 'Our Common Future' (the Brundtland Report).

The WCS was launched in 1980 with three main objectives.

1. To maintain essential ecological processes and life-support systems.
2. To preserve genetic diversity.
3. To ensure the sustainable use by us and our children of species and ecosystems.

In the UK an amalgam of organizations and individuals used the WCS to produce a Conservation and Development Programme for the UK. This argued that if the objectives of the WCS were to be built upon and extended to the UK, action was required in three broad areas.

1. Integrating conservation of both living and non-living resources with development.
2. Developing a sustainable society in which both physical and psychological needs are fully met.
3. Developing a stable and sustainable economy through the practices of resource conservation in all spheres of activity.

In a separate report O'Riordan (1982) continues the theme of sustainability by putting forward two general principles.

1. Optimizing the use of countryside resources so that they will be permanently productive while minimizing external inputs and environmental damage.
2. Conserving visual beauty, protecting yesterday's heritage and creating tomorrow's heritage to give people a sense of belonging and identity, and the opportunity to live satisfying and fully occupied lives.

O'Riordan then proposes a number of recommended courses of action to achieve these principles, notably: maintaining sustainable utilization, integrating conservation values with resource use; reconciling productive sustainability with the protection of heritage values; incorporating community enterprise; and providing education for countryside care.

In more detail O'Riordan also proposes a threefold classification of the countryside into heritage sites (10%), conservation zones (20%) and agricultural and forestry landscapes (70%), and a quinquennial review of all major rural-resource requirements.

However, in their response to the WCS the UK Government (Environment, 1986a) ruled out any radical changes in policy claiming rather optimistically that the philosophy of the WCS had already been applied in the UK.

In a further development of the WCS the World Commission on Environment and Development (1987), a United Nations organization consisting of 23 commissioners drawn from all parts of the world, has set out a series of principles for the year 2000. These are based on the fundamental principle of sustainable development and Principle 1 of the 1972 Stockholm Declaration: 'Man has the fundamental right to freedom, equality and adequate conditions of life in an environment of a quality that permits a life of dignity and well-being.'

After a review of the global situation the Commission declared that individuals and states had reciprocal rights and responsibilities if both sustainable development and quality of life were to be achieved together. In more detail the commissioners recommended the implementation of measures to:

- maintain ecosystems and related ecological processes essential for the functioning of the biosphere
- maintain biological diversity by ensuring the survival of all species of flora and fauna in their natural habitats
- observe the principle of optimum sustainable yield in the exploitation of living natural resources and ecosystems
- prevent or abate significant environmental pollution or harm
- establish adequate environmental protection standards

- undertake or require prior assessments to ensure that major new policies, projects and technologies contribute to sustainable development.

In order to prevent their report becoming another worthy tome like the WCS the Commission called on the UN to transfer the report into a UN programme of Action for Sustainable Development, with a set of 22 legal principles, in order to achieve the changes in attitudes needed and a reorientation of policies and institutions.

In their response to the 'Brundtland report' the UK Government (Environment, 1988a) did not announce any new policies but reaffirmed their 1986 commitment not only to sustainable development but also to the 'polluter-pays principle' and the concept of the 'Best practicable environmental option'.

However, to deep ecologists or really radical thinkers these reports are cosmetic and Redclift (1984) a Marxist environmental scientist has argued that: 'It is an illusion to believe that environmental objectives are other than political or other than redistributive' (p. 130). The challenge thus is not to protect the natural environment from humans but to alter the global economy in which our appetites press on the 'outer limits' of resources. This can only be done by giving the people of the Third World a greater share of the world's resources, and thus the developed world a smaller share. If this is to be achieved, however, there will need to be a massive shift of public opinion in the developed world including the UK. Attention is thus now directed to the UK.

UK proposals for holistic environmental strategies

At the heart of most radical environmental policies one will find proposals for the de-industrialization and decentralization of society. This is not a new concept, for example, William Moriss' 'Arts and Crafts Movement' at the end of the 19th century. In the 20th century, however, much inspiration has come from Kropotkin's (1912) classic view of a society which combines labour-intensive agriculture and small-scale industry both producing for local needs. In a decentralized pattern of settlement the division of labour would be replaced by the integration of brain work and manual work.

Kropotkin advocated such a society largely because he was an anarchist, but also because of the inhumane conditions existing in factories at the turn of the century. Today the imperative for change comes from the growing realization that the world's resources of energy and raw materials are finite. Therefore, instead of converting self-sustaining communities in the Third World into horrendous industrializing slum cities, the developed world it is argued should begin to reverse the process of industrialization if the planet is to survive.

Table 4.1. Deep ecology contrasted with modernism.

Modernism	Deep ecology
Domination over nature	Harmony with nature
Nature a resource; intrinsic value confined to humans	Natural environment valued for itself
Human supremacy	Biocentric egalitarianism
Ample resources/substitutes	Earth supplies limited
Material economic growth a predominant goal	Non-material goods especially self-realization
Consumerism	Doing with enough/recycling
Competitive lifestyle	Cooperative lifeway
Centralized/urban centred	Decentralized/bioregional
National focus	Neighbourhood focus
Power structure hierarchical	Non-hierarchical/grass roots democracy
High technology	Appropriate technology

Source: Sylvan and Bennett in Goldsmith (1988, p. 149).

Examples of such movements are, however, rather isolated. One can cite the Dartington Hall experiment begun in the 1920s, the Kibbutzim system in Israel developed after the Second World War, and the Town and Country Planning Association's Lightmoor experiment. As a transition phase, however, Kropotkin's vision of small self-governing societies could be adapted as shown below:

More stress on	**Less stress on**
Intrinsic satisfaction of work	Maximum consumption
Durable artefacts	Inbuilt obsolescence
Craft apprenticeships	Activity rates
Quality of environment	Increase in GNP
Balanced community	Physical mobility
Devolution of government	(Alleged) Economies of scale

A more detailed and updated version of Kropotkin's alternative view of life is provided by Sylvan and Bennett in Goldsmith's (1988) edited collection of essays on rethinking man's relationship with nature as shown in Table 4.1.

Elsewhere in the same volume Goldsmith (1988), co-editor of the *Ecologist*, and a true radical, has attacked the most pernicious myth ever entertained by man – that of modernism. According to this myth the world is imperfect, random, chaotic and aggressive. Man's natural role is thus to transform this chaotic world via science, technology, industry and the various institutions of the Nation State to bring about the miraculous process called 'economic development' or 'progress'. According to Goldsmith this man-centred view of the world is ultimately self-defeating. This is because it destroys the biosphere, by consuming its resources, and polluting what is left and replaces it with an unsustainable technosphere, it does not matter if this is done by capitalism or by any other political process including Marxism, because the end result is the same.

Current policies which seem to ameliorate this process are, according to Goldsmith, equally self-defeating since they still subscribe to the myth of exploiting the biosphere. The only solution is truly radical and is to abandon modernism in favour of creating a new society that is structurally and cognitively geared to the achievement of a very different goal from that of the society we live in today: Goldsmith (1988) in a separate text therefore advocates a six-stage return to primitive self-regulating communities in which ecology is paramount. Key stages of this return involve the phasing out of labour-saving processes, the withdrawal of consumer products, the decentralization of society, a return to family and community groupings, and the adoption of appropriate technology. In essence this means building up our biological, social and ecological wealth, the only wealth that satisfies the real needs of living things, including humans. It also means accepting the principle of 'Gaia' in which the earth is seen as a cybernetic system capable of acting as a single unit for the purpose of maintaining its stability in the face of environmental challenges.

This view of 'Gaia' has been created by Lovelock (1979, 1988) a renegade scientist in a brilliant and radical view of the planet Earth as a living self-correcting organism. According to this view humans are but a small part of this greater system. As such, there can be no prescription, no set of rules, for living within Gaia, only an acceptance of the fact that to our different actions there are only consequences. However, this does not prevent Lovelock from painting his vision of a 'Jerusalem' England in contrast to the dark satanic millscape created by modern agriculture, which is likened to ecocide.

In this vision there would be a return to small densely populated cities, never too big, so that the countryside was only a walk or bus ride away. At least one-third of the land would revert to natural woodland and heath, about half of this land would be open for recreation but the rest should be left to nature. Farming would be a mixture of intensive production where it was fit to be and small unsubsidized farms for those with the vocation of living in harmony with the land.

If, however, we continue our present ways, Gaia will strike back, because though she is not anti-human, she is against any force which threatens her. As an example of such a reaction Lovelock asks us to think how we would feel if we drilled for blood through our skins in the way we drill for oil through the skin of the earth. The blame for this type of action is placed by two ecologists (Goldsmith and Hildyard, 1986) on the cock-eyed view of economists who seek to maximize short-term returns while not costing in the so-called free environmental goods, air, water and climate.

These arguments are, however, those of individuals, and although persuasive they have no political authority in their own right. More overtly political statements have been provided by Porritt and Winner (1988), the well-known environmentalist and a journalist, in a popular book tracing the coming of the 'Greens'. In this they agree that the 1980s witnessed a remarkable greening of all walks of life, albeit at a superficial level. For example, all political parties at various times throughout the 1980s espoused green issues at least rhetorically, although they still saw economic growth as the only way of solving them. Nonetheless, to Porritt and Winner this was an important first step onto a long road, significant because the road had at least been stepped onto. For the future, Porritt and Winner believe that a mass movement to green policies can only arise via individuals gradually acting in a more green way and then demanding that politicians impose green controls in the general interest. They, therefore, see a grass roots development as the way forward, since at the moment the only way to persuade world governments and policy makers to take effective action is to hold then over the brink of disaster and let them stare into the abyss in order to shock them into pulling back in time, as in the case of CFCs and the thinning of the ozone layer.

However, in the case of CFCs although they were rapidly withdrawn from supermarket shelves in the late 1980s, this was not so much by government decree, but because individuals and businessmen collectively decided that their sale was no longer acceptable or profitable. According to Porritt and Winner this is an example of the grass roots revolution that they hope will sooner or later dawn on more and more people as the only way of solving the planet's problems.

At the moment, however, the grass roots revolution, as represented by actual membership of the Green Party, is still small. This is not for lack of information or policies. For example, in a popular and rhetorical statement of the Green Party's views, two party activists (Irvine and Ponton, 1988) writing personally rather than for the Party, have spelt out a 'Green Manifesto'. According to Irvine and Ponton, Greens are guided by four fundamental assumptions.

1. Life on earth should continue.
2. Human life on earth should continue.
3. Natural justice should be done.
4. There is a quality of life worth pursuing independent of material well-being.

From these assumptions there follow 12 principles: put the earth first; live within limits; think in terms of self-sufficiency; tread lightly; defend diversity; respect our descendant's rights; design with nature; keep things in proportion; balance rights and responsibilities; decentralize and democratize; tread carefully; and always remember that bad means produce bad ends. In essence the Green goal is to allow everyone the opportunity to live a fulfilling life, caring for and sharing with each other, future generations and other species, while living sustainably within the capacities of a limited world.

The manifesto then considers the major issues facing the earth and the Green response to them. By its very nature the approach is therefore global since if USA rates of consumption were spread to the rest of the world there would need to be a 130-fold increase in the consumption of resources. A clearly unsustainable situation. The basic solutions proposed by the Greens are thus to consume less so that resources are sustained. In order to make this process easier a major programme of draconian measures to reduce population is proposed. Fewer people, consuming fewer goods is therefore the long-term goal at the global level. In these terms the present approach to conservation is akin to a finger in the dyke while the tide of pollution and destruction threatens to break the whole dam. UK responses can then only be helpful but not provide the whole solution.

Given that the Green Party is unlikely to come to power in the near future it is more realistic to turn to those policy measures that seek to achieve sustainable development by less radical means, via economics or environmental assessment.

Conventional policy measures

Economics

If economic growth is the root cause of environmental problems then it seems only logical to turn to economics for the solution. Unfortunately as Underwood and King (1989), two Americans writing in the first issue of *Ecological Economics*, have pointed out modern economies necessarily consume and degrade the very resource that sustains them. Accordingly, contrary to the assumptions of neoclassical economic theory substituting one resource for another or even recycling is only a stop-gap on the road to scarcity, and ignores the key debate about the Earth's true carrying capacity and resource potential.

It is therefore necessary to look at a wider range of economic measures for controlling pollution and increasing the quality of life. Baumol and Oates (1988), two economists, have concluded that there is no one proposition or rule of economics that is applicable to the many difficult and complex trade-off decisions to be made. Instead they analyse four possible measures: first, the imposition of taxes on polluters; second, a system of marketable emission permits; third, subsidies to prevent pollution; and fourth, the imposition of direct controls. They note that marketable permits may be the best compromise between increasing costs for everyone and at the same time cutting pollution.

O'Riordan (1985a), in a variation of this idea, has proposed an extension of the 'polluter pays' principle, under which those who exploit environmental resources in a damaging way should by means of transfer taxes and payments, subsidize those who use environmental resources frugally and benignly. O'Riordan (1985b) has also proposed tax reliefs for those managing land with a heritage value, and 'environmental bonds' for those proposing major land use changes which would be paid as surety against any loss in landscape value.

However, Pearce *et al.* (1989) argue that the price mechanism is the most effective policy measure available, but only if the true values of environmental services are reflected in prices, rather than in treating them as 'free goods'. Nonetheless, Pearce *et al.* agree with Baumol and Oates that tradeable permits for the use of environmental goods are needed to supplement prices.

The use of market prices, but at the point of sale, has also been advocated by two green authors (Elkington and Burke, 1987) in their study of green capitalism. From this they list ten steps to environmental excellence which companies can take in the 1990s, for example, developing and publishing an environmental policy, preparing action programmes and contributing to environmental programmes. Looking towards the 21st century they foresee green growth and green consumerism developing further, and more significantly, the death of socialism as an economic theory and its replacement by green ethical capitalism.

In an attempt to provide an alternative method to straight economics an interdisciplinary team of planners, scientists and philosophers (Attfield and Dell, 1989) have concluded that a revised form of cost–benefit analysis could form a basis for sound decision making in environmental matters. Proposed revisions include monetary measures with units of welfare where appropriate, and by weighting different elements of the equation according to different groups. Such a system would provide according to Attfield and Dell the technical means for the better evaluation of and greater use of environmental assessments by politicians.

Environmental Assessment

Environmental Assessment (EA) as has been shown in Chapter 3 was introduced into the UK in July 1988. Wood and McDonic (1989), an academic and a former country planning officer, have argued that the already considerable experience in using *ad hoc* environmental impact assessments mean that it offers not a radical but an evolutionary method for improving environmental management in the 1990s, largely by integrating professional evidence, and by anticipating environmental problems, and also according to Haigh (1987) by extending the range of environmental effects to be considered.

Further improvements according to Wood and Lee (1988), co-Directors of the EIA centre at Manchester University, could be made by extending the amount of information needed to undertake satisfactory environmental assessments, and by providing for more effective consultation and public participation.

These pragmatic improvements to EA are a far cry from those proposed by a Canadian environmentalist (Rees, 1988), whose model is radical because it explicitly accepts ecological constraints on human activity, and thus recognizes that we rather than the environment are the problem. If Rees' model is to be successful it depends on a shift in societal perceptions away from seeing the Earth as a treasure chest to be plundered.

Cautionary concluding comments

This chapter has encompassed a wide span of policy proposals, from those of deep ecology to the narrowly pragmatic approach of environmental assessment. It is now time to ask whether any of the more radical views are likely to be implemented. In a reply to this question Blowers (1990), an academic social scientist, has argued that there are nine political reasons which will prevent or deter fundamental action to arrest and reverse environmental destruction. First, the complexity of the issues; second, their interrelatedness; third, their long-term nature; fourth, the invisibility of the problem; fifth, the transboundary effects of environmental processes; sixth, inequality between nations; seventh, the matter of cost; eighth, because political parties all agree that green issues are OK they can form a do-nothing cartel; and ninth, the political implications of shifting society to a lower rate of consumption are so awesome that it is difficult to imagine the fundamental changes that will be necessary.

In a further negative view, O'Riordan (1989) has claimed that though the arguments in favour of a pro-active environmental policy regime are now generally recognized it is doubtful if such regimes will come into operation quickly, largely because of jealously guarded jobs and resources, and the sheer difficulty of persuading people to act ahead of scientific proof.

The greenhouse effect provides a perfect example, for not only do some people disbelieve the science but even the estimates of warming by themselves do not seem too disastrous. For example, Parry and Porter (1990), of the Climate Impacts Review Group at the University of Birmingham, have stated that the best estimates of greenhouse effect type warming could be a rise in average temperature of 0.5°C by 1995–2005, and 3°C by 2050–2100. This seems fairly harmless until it is set against a fluctuation of only 1 or 2°C in the past 1000 years. Indeed, Parry and Porter warn that the effects could be dramatic with: (i) the migration of species northwards and upwards; (ii) an upward rise of 650 feet in the height of cultivation; and (iii) a longer growing season, and the extension of grazing and afforestation to even the highest altitudes. In the south, the agriculture of France could take over with maize and sunflowers becoming commonplace, and drought-resistant species appearing on wildland. Around the coast, there could be a substantial loss of mud flats and salt marshes.

Similar forecasts have been provided by a group of scientists working for the Department of the Environment (Environment, 1988a). They assumed a temperature rise of 3°C to forecast that a wider range of trees, notably broadleaves, could be grown more quickly except for those conifers best suited to cool damp climates. The forecast for wild plants was less optimistic, however, with woodland, heathland, wetland and montane species expected to show a decline.

Although science can be a useful guide to policy Sandbach (1980), an environmental academic, has stressed that capitalism has misused science so much that what society accepts, as science, is actually ideology posing as science. The solution to environmental problems is thus not a scientific one but one of who controls the science.

In a counter view Whelan (1989), a freelance author in a booklet for the Institute of Economic Affairs, has made a savage attack on the Green movement for being far too pessimistic about the environment and wildly exaggerating the threats to its survival. He also claims that the Greens are basically anti-people and that the controls they wish to impose would plunge free-market western economies into the slow growth cycle of communist countries. Finally, he argues that only industrial countries can pay for a clean environment and that the Third World cannot pay for sanitation because it is poor and unindustrialized. Whelan concludes that friends of the Earth need not be enemies of the people.

Despite these cautionary comments proposals have been made which steer a course between utopian radicalism and overcautious pragmatism. For example, Turner (1988b) an environmental scientist has argued that since there is no requirement for radical deep ecology, an ethic for the use of the environment could be devised which would offer adequate environmental safeguards. This ethic would need a modification of existing individualistic views of utilitarianism and conventional economic thinking, especially with regard to present generations recognizing an obligation to maintain a stable flow of resources for future generations. Turner believes that such a shift could be achieved by adopting three conservation rules for sustainable growth; namely:

Rule One: Maintenance of regenerative capacity of renewable resources and avoidance of excessive pollution;
Rule Two: Encourage technological research allowing a move from non-renewable to renewable resources; and
Rule Three: Switch wherever possible in a phased way from non-renewable to renewable resources.

5 Policy Proposals for the Countryside as a Whole

Chapter 4 dealt with the environment as a whole and though many of the proposals considered there are of direct relevance to the countryside, they were not always countryside specific. In this chapter, only those proposals which deal with the countryside as a whole are considered. Proposals for specific activities in the countryside are considered in later chapters. For the sake of convenience the proposals are divided into the type of organization making them as follows: political organizations; government agencies; professional organizations; pressure groups; academics and professionals; and individuals.

Before embarking on this survey, however, it is useful to remind ourselves of the problems facing the countryside in the 1990s. A useful review has been provided by the European Communities Commission (1989). This divides rural areas into three standard problem areas as shown in Tables 5.1, 5.2 and 5.3. Namely, rural land areas under pressure from expansion (e.g. South East England), rural areas in the lowlands suffering from decline as agricultural employment declines (e.g. West of Scotland) and rural areas in the marginal mainly mountainous areas (e.g. Highlands of Scotland).

Political proposals

As Chapter 1 has demonstrated politicians make policy proposals for a variety of reasons. It is therefore advisable to review these motives before embarking on a consideration of the proposals themselves. For example, Brotherton (1986a) has demonstrated that although all the main parties had espoused conservation as a legitimate policy goal by the 1980s this goal was still subordinate to other more important aims and ideals. In particular, some

Table 5.1. The European Community's first standard problem area.

	Agriculture	Woodlands	Environment
Type of problem	Pressure of demand for land. Land fragmentation. Various types of pollution	Woodlands are subject to particular pressure: (i) over-use by the public; (ii) pollution	Peri-urban pressure (damage to green spaces). Intensive farming (pollution with fertilizers and pesticides, destruction of biotopes)
	Services		Industrial activities
Type of problem	Competition/attraction of urban nucleus. Quality of life, linked to the disadvantages of outlying urban areas (dormitory towns etc.)		Congestion of towns, absence of alternative activities, empty space around towns (in southern regions of the Community)

Table 5.2. The European Community's second standard problem area.

	Agriculture	Woodlands	Industrial activities
Type of problem	Structural handicaps. Migration to medium-sized towns. Abandonment of marginal land	General: increase in area of land in a state of abandon and insufficient alternative jobs. Forestry: (i) underexploitation of woodlands; (ii) large quantity of low-value, second-grade timber; (iii) fragmentation of woodland property; (iv) low geographical concentration of woodlands	Ageing production plant. Economic isolation. Insufficient analytical and managerial capacity. Limited credit possibilities, with most available credit channelled into agriculture

	Services	Training	Infrastructure
Type of problem	Restructuring of supply of public services. The business back-up services currently on offer to firms are of inadequate quality. Slow adaptation process due to underdevelopment of alternative activities	Basic training still inadequate. Less education available than in urban areas. Relatively little demand for education. Cultural isolation	Basic infrastructure and business back-up services often inadequate (transport, telecommunications, industrial and craft areas, multi-service centres). The situation is particularly bad in structurally backward regions

Table 5.3. The European Community's third standard problem area.

Type of problem	Agriculture	Woodlands	Industrial activities
	Poor agricultural structures. Difficult production conditions. Difficult living conditions	Inadequate forestry infrastructure. High exploitation costs (including transport costs). Restrictions on exploitation for reasons of environmental protection. Location of the wood-processing industries	Depopulation (hence absence of nearby markets). Excessive cost of modern, efficient infrastructure
Type of problem	Tertiary activities	Education and vocational training	Infrastructure
	Insufficient basic services for individuals (administrative, health, education and transport services). Absence of business back-up services. Excessive cost of a permanent supply of services due to small population	The relative importance of agriculture imposes the need for conversion and therefore for vocational training. The rural exodus and the ageing of the population result in schools being closed down and in infrastructure problems. Cultural isolation and the cost of infrastructure	Investment and infrastructure do not become quickly profitable

Conservatives are theoretically said to favour some sort of planning controls over forestry since this would increase the power of landowners and farmers, as elected councillors, over the Forestry Commission and urban-based forestry companies, thus restoring power to their rural representatives. In contrast, the Labour Party and SNP are theoretically in favour of planning controls over agriculture since this would reduce the power base of farmers, but at the same time advocate public afforestation schemes rather than planning control over private forestry, again largely for ideological and power structure reasons (Brotherton, 1986b).

In contrast, Flyn and Lowe (1987) conclude that the central themes in both Conservative and Labour attitudes to conservation are dominated by their basic ideologies of *laissez-faire* and centralized intervention respectively, and not by any deeper motivation or hidden agenda aimed at disturbing rural power structures. In a spirited defence of his original position, Brotherton (1987a) argues that these notions of *laissez-faire* and intervention are not only meaningless but also unhelpful, and points not only to the many interventionist initiatives of the Conservatives in the 1980s but also to the fact that Labour, when in power resisted intense pressures to extend planning controls to afforestation in the early 1970s, but then espoused planning controls over agriculture in 1982 for political advantage in opposition.

Bearing these cautionary comments in mind the next section considers political proposals in turn beginning with the semi-political Committees of the Houses of Parliament and then proceeding to the Conservative, Labour, Centre and Green Parties.

Committees of the Houses of Parliament

Apart from providing a mass of evidence on all sorts of issues, the main contribution of the Committees has been to consider the matter of integrated rural policy and whether there should be a Minister of Rural Affairs. For example, the House of Lords Select Committee on the European Communities (1979) has argued that it is unrealistic to talk of integrated rural policy in the sense of one single common rural policy that would apply uniformly across all the countryside.

In contrast, the integrated approach has been advocated by the Agriculture Committee of the House of Commons (1982). In addition they have also proposed that a new Minister of State (not necessarily attached to MAFF) should be made responsible for the coordination of rural policies.

Conservative Party

Because the party has been in power since 1979, most of their proposals have already been covered in Chapter 3. However, from time to time a number of dissenting views are put forward even by Conservatives normally noted for their loyalty to the party line. Perhaps because of this many of them are not exactly controversial, for example, Waldegrave, a Conservative politician and a possible leader in the 1990s, has set out two primary policy principles (Waldegrave *et al.*, 1986). First, the need to find alternative uses for the surplus land released from agriculture using transfers of money from the taxpayer. Second, the need to continue to protect the countryside from development, since it would be silly to move our nearly stable population into an undamaged countryside. The challenge to our skills is instead to revitalize the cities.

More controversially the Tory MP Carlisle (1984) has argued that the party must be seen to respond more constructively to the political importance of the environment groups and their millions of members. Accordingly, Carlisle suggests planning controls for large blocks of forestry and a review of those fiscal incentives which could encourage good conservation practices both on heritage land and in the wider countryside.

In contrast to Carlisle's left-of-centre Toryism, Bracewell-Milnes (1988), in a report for the Social Affairs Unit whose advisory council contains a number of 'New Right' figures, places much of the blame for current countryside problems on government intervention. This he believes to have been more a liability rather than an advantage. First, because the costs of intervention in terms of the executives employed and the costs imposed on the free market by constraining its behaviour are too high; second, the short time horizon of politicians and bureaucrats is too short for the environment where decades and centuries have to be taken into account; third, urban-based decision makers do not understand the countryside; fourth, the sectoral and unintegrated nature of government bodies artifically divide the countryside into separate issues; and fifth, public land ownership is not subject to the safeguards imposed on private property.

Bracewell-Milnes therefore suggests returning responsibility for the countryside to where it formerly rested, the rural community and landowners and developers. He suggests that a number of checks and balances would ensure that land was better managed. First, most employers now know that sustainable utilization of resources makes economic sense, costing less in the long-run than short-run exploitation; second, most employers now know that there is a market for conservation either directly on the farm or in the 'green nature' of their product; and third, the desire to pass on, a thriving business and a good landscape, is endemic in the motivation of private entrepreneurs who see their own life's work being passed on as a dynasty in a form of stewardship, and this engenders a sense of commitment rare in public officials.

In order to aid these factors, Bracewell-Milnes proposes that public officials are given longer assignments in order to develop their loyalty to the countryside, that financial assistance for conservation be a positive plank of policy with the aid being given in the form of tax relief rather than subsidies (thus reducing taxation and government expenditure), and that conservation aid be paid for results achieved, e.g. the number of wild flowers counted in a wood or meadow.

The central theme of Bracewell-Milnes' proposals, however, is one of reducing government expenditure rather than increasing it as so many people advocate, and to this end he proposes abolishing inheritance tax which he argues is the greatest disincentive for landowners to invest in the long-term value of their environment, notably, woodland. Thus placing responsibility for the countryside firmly on those with a direct and long-term interest in it and those best suited to manage it by living and working in it, rather than in a suburban home and city centre office.

In a similar attack on planning Mount (1987) writing in *The Spectator* (the weekly magazine for Conservatives) has called for a rural revolution to cut back the ownership of land by public authorities, to reduce the armoury of planning instruments, and to minimize the subsidization and taxation of the land.

In more detail, Mount proposes that the Government should re-emphasize its commitment to the Green Belt and all other protected areas but elsewhere, outside preserved areas, there would be a presumption in favour of applications for fishing, golf and other leisure schemes; and farmers on grade three land would be free to put up schemes for developing new villages of 1000–10,000 houses. Every county would be required to approve a certain number of these applications, but could of course, choose the most suitable applications. Farmer's profits would be limited by a requirement that they bear the costs of access, drainage and landscaping. Council estates would be converted into independent housing trusts whereas the abolition of mortgage tax relief would reduce house prices, and thus the need for subsidized housing. In the primary sector the Government should encourage more fallow land, and adopt the NFU scheme for semi-ornamental/semi-economic broadleaved trees and hedges in the lowlands. In the uplands new afforestation schemes would only be approved in exceptional circumstances, and tax concessions would be replaced by maintenance grants.

Labour Party

The Labour Party's policy for rural areas has evolved through the 1980s in a response both to changing conditions and the rightward shift in the Party in order to become electorally credible.

In the heady days of government in the late 1970s the Party (Labour, 1979) began work on a major statement on rural areas. By 1979, however, only employment and services had been covered. Policies for these areas included expanding the work of the Development Agencies and re-establishing

Rural Development Boards and providing more grant aid to rural tourism in a bid to diversify jobs. Powers to encourage the Forestry Commission to process its timber and thus provide profits were also seen as a way of publicly developing the economic base of rural areas. In terms of services the Party advocated subsidized transport and the creation of core service centres to which various services could plug in on a fixed or mobile basis. Politically, the Party advocated an attack on entrenched representation via farmers but did not advocate the creation of a Ministry of Rural Affairs.

The review was completed in the early 1980s, and the resulting document (Labour Party, 1981) contained 67 proposals. Significantly 44 of these were in the area of service provision and most involved extra public spending, but only five involved agriculture. Changes or additions to the 1979 interim statement included proposals to slow down the loss of jobs, by examining agricultural practices, farm amalgamations and the development of unconventional forms of agriculture. Another new proposal w s to appoint a coordinating Minister for Rural Affairs.

In the run up to the May 1983 election the then Labour leader, Michael Foot promised to introduce planning controls over everything in the countryside including hedgerow grubbing, ploughing up permanent grassland and buildings. He also promised to pull Britain out of the EC and introduce a farm policy based on deficiency payments and cheap food imports.

Following a second election defeat in 1983 the policies were reappraised and re-emerged as the Labour Charter for Rural Areas (Labour Party, 1986a) which was strong on promises but weak on detail.

The ten point plan included the following proposals.

1. Initiate a major drive to create worthwhile jobs.
2. Provide jobs in construction, woodland management, leisure services, the environment and light industry.
3. Give high priority to providing pre-school education and keeping local schools open.
4. Ensure proper support and regulation of public transport.
5. Back local people fighting to retain village services.
6. Improve housing provisions through more house building, repairs and renovation.
7. Introduce measures to improve the availability of low cost property to rent.
8. Implement a comprehensive environment policy to ensure all the countryside is properly catered for.
9. Improve access to the countryside by clearing footpaths and opening up common land.
10. Guarantee local people an effective voice by devolving decision making to the local level.

In more detail the charter called for a more extensive agriculture to create jobs, and for EC aid to be switched from the CAP to a diversification programme for the rural economy, and for the creation of a Land Bank system to help people enter or expand small farms. Further jobs would be created by environment improvement programmes. In the area of houses, the proceeds of council house sales would be ploughed back to help an expanded programme of new houses to be built for rent. In areas with a high proportion of second homes, local authorities would have a right of first refusal when such homes came up for sale. In the environmental area a long-term proposal of moving toward the production of more natural and nutritious food would be begun and planning controls would be introduced for farm buildings, forestry and in important landscape and wildlife sites. Finally, a legal right of access would be brought in for 'open land' areas.

In essence the charter proposed an integrated approach based on local people drawing up Rural Development programmes, the provision of resources, the investment of money and the creation of jobs.

In a response to the growing green movement the Labour Party (1985) also produced a Charter for the Environment which was centred on three principles: sustainable growth; prevention of pollution and environmental damage; and increasing democratic controls over the environment.

To many Labour supporters these proposals were not radical enough and in a statement to the Party Conference a year later (Labour Party, 1986b) the creation of a Ministry of Environmental Protection, and two new national agencies, an Environmental Protection Service and a Wildlife and Country-side Service, were added to the 1985 Charter.

Following a third defeat in 1987 the Labour Party embarked on a major policy review in another attempt to capture the middle ground. As part of the review, seven topic documents were produced, including one on the Physical and Social Environment (Labour Party *et al.*, 1988). The basic premise in the review was the need to develop a new planning system for the 1990s which would be:

- Fully responsive to the needs and demands of ordinary people
- Capable of resolving conflicts between strategic necessity and local and individual concerns
- Innovative rather than conservative
- Simple in concept and application

In essence the proposals were of planning for people, who it was claimed have three rights: first, the right to live and work in a safe, healthy and pleasant environment; second, the right to decent, reasonably priced accommodation; and third, the right to a varied, wholesome and reasonably priced diet. The review was, however, sketchy in detail and omitted any detailed proposals for agriculture, nature conservation and forestry.

The next stage in the policy review was the document Meet the Challenge: Make the Change (Labour Party, 1989). This included a major section on the environment which began with the following assertions:

> Protecting our environment is the greatest challenge we face.
> It can't be left to the 'free market'. Government has to act
> on behalf of the whole community and of generations to
> come. Protecting the environment isn't a matter of cleaning
> the damage up after it has been done. Concern about the
> environment has to be integrated into economic, industrial,
> energy, transport and social policies so that individuals,
> industry and government all work together (p. 67).

Key proposals included setting up a Ministry of Environmental Protection, a Ministry of Rural Affairs, an independent Environmental Protection Executive with a Wildlife and Countryside Service branch within it, and a more powerful Rural Development Commission.

In the farming sector, MAFF would give priority to food not farming, the CAP price support system would be based on lower guaranteed prices for limited levels of production, Countryside Management Agreements supported by Green Premiums would be made available to protect and create the countryside and to encourage organic farming. Major land use changes would become subject to planning controls, and there would be a prescription against large-scale afforestation in the uplands and the disturbance of rare and declining habitats such as lowland heathland. Other measures would include the introduction of Hedgerow Protection Orders and Landscape Conservation Orders, extending the legal right of access to common land, mountain, moor and heath, and increasing the number and quality of National Parks.

In the wider environment the document proposed zero energy growth, a presumption against pollution, adoption of the polluter-pays principle, a Clean Water Act to improve water quality and a greatly extended programme of environmental impact assessment.

In terms of planning, a subsidiary document (Labour Party, 1990a) proposed: the reorganization of planning to regional, district and community-based organizations; widening the scope of local plans to include energy conservation, ecology, landscape and design; giving local authorities the option of deciding whether second homes will need planning consent and introducing the concept of 'Public Action Zones' where local authorities will buy land in advance of need and become the major owner and developer of this land.

The culmination of all these policy documents was a new look document, Looking to the Future (Labour Party, 1990b). This was full of pious hopes and generalities but detailed policy proposals were almost totally absent. However, commitments were made to improve the quality of life, to aim for active and viable communities, to provide good public transport, wider job opportunities and resources for houses for locals and at the same time preserve the countryside from development. The only specific proposal was to provide devolution to Wales and Scotland, and set up regional authorities and regional development bodies in England.

In summary, all the proposals tended to use intervention in the market as the main means of policy, either by negative controls or via subsidies, and administered by new or expanded agencies.

Centre parties

In the middle years of the 1980s the Liberal Party (1984a) espoused policies very similar to the Labour Party. For example, the 1984 Manifesto defeat called for reform of the CAP in order to cut back surplus production and prevent damaging environmental farming systems. In addition it called for the creation of a 'Land Bank' not for land acquisition as under the Labour proposal but to provide financial credit for new entrants to farming. Other aid for employment would be provided for by the creation of a Rural Development Agency based on an expanded Development Commission. Similarly, in the area of housing, the manifesto argued that the proceeds of council house sales should go to the construction of new houses, that more areas should be designated where the resale provisions of the 1980 Housing Act should apply and that Section 52 could be used to restrict the sale of new houses to locals only. The only real differences came in the area of politics where the manifesto recommended not only the creation of a Select Committee on Rural Affairs to act as a watchdog on Ministers and Departments but also the creation of a Proportional Representation system of elections so that the safe inactive seats held by so many rural Tory MPs would be discontinued.

Rural policies for the Social Democratic Party were at the same time outlined by Sinclair and Heppel (1986). These included policies for the creation of a Land Bank into which farmers could sell land, for other farmers to purchase as and when appropriate; the creation of Credit Schemes to fund initiatives in all sectors of the rural economy; and the creation of 15-17 Regional Development Agencies in the UK along the lines of the Highlands and Islands Development Board. In terms of managing agriculture Sinclair and Heppel proposed a setaside scheme for a minimum of 200,000 hectares and the creation of a system of 'freeway prices'. These would be set between 97% and 106% of the costs of production to provide a floor support for farming, with the median freeway price being used to set the import threshold price.

After the 1987 general election the Liberal Party merged with the Social Democratic Party (a rump of which survived until its dissolution in May 1990) to form the Social and Liberal Democratic Party (1988). In their initial one-page policy declaration they supported sustainable growth. More detail was added one year later (Social and Liberal Democrats, 1988) in an alternative 'Environment Bill', which proposed the following.

1. The creation of an Environment Protection Agency.
2. Reform of agricultural policy to encourage farmers to adopt non-intensive, organic methods. Consultation with farmers to introduce premium grants for positive management of sensitive sites, namely: wetlands; limestone grassland; heathland; moorland; and hay-meadows. To qualify farmers would have to submit whole-farm plans to their local authority.
3. Planting incentives for deciduous trees under the Farm Woodland Scheme to be increased.
4. Forestry and farming to come under planning control.
5. Evaluation of the present system of designated areas to consider the possibility of a simplified system of environmental contracts.

In February 1991 the Liberal Democrats – the Social part having been quietly dropped – produced a draft manifesto which promised a wide-ranging pollution tax including higher petrol taxes to reduce private car use, but offset by the abolition of Vehicle Excise Duty thus reducing the impact for those in rural areas.

The Green Party

The Green Party (1986) (between 1973 and 1985 the Ecology Party) in a review of the green position of the other political parties has claimed that there was no substance to the Conservative Party's claims to be green, dismissed the SDPs stance as opportunism, and rejected Labour's green credentials because of its opposition to Proportional Representation which would let a green vote grow in importance. The Liberal Party was thought to be nearly green but the failure to espouse policies on sustainable economic development continued to preclude it from being fully green (however, see the declaration made by the Liberal Democrats in 1988 set out earlier).

In terms of the Green Party's own position, its policies are in essence based on sustainability, human welfare and a healthy environment. Its environment policy calls for the following.

1. Conservation of resources and promotion of their more efficient uses, reuse and recycling, aiming at the sustainable use of renewable resources and minimum throughput of non-renewables.
2. Preservation and enhancement of the urban and rural environments, seeking a maximizing balance between beauty, ecological diversity and public amenity.

3. Stringent control of environmental pollution of all kinds.

It is in the field of agriculture that the policies are really radical and the following passage is worth quoting at length:

> The purpose of an ecological agriculture is to provide
> healthy food at reasonable cost in a way that maintains
> long-term fertility; to provide good work in a way that
> underpins rural communities; and to conserve and enhance a
> beautiful, diverse rural environment to which there is ample
> public access for recreation.

So far, not very radical but then the policy continues:

> To achieve these objectives our agriculture needs to be
> almost completely restructured, not least in terms of
> establishing new systems of land tenure that will greatly
> increase opportunities for new entrants to farming. In
> addition, big, highly-mechanised, single crop farms, relying
> on a large input of fossil fuel, fertilizers, pesticides and
> herbicides and employing few people, will have to give way
> to a regime of many more small farms using smaller
> machinery, mixed cropping, labour-intensive and
> predominantly organic farming methods. To achieve such a
> transformation, the enormous public subsidies to agriculture
> would be redeployed to provide income support,
> conservation grants, subsidies for conversion to organic
> systems, premium prices for organic produce and a
> comprehensive programme of research into organic
> agricultural methods. The use and application of chemicals
> would be far more strictly controlled and the use of animals,
> in agriculture and elsewhere, drastically curtailed. Such
> policies would return agriculture to the status of an integral
> part of the culture of our society, instead of it being a
> dehumanised, denaturised, profit orientated rural outpost of
> heavy industry as at present (p. 23).

In conclusion, the three main parties are now cosmetically green but there are still deep differences in opinion between the depth of greenness and the mechanisms to be employed to bring greenness about, both between and within the parties.

Proposals from government agencies

Not surprisingly most of the proposals here come from the Countryside Commission. In the second half of the 1980s the Commission undertook a

Table 5.4. Reshaping Countryside Commission policy 1986–1990.

Countryside Policy Review Panel: Set-up in 1986 Report published in 1987 as 'New Opportunities for the Countryside' CCP 224		
Overall Response by Countryside Commission in 1987: 'Shaping a new countryside' CCP 243		
Evolution of policy for agriculture in CCP 262, 'Incentives for a new direction in farming' published in 1989* Evolution of policy for forestry in CCP 245 'Forestry in the countryside' published in 1987*	Evolution of policies for town and country planning in CCD24, 'Planning for change: Development in a green countryside' published in 1988, and in CCP 264, 'Planning for a greener countryside' published in 1989	Evolution for policies on access and recreation in CCP 225, CCP 234, CCP 235, 'Recreation 2000' published in 1987 and in CCP 253, 254, 265, 266 and 273 on Rights of Way and Paths, Routes and Trails published in 1988, 1989 and 1990*
Integration of policy review in 'Ten Critical Years: An agenda for the 1990s' CCP 282 published in 1990		
Followed by Consultation paper 'An Agenda for the Countryside, CCP 336, April 1991		

*Examined in separate chapters.

major review of their policies (Table 5.4). This process began with a thorough and radical review by the 13 member Countryside Policy Review Panel (1987). The panel's remit was to assess the changing situation in agriculture and forestry, to identify the opportunities for conservation, recreation and socio-economic factors and to make recommendations. In developing their proposals the Panel used three principles.

1. Countryside policies should whenever possible be integrated.
2. New initiatives are best achieved by encouragement and leadership with minimal recourse to statutory controls and new legislation.
3. Rural wealth is best advanced through the conservation of the land and its resources.

The panel began with the assumption that up to 4 million hectares could be surplus to requirements by the year 2000 (Edwards, 1986), and then proposed alternative uses for 2 million of these hectares (Table 5.5).

Table 5.5. Possible options for diversifying rural land use.

Land use with bias towards	Short term < 5 years	Medium term 5–10 years	Long term > 10 years
Agriculture	Rotational fallow	Alternative crops Organic farming	Lower input farming including permanent grassland
Landscape and wildlife conservation	Headland fallow, small-scale conservation planting and management	Integration of conservation into agricultural systems including ESAs	New nature reserves New woodlands
Recreation and alternative enterprises	Picnic sites and other public access measures	Improvements to rights of way	New Country Parks New woodlands Urban or urban induced uses

Source: Countryside Policy Review Panel (1987).

In more detail the Panel made over 100 specific recommendations, which they divided into eight themes. Some of these are set out in Table 5.6 together with the Countryside Commission's (1987a) response.

The Panel also costed out their programme (Table 5.7) and estimated that the £320 million needed would create 150,000 jobs by the year 2000 compared with the £2500 million spent on subsidizing agriculture, with its 500,000 or so jobs. In their response the Commission did not attempt to cost out their own proposals but merely pointed out that each hectare of land taken out of cereals could save the UK exchequer at least £240 per annum if the land was transferred to woodland conservation.

In a separate review of policies not covered by the Countryside Policy Review Panel, for example, housing, the Countryside Commission (1988a) produced a consultation paper directly aimed at influencing Ministers. This set out ten policy issues as follows.

1. The maintenance of a strong and effective system of town and country planning to which needs to be added guidance at the National and Regional levels and a more active role to be played by the District Councils.
2. The conservation of natural beauty and regional diversity by bringing afforestation under planning control and using landscape conservation order type schemes in the National Parks and similar areas.
3. The creation of new countryside.
4. Using conditions and Section 52 agreements to obtain more environmental benefits from development.
5. An enhanced role for green belts.
6. New housing in the countryside should be resisted in the open countryside but there is scope for expanding small towns and villages and even for creating entirely new settlements.
7. Rural enterprise to replace agricultural work should only be encouraged where it will not detract from the surroundings.
8. Large-scale developments should be resisted in all the protected areas, and environmental assessments should be used to control other operations for example, open-cast coal mining.
9. Better cooperation between countryside agencies.
10. Complementing countryside planning with countryside management.

Following on from this paper the Countryside Commission (1989a) produced a statement intended as advice to Ministers and all concerned with 'Planning for a greener countryside'. The Commission's aim is to produce a sustainable, multi-purpose countryside to be achieved by observing the following seven principles for town and country planning.

1. Natural beauty and landscape diversity should be conserved.
2. New countryside should be created wherever possible.
3. Green belts should serve a wider purpose.

Table 5.6. Some of the recommendations made by the Countryside Policy Review Panel, and the response from the Countryside Commission to these proposals.

Countryside Policy Review Panel proposals	Countryside Commission responses
Agriculture	
There should be a shift away from food production	Government should seek to ensure that any new schemes introduced to deal with agricultural over production make a positive contribution to conservation, and its enjoyment by the public as well as to the social and economic well-being of the farming community
Less intensive farming systems should be encouraged	
More effort should be put into alternative crops and organic/low input farming	
There is a place for price restraint in any package designed to control surpluses	Setaside and extensification should not be seen as mutually exclusive
Measures should be taken to control use of and pollution by nitrogenous fertilizers, including a modest levy and the establishment of water protection zones	Setaside schemes should take into account all other land on the farm and neighbouring land to ensure setaside conservation gains are maximized and not offset by losses elsewhere
Any proposals to take land out of production should encourage the creation of new wildlife habitats and reserves	
Forestry and farm woodlands	
The introduction of woodland management allowances	The introduction of a policy for multipurpose forestry
More support for broadleaved planting especially in Eastern England	A review of the incentives available in order to encourage multipurpose forestry
County council forestry strategies and Forestry Commission planting licences to control afforestation	County council forestry strategies and afforestation to be brought under planning control
New outlets for woodland products	New forests to be planted in the lowlands and in the urban fringe. (Also see CCP 245)
More involvement by local communities	

Table 5.6. *Continued.*

Countryside Policy Review Panel proposals	Countryside Commission responses
Recreation and access	
Public enjoyment would rank in importance with food and timber production as a land use	The rights of way network to be maintained properly and made more accessible
More public money should be spent in making the countryside accesssible	All concerned to be made aware of their rights and responsibilities about access
Farmers should be paid to keep rights of way in good repair	A new Common Land Act to safeguard Common Land and access to it
Farmers should be encouraged to diversify into recreation	More long-distance footpaths
	Extending Countryside Management schemes to further areas
	Local authority strategies for recreation
Also see CCP 225, 234, 234, 235, 254, 254, 265, 266, 273.	
Pressure from the towns	
Central Government should provide a nationally coordinated urban fringe policy for elboration in Structure and Local Plans	Government should produce a national policy for the urban fringe
	Initiative like the Groundwork scheme should be further encouraged
New areas of publicly usable space should be created in the urban fringe including new woods, nature reserves and wildlife sanctuaries	Local authority policies should reflect the special role urban fringe land can play in recreation
Integrating farming and environmental conservation	
Provide more support for environmental conservation and recreation by replacing the 'Agricultural Improvement Scheme' by a new 'Farm and Countryside Scheme'	The Agricultural Improvement Scheme should be replaced with a more broadly based scheme offering a wide range of conservation and recreation management incentives which can be built into normal farm practices
Increase the number and widen the aims of ESAs	

Table 5.6. *Continued.*

Countryside Policy Review Panel proposals	Countryside Commission responses
Introduce variable Hill Livestock Compensatory Allowances in the Less Favoured Areas to encourage stocking rates which enhance the natural beauty and wildlife interest of the uplands	A vigorous expansion of ESA designations and a review of their operations
	A new scheme for Hill Livestock Compensatory Allowances should be introduced which reflects conservation needs without penalizing farmers' incomes
Note: All of these would require EC approval.	
Encouraging rural enterprise	
Government should require a coordinated national programme by its agencies working in rural areas	The Government should discuss with its agencies means of achieving a better coordinated approach to national policy for the countryside
County Councils should propose rural development strategies	County Councils should be asked to prepare a rural development or countryside strategy for their areas, as part of the strategic planning process
More public funding for rural development agencies	
Funds should be available to relocate businesses where environmental considerations dictate	
Taxation arrangements should be made to encourage farmers to diversify	
The Housing Corporation should receive special financial incentives to develop rural housing programmes	
Putting the pieces together	
All advisers in the rural planning sector should get together to set up gatekeepers for different sorts of advice and should meet regularly	Land managers should be encouraged to prepare multipurpose farm plans which should be subject to grant aid
	All staff in the advisory services should get together at the national and local level to coordinate their work and participate in training programmes

Source: Countryside Policy Review Panel (1987) and Countryside Commission (1987a).

Table 5.7. The cost of the initiatives proposed by the Countryside Policy Review Panel in 1987.

Initiatives	Investment £ million annually
1. Land use diversification	150
2. Additional ESAs	20–30
3. Woodland management allowance	40
4. Picnic sites	20
5. Conservation grants under the Farm and Countryside Scheme proposal to replace the Agricultural Improvement Scheme	10
6. Redundant farm buildings	5
7. Countryside management	10
8. Relocation of business in sensitive locations	20
9. Rural initiative programmes, rural development officers and rural enterprise	45
Total	320

Source: Countryside Policy Review Panel (1987).

4. Maximum environmental benefits should be served from development that has to take place in the countryside.
5. New housing in the countryside must make a positive contribution to the rural scene.
6. Rural enterprise is welcome if it is developed harmoniously with the countryside.
7. Major development in the countryside should be strictly controlled and of the highest standard of design and landscaping.

Returning to the countryside as a whole the Countryside Commission (1990a) began the decade by producing a two-page leaflet entitled 'An Agenda for the 1990s', part of which is reproduced in Table 5.8.

Only a year later, however, the Countryside Commission (1991) published a follow-up consultation paper 'An Agenda for the Countryside'. This promoted a vision for the 21st century based on an environmentally healthy, beautiful, diverse, accessible, and thriving countryside of quality, managed in a multipurpose way to sustain its environmental qualities. Creating this vision according to the Commission will need 14 guiding principles, for example, integrating conservation into mainstream activities and a new national strategy for the use of rural land. As part of the development of this strategy, the Commission plan to draw up a 'new map of England' by the mid 1990s, in order to provide a regional component for the national strategy.

Turning to specific sectors the Commission called for: a further development of incentives to manage farmland; a further reappraisal of forestry

Table 5.8. Countryside Commission's Agenda for the 1990s.

The 1990s will be critical years for the countryside of England and Wales. Both the threats and the opportunities are greater than ever. Global environmental problems and cosmetic pressures for development are likely to focus increased attention on our countryside as a scarce and precious resource. But the current food surpluses backed by public interest in the environment, mean that we have a unique opportunity to get things right: to bequeath to future generations an environmentally healthy, beautiful and accessible countryside fit for the needs of the next century.

The Countryside Commission sets out these ten points as an agenda for countryside policy for the 1990s.

1. Conservation means creation as well as preservation . . . We need an approach to conservation which both safeguards the best of our existing natural heritage and sets out to create a more beautiful countryside for the future.

2. Cherish the wild places . . . We need stronger commitment to defend and where possible extend our wild places – especially in our national parks.

3. Conserve through farming . . . We need a system of incentives and advice to help farmers meet people's need for an environmentally healthy, beautiful and accessible countryside, food for the spirit as well as for sustenance.

4. Create a new face for forestry . . . We need a multi-purpose approach to forests, to produce timber, jobs, a better environment, and opportunities for recreation.

5. Make the countryside more accessible . . . We need a fully accessible, well maintained and well publicized path network throughout the countryside.

6. Avert damage from visitor pressure . . . We need a recreation and tourist industry that adopts environmental objectives and supports conservation measures.

7. Set a new direction for transport . . . We need new transport policies which give much higher priority to environmental conservation.

8. Establish a new role for planning . . . We need the planning system to be linked to positive programmes for environmental improvement.

9. Build on popular support . . . We need to raise public awareness of how to achieve a well managed countryside and to show how individual citizens can make their own contribution to resolving environmental problems.

10. Government must give the policy lead . . . We need government to spell out the importance of the countryside and to provide clear directions for public policy.'

Source: Countryside Commission (1990a).

policy; the re-creation of relatively wild places; the better management of common land; a presumption that 'open country' should be accessible for quiet recreation; and a review of policies for special areas, notably the need to protect all the countryside not just the National Parks and AONBs.

In conclusion the 'Agenda' called for a new Countryside Act for the mid-1990s to redefine the role of National Parks and AONBs in light of the 1991 report (see Chapter 10), to strengthen powers over the wider countryside, to redefine coastal and forestry policy, and to enable the creation of new boundaries for re-creating the habitats of degraded areas, e.g. the new National Forest.

Proposals from professional organizations

In a report for the Association of County Councils, the County Planning Officers Society (1987) has concluded that rural planning is no longer about devising 'ways of constraining a vast subsidised juggernaut from rolling thoughtlessly over the environment' (p. 13) but one of deciding how to integrate change in the agricultural industry into the total rural scene. In order to achieve this integration aim the Society made the following nine recommendations, which in some cases were modified by the Association.

1. The Government should be encouraged to examine on a comprehensive basis the new economic, physical and social pattern which is emerging in the countryside with a view to establishing integrated guidelines for the various agencies involved.
2. Consideration should be given to the creation of a Ministry of Rural Affairs charged with the responsibility for all matters relating to the countryside. It should absorb the present Ministry of Agriculture.
3. At the local level, County and District Councils should work jointly to coordinate the policies and actions of the many agencies involved in rural areas.

The ACC modified these three recommendations as follows:
The Government should issue a Green Paper:
a. examining comprehensively the new economic, social and physical pattern which is emerging in the countryside with a view to establishing integrated guidelines for the various agencies involved;
b. reviewing comprehensively the allocation of responsibility for agriculture and other countryside matters within Government, with a view to greater coordination, within and between, the various aspects of the economy, and its development on the one hand, and conservation and environmental matters on the other; and
c. examining the possibilities for joint working at County and District Council level to coordinate the policies and actions of the many agencies involved within their respective established spheres in rural areas.

The remaining six recommendations were accepted except for the changes shown in italics.

4. Care should be taken to ensure that any further fall in farm incomes is neither so great nor so swift that it undermines the basic financial viability of farm business, *and special attention should be paid to the needs of small farms.*
5. The desirability of maintaining small farm buildings should be recognized in any future schemes for capital grants or revenue support.
6. A greater effort should be made to relate grants given to support agricultural production and those given to support conservation practices. One way of doing this would be to require any farm improvement plan to include proposals for both objectives. Any production grants would then rest on an undertaking to follow both acceptable farming and conservation policies.
7. Support should be given to schemes which encourage the planting *in appropriate cases* of new broadleaved woodlands or/*and* the better management of those which already exist.
8. A form of selective control over countryside changes should be available to be used as a last resort in areas of special sensitivity where threats are believed to exist. It should be operated by local authorities but any compensation costs should be borne by a central fund. *A form of selective control over countryside changes should be available to be used as a last resort in areas of special sensitivity where threats are believed to exist, such control to be operated by local authorities but subject to suitable financial agreements with Central Government and that appropriate parliamentary and other opportunities be taken to pursue this proposal.*
9. *The Association notes that local authorities* have an important practical role to play in the countryside which requires competent trained staff.

The report also contained an Appendix regarding the extension of planning control to agricultural buildings via notification rather than through the full procedure of control. With regard to the control of farm operations the report considered that this should be approached with caution because it would be costly to implement and probably not be as effective as people hoped.

Proposals from pressure groups

The Town and Country Planning Association has for most of this century been the source of many radical views on planning and so it was no surprise when in (1984) they advocated a new approach to planning and democracy based on three vital elements: more local initiative; maximum decentralization; and a stronger but more flexible planning framework, and on four essential functions: (i) coordination; (ii) foresight; (iii) the selection of priorities; and (iv) a vision of a better future.

The Association thus believed that two main changes to the planning system were required, first, a clear regional framework for all major developments underpinned by a stronger emphasis on closely integrated structure plans, and second, provision for action area plans at neighbourhood level to be prepared by local communities with assistance from the district authority.

In a wider debate on the future of rural areas the director of the Town and Country Planning Association (Hall *et al.*, 1988) has argued for a new set of principles for the countryside, not based on agriculture but on a more holistic view of rural areas. They would include defining minimum acceptable standards for quality of life; protecting rare and unique natural environments; reducing pollution to an acceptable minimum; providing reasonable access for recreation; and accepting that a different mix of land areas is not only inevitable but also desirable.

Hall argues that the area of land that will become surplus to agriculture is so enormous that no one set of alternatives, for example, forestry, housing and recreation can make any real impact. Instead, he advocates that most of it should be allowed to revert to its natural ecological state. However, in a response to Hall, O'Riordan argues that 1992 will see a splintering of the CAP and the creation of a chauvinistic and nationally politicized Farm Survival Policy. Under such a scenario O'Riordan forecasts two types of land use. First an intensive area farmed by 20,000 holdings (10% of the total) producing some 75% of all UK agricultural output on farms farmed by 'accumulators' self-reliant, well capitalized and efficient people. In contrast as many as 100,000 'survivor' holdings could face a rough future since the Government will not have the will or funds to subsidize them any further or to extend setaside schemes to the majority of farmers.

The Town and Country Planning Association's main proposals have, however, come from a working group set up to look at the future planning needs of the countryside (Green *et al.*, 1989). The main premises of the group are that the city and the countryside are now interdependent. The countryside can thus no longer be seen as a resource which can be exploited without taking into account the external costs involved. Before outlining their own policies, the authors discuss four possible policy scenarios; first, a continuing trend scenario in which *ad hoc* planning muddles through; second, a stronger market scenario in which current trends are given freer rein. Under both these scenarios the countryside of Southern England would be put under severe pressure. In the third scenario, a social scenario, these pressures are accommodated but the added development value of allowing development is made available to the wider community, while in a fourth scenario, a resource-based one, most of this extra value is directed towards creating a more sustainable environment.

The group believes that both the first two scenarios will ultimately lead to a crisis and that they will thus in due course develop into the third or fourth scenarios, or preferably into a combination of the third and fourth scenarios which the authors favour.

Turning to their own policy prescriptions the authors put forward a 16 point plan which in terms of radical policy options can be grouped as shown below.[a]

1. There needs to be a radical reorientation of countryside policies, combining the sustainable use of environment and its resources with the extension of choice of living place, work and lifestyle.

2. A nationwide Countryside Resource Audit is needed, co-ordinated by County Councils in collaboration with all levels of government and other organizations involved with the countryside.

5 and **6**. As a general principle the external costs of all developments or land uses should be met by the developer/user. The costs involved would be monitored by a Commission for Environmental and Social Accounting.

7, 8, 9 and **12**. There should be a substantial increase in development land allocations outside the South East of England, thereby shifting the planning process from one of control by responding to demand to one of leading by supplying land. Enough land should be allocated to allow a significant programme of new settlements of various sizes to enhance dispersal from major urban centres. A release of 150,000 hectares over 10 years is suggested against a possible farmland surplus of 6 million hectares. Land should be acquired at existing use value thus allowing the community to retain the added value created by the development. The key village concept should be abandoned but services should be located in towns.

13, 14 and **4**. Major changes in agriculture and forestry use should be the subject of planning control. ADAS should be made responsible for introducing and supervising farm land management plans in consultation with other agencies. The case for an environmental tax on all agrochemicals should be considered as a way of moving towards more ecologically sensitive farming practices.

16. Encouragement should be given in suitable locations to mixed rural enterprises embracing leisure, forestry and farming.

In a series of ten articles on the Association's proposals (Green *et al.*, 1989) widespread agreement is expressed with a view that the 1990s presents a time for both radical and positive action. Only two authors really dissent. First, Bate for the CPRE regrets the omission of two options, namely, that of making cities into places where people want to live by extolling the virtues of high density living, and option two, questioning more closely the benefits claimed for dispersal into rural areas. Second, Dean for the House Builders Federation queries the wisdom of providing the carrot of providing building land away from the South East, because that is where people actually want to build.

---

[a] Only the 'radical' points are listed here.

Another pressure group, the Council for the Protection of Rural England (CPRE) (1989a–c), has argued that it is difficult to underestimate the long-term political significance of the Single European Act and the increasing influence that European legal decisions will have from 1992 onwards. Accordingly the Council has proposed that the EC should introduce measures to protect individual features such as hedgerows; discrete habitats, such as fern, woodland and meadow, and landscapes such as moorland. This should be backed up by a requirement to compile an inventory of such habitats by, for example, using remote sensing.

In another pro-active role the CPRE (1990a) laid out a green manifesto for the 1990s, in advance of the Government's White Paper on the environment. As matters of central principle the manifesto accepted the philosophy of 'sustainable development', and the linking of global and local issues. Key requirements for the White Paper were thus listed as: environmental integration; improving the quality of life; adding quality of life to the definition of progress; looking afresh at the best mix of regulation, underlying incentives and economic instruments; minimizing environmental damage while maximizing environmental benefit; and effective public participation.

The CPRE then made a series of proposals in a number of sectoral policy areas as follows. In the area of *Planning Policy* the CPRE called on the Government to: (i) reaffirm the commitment to restrict urban sprawl; (ii) integrate policies and proposals of other relevant departments, e.g. Energy, Transport, Agriculture and the Treasury; (iii) strengthen the rights of third parties by giving them a right of appeal; (iv) restore the power of County Councils to direct District Councils to refuse planning applications which conflict with strategic policies; (v) extend planning controls to farm buildings and new afforestation; and (vi) remove the presumption in favour of development set out in DOE Circular 22/80.

In the area of *Landscape Protection and Enjoyment* the CPRE called on the Government to: (i) support the EC Habitats Directive; (ii) strengthen protection for SSSIs; (iii) strengthen the financial and legislative support for National Parks; (iv) establish a new National Park for the New Forest; (v) accept that landscape features such as hedgerows need the same level of protection as trees and listed buildings probably by the use of Landscape Conservation Orders not just for National Parks but for all areas; (vi) bring forward a Common Land Bill along the lines recommended by the Common Land Forum; (vii) provide enough resources to ensure that all legal rights of way are accessible by 2000; (viii) reform the basis of negative compensation under the 1981 Wildlife and Countryside Act into positive payments for positive management; and (ix) introduce measures for the long-term re-creation of wildlife habitats and landscape features as opposed to short-term setaside policies.

In the area of *Environmental Assessments* (EA) the CPRE called on the Government to: (i) make EA a central process at all levels of decision making throughout government both national and local; (ii) extend the powers of the EA Directive to other activities, for example, the cultivation of semi-natural areas; (iii) remove the anomaly whereby the Forestry Commission acts as both judge and jury in the EA process.

In the area of *Agriculture* the CPRE called on the Government to commit itself to achieving a programme of radical reform to the CAP embracing in particular:

- a continued reduction in guaranteed prices
- a switch to support which is decoupled from production
- an acknowledgement of the need to maintain farm structures for environmental reasons
- replacement of setaside with a policy for the re-creation of lost habitats and wildlife
- introduction of an environmentally based extensification policy
- support for organic farming.

In the UK arena the CPRE called for: the reintroduction of free ADAS advice on conservation clearly separate from its commercial work; make ESA type payments available to all farmers in return for a whole farm management plan; revise the Hill Livestock Compensatory Allowance Scheme on an area rather then headage basis in order to reduce overstocking; change the emphasis from diversification to land management which encourages conservation and public enjoyment of the countryside; introduce Nitrate Sensitive Areas (NSAs) in ways which preserve the polluter pays principle and finally, reduce nitrate use.

In the area of *Forestry* the CPRE called on the Government to replace the existing muddled and incoherent policies with a new set of objectives including protection of existing woodland, landscape enhancement, nature conservation, public enjoyment, timber production and CO_2 absorption. In more detail the CPRE advocated: the separation of the Forestry Enterprise and Authority to develop a new stronger State Forest Service; the introduction of management grants for woodland; a requirement for County Councils to prepare County Woodland Strategies; and the extension of planning controls over new afforestation.

In the area of *Institutional Structures* the CPRE favoured retention of the DOE and rejected the idea of a Ministry of Rural Affairs, but advocated the creation of a new independent Environmental Protection Commission, as an advisory and research body. Regulatory bodies should be separate and strong according to the CPRE, including a restructuring of the NCC and Countryside Commission but not along the lines set out in the Environmental Protection Act. Instead they proposed the establishment of a new body with a clear UK perspective, charged with the protection of the UK's natural, visual and cultural heritage and its enjoyment by the public.

In December 1990 the CPRE published an 'Agenda 2000' in the form of a folding leaflet (1990b). This leaflet covered nine policy areas, and not only carried forward the proposals made earlier in the year but also added: proposals for a 'Charter of Rights' to enable the ordinary citizen to play a fuller part in the planning process; proposals for non-production related Environmental Management Payments to encourage environmentally friendly farming throughout the countryside; a proposal to scrap setaside and to replace it with a specific encouragement for less intensive farming; and, in forestry, a proposal to replace commercial forests in the uplands with new planting and natural regeneration based on more appropriate species.

The TCPA and CPRE are of course outsiders looking in and thus happy to impose controls on rural land users. In contrast the Country Landowners Association (CLA) who represent large long-standing landowners are less likely to argue for such control. For example, in their (1983) examination of planning controls in the countryside they reject them for three basic reasons. First, they would be too standardized and would reduce diversity, second, they would undermine the economic function of the countryside, and lead to shabby neglected landscapes, and third, they would be too negative for a living countryside, since preventing the clearance of a hedgerow does not preserve or manage it. Instead the CLA advocated a healthy rural economy with agriculture as its mainstay backed up with management agreements and other voluntary mechanisms which are both well resourced and staffed by able people.

This fundamental belief that only landowners and managers can manage the countryside, was restated at the end of the decade when the CLA (1989) proposed the introduction of an Environmental Land Management Scheme under which landowners would voluntarily offer to provide various services, for example, access to woodland, in return for a contract where taxpayers' money was involved. This fairly radical idea was, however, only sketched out in the most general of terms, but later in the year *Environment Digest* (November 1989, issue 30, p. 2) reported that the idea had been extended to cover all types of landscapes and habitats that the Government wished to conserve. Under the proposals individual landowners would contract to manage these sites with any organization who wished to conserve them, public or private.

More specific proposals, including some surprising concessions, related to the following.

1. A single ministry for countryside policy with responsibility for rural agencies including MAFF, NCC, The Countryside Commission, Rural Development Commission, Forestry Commission and the Rural Directorate of the DOE.

2. Revision of the GDO bringing all farm buildings, whether agricultural or for other purposes, above 465 m^2 under full development control.
3. The provision of National Guidelines for protecting high quality land, providing housing and transport, conserving the environment and promoting the rural economy.
4. Limited expansion of self-contained villages and small towns.
5. Help for local housing needs by offering land at less than full market value.

Proposals from academics and professionals

Proposals from academics and professionals can of course range from eccentric to idealistic, since they are not rooted in any power base or restricted by membership of a group. They do, however, often represent ideas ahead of their time. For example Holliday (1986), a planning consultant, has produced a challenging book on the new movements and possible outcomes that could arise if a post-industrial global village type world emerges as a result of accelerating changes in social values, in advances in science and technology, and the widening plurality of economic structures and growing conflicts between centralized power and decentralized life.

Holliday then translates these possible global changes to the British context which he believes will almost certainly lead to a need for new political systems and new ways of tackling problems to be found, based on a better appreciation of the physical world.

It is not, however, Holliday's purpose to set out detailed reforms or land policies but in broad terms he argues for a decentralized post-urban landscape of new country settlements, which can accommodate the demands for decentralization from both work and non-work activities which the 1990s will bring. This in turn will demand new forms of settlement structure and new approaches to land management.

A similarly radical writer is Shoard (1980, 1987), a freelance author and part-time academic, who in 1990 became a full-time academic planner. In her two major books she paints a devastating canvas of the damage wreaked by farmers, but it is her proposals that make the books so radical, the second one even more so than the first, for as the 1980s unfolded Shoard became convinced that the earlier medicine was not strong enough.

In the first book Shoard, after accusing, and in most peoples eyes, proving, farmers of the theft of the countryside, made three radical proposals.

1. The introduction of planning control over major changes to farmland.
2. The creation of nine regional countryside planning authorities, made up of nominated members who would draw up countryside plans which would set a framework for the general use of each subregion; provide guidance for

the management of specific areas; make proposals to reconstruct the land-scape of certain areas; and encourage recreational use overall as well as in specific areas.

3. Create six new National Parks in the Wye Valley, Somerset Levels, Dorset Downs, West Downs (Sussex), the Chilterns and the Broads.

Apart from the creation of the Broads Authority none of these proposals had come to fruition by the time of the much larger book in 1987. This second book was basically a plea on behalf of the landless to regain control from landowners, using precedents from history and around the world, to show that the land belongs to the people not the owner.

Previous attempts to do this have so far failed. For example, the 'Social Contract' of the 1947 Attlee government to provide local community control over the environment, according to Shoard, lies in ruins, and the attempt to impose national control over our most valued landscapes, for example, the National Parks has turned sour.

Accordingly, Shoard turns to a list of possible radical options to deal with the causes and not the symptoms of the malaise. Five main options are rejected. First, the nationalization of either agriculture or just land is ruled out as politically impossible as well as unwise. Second, restricting ownership to certain groups is rejected as being too narrow in its scope. Third, funding other owners, for example, conservation groups, is rejected as continuing the pocket compartmental approach. Fourth, reform of the CAP will not be enough by itself, and fifth, neither will be all the schemes to divert farm subsidies to conservation.

Having rejected these five options either in part or whole Shoard reiterates the proposal for introducing planning controls but this time widens the scope to changes having a significant impact on the rural environment.

Shoard then proposes what could be considered an 'extremely radical' (p. 553) proposal for a Land Tax. This Land Tax would be either positive (a payment to the landowner) or negative (a payment by the landowner) and would replace all other taxes, grants or subsidies concerned with land. The tax would be set nationally at different levels for each type of land use. For example, a wildlife rich meadow would attract a payment of say £x per hectare, whereas an environmentally damaging use would be subject to a tax of say £y per hectare. Each farmer would be assessed an aggregate tax level depending on a land plan which he would submit to the appropriate authorities. In addition Shoard also proposes an Act of Parliament giving right of access to all woodland, parkland, rough grassland, lakesides, river-banks, coastlines, field edges, farm tracks and forest paths.

In a less radical view Lowe *et al.* (1986), a group of social scientists, geographers and freelance authors, have made a series of coordinated proposals based on four case studies and on four prerequisites: sustainability, cost-effectiveness, social justice and political attainability. To these can be added the idea of producing a system of 'sticks and carrots' which are mutually reinforcing, as the following list of their proposals makes clear.

1. The replacement of production-orientated farm (forestry) grants/ subsidies with more widely based integrated grants and management plans for both farming and forestry in both the uplands and lowlands. All grants would be conditional on the preparation and implementation of a comprehensive farm management plan. In the uplands a new upland management grant would be available for unprofitable but necessary action to provide conservation or recreation benefits. Underlying the schemes would be a transfer of aid from richer bigger farms to poorer smaller farms, and from the agricultural budget to the conservation budget.

2. The introduction of landscape conservation type orders under which farmers would be required to give notice to the relevant authority if they intended to remove or alter a specified feature. The authority would then have time to seek a financial management agreement if necessary with back up powers to impose an agreement as a last resort. Lowe *et al.* reject planning control as being too blunt and negative a procedure, but call for the repeal of compensation paid for any loss of land value.

3. The introduction of planning controls over forestry as a necessary stick, but more importantly a carrot in the form of grants and other aid to establish multipurpose, mainly hardwood forests in the lowlands, integrated with conservation recreation and farming, which could in due course provide half of Britain's hardwood timber.

4. A restructuring of MAFF, ADAS and the DOE so that they can work more closely, without actually forming a Ministry of Rural Affairs. Some powers would be devolved to county councils. A new ethos centred on conservation would be the *raison d'être* of the reorganized structure.

5. The replacement of the present complex of landscape/conservation designations with a three-tier system of 'heritage sites', 'conservation zones' and 'agricultural/forestry landscapes'.

6. An increased rate of purchase of key conservation sites which would be leased back to voluntary conservation bodies for day to day management.

This theme of positive aid has also been taken up by Mowle (1988), an NCC officer, who has argued that only positive action can ensure the survival of the wildlife heritage. Experience, according to Mowle, tells us that designations cannot alone guarantee sensitive land management, whereas comprehensive blueprint-type planning has been discredited. The 1980s have taught us that although market forces have a role to play, the balance must now shift in favour of non-market environmental goods. Taking these three strands together Mowle proposes a three-tier methodology for evaluating and placing land use conflicts in context with one another.

At the policy level, where overall goals are set and policy implementation is monitored, sectoral agencies should get together to set environmental standards defining acceptable management in agriculture, forestry and other countryside activities. At the moment sectoral policies and programmes impede this kind of integration and send confused signals to the practical farmer or forester.

At the programme, local and regional level of policy implementation, feedback is required to condition flexibility of response and integration of purpose. For example, regional indicative strategies, in the form of explicit frameworks spelling out the relationship between different land use interests are needed to provide a basis for local interpretation in achieving the 'reasonable balance' required by legislation between conservation and development.

Finally, at the practical level on the farm, the adoption of a managerial ethic is essential based on farm plans which balance financial concerns with the maintenance of environmental quality. This will depend on price and other signals from above which favour environmentally sensitive management while still responding to market forces.

Finally, Sinclair (1988), an environmental consultant in a short but thought-provoking paper, has criticized most of the current debate about land use change as being too short term and adversarial. Instead he suggests we get to the root of the issues and proposes five main considerations for a radical but integrated land use policy: (i) farming and forestry should remain the key uses of the countryside; but (ii) the principles of multiple land use should be embodied in both farming and forestry, encouraged (iii) by farming and environmental policies acting in unison to produce lower input-lower output systems with a greater labour need. At the same time (iv) measures would need to be taken to sustain and create suitable forms of rural employment, and finally (v) a new Ministry of Agriculture, Rural Land Use and Natural Resources should be set up with a Minister in the Cabinet. A Land Use Strategy Section of this Ministry supervised by a Department of Environmental Protection would lead to five policy section areas each having its own Minister of State, Agriculture, Forestry, Conservation, Rural Affairs, and Natural Resources with three main tasks.

1. To define broad food and timber production targets and to align incentives accordingly.
2. To define optimal geographical areas for production in which local authorities would formulate plans for integrated land use, sector by sector.
3. To assess the importance of non-productive factors especially in multiple land use systems.

Gilg (1978a, b) is another who has advocated the development of a national land use strategy setting out priorities within a multiple land use context. Such a strategy would be reviewed and revised every year by an 'Annual Review of Countryside Resources' carried out by a new Ministry for Physical Resources (modelled on the Scottish Development Department and to include MAFF, DOE and the Department of Energy and Transport).

Below this tier, newly created Regional Planning Authorities would review Regional Resource Plans annually, and at the executive level, the existing District Councils would produce District Reviews of area-based local plans. These reviews would be short statements based on existing data sources and would form the focus for an annual debate by the rural community.

To some extent integration at the local level already exists. For example, Selman and Barker (1989) two environmental scientists have made a study of five areas, Somerset Levels, Loch Rannoch, Glen Lyon, Loch Lomond, Islay and Fetlar, in which multi-agency fora have been established, to resolve local land use and economic development issues. They concluded that although their performance is imperfect there are areas in which progress may be made towards the creation of genuine integrated policies at the local level. One of the main achievements has been that via fora facilitated informal contact, increased mutual understanding has fostered progress rather than conflict, and consensus rather than class war.

Finally, the need for such new partnerships between farming and conservation fostered by a modified Ministry of Agriculture has been advocated by Wibberley (1982, 1985) from a lifetime's experience of rural planning. In his recast Ministry, conservation would become a normal part of its policy and operations and would be built into all forms of grant aid and advice. At the local level, County Agricultural and Rural Conservation Committees based on the wartime Agricultural Committees would monitor policy. Wibberley defends the use of MAFF since it is the only government department trusted by farmers, and thus the only way to get conservation in from the cold to the warmth of everyday farm husbandry.

Proposals from individuals

In conclusion, we can look at proposals from individuals ranging from the considered to the romantic. Pye-Smith and Hall (1987) a freelance author and chairman of the Ramblers Association have produced a manifesto for the countryside we want in the year 2000, based on the views of an eight-man committee. The central ideal they wish to achieve is a countryside in which humans manage their activities in such a way as to allow the maximum possible use of the land to other creatures. In order to attain this ideal their detailed policy proposals include the following.

1. *Agriculture.* A freeze on all tenancies, the abolition of export subsidies, reducing price support, and phasing out production grants. On the positive side they wish to encourage mixed farming by taxing fertilizers and pesticides and abolishing intensive livestock units which depend on outside food inputs. More radically they also suggest the creation of a Land Bank Order under which 5% of all land would become publicly owned and used for non-

agricultural purposes such as conservation, deciduous forestry, recreation and so on. Another 5% of all land would also be taken into public ownership and broken up into smallholdings. This together with the radical restructuring of agriculture to lower-intensive mixed farming would create thousands of full- and part-time jobs and the type of rural economy enjoyed in Bavaria.

2. *Forestry*. The manifesto proposes the abolition of the Forestry Commission and all forms of grant-aid and tax relief for coniferous afforestation. Existing estates would be transferred to county councils, and regulatory functions would be passed to a central government environmental agency.

3. *Planning controls*. The manifesto proposes that land drainage, the removal of trees, hedges or woodlands, the conversion of deciduous woodland to other uses, the ploughing up of moorland, marshland or heath and the use of agrochemicals in previously untreated land would be subject to planning control. To back-up the system a new register of the countryside would need to be created by a comprehensive survey conducted at parish level.

4. *Land management payments*. These would provide a new source of income for farmers prepared to manage their land for conservation. They would be more comprehensive than ESAs and if one assumed a payment of £100 per hectare, one-third of the agricultural area of the country could be covered for a cost of £700 million compared with public spending on agriculture in 1982/83 of £1333 million much of which would be saved under the proposed changes to agricultural policy.

5. *Housing*. Housing Stress Areas should be created in which the sale of new and existing property would be restricted to local people. The supply of local housing could also be bolstered by financing the building of homes for sale or rent via the rating (poll-tax) system.

6. *Transport*. By the end of the century the manifesto suggests the really radical proposal of seeing a countryside in which the main means of getting about will be by public transport.

7. *Access to the countryside*. The manifesto proposes creating a 'Right of Common Access' similar to the Swedish system in which subject to certain rules such as not walking over growing crops, people would have access to all parts of the countryside.

Sinclair (1990) a freelance author in a popular book proposes.

1. Taking surplus land into public ownership by offering to buy out those farmers who wished to retire or who were in financial difficulties. The land could then be transferred to local communities, the outdoor leisure industry, conservation groups, or to developers.

2. Accepting that post-war farming policy has 'had its day' and should be reformed to a consumer-led rather than technology-driven system. One method to achieve this would be by replacing price guarantees with production entitlement guarantees which would limit price guarantees to a percentage of the farm's output on a sliding scale. Small farmers would receive the most, large farmers, the least.

3. Re-creating lost habitats by man-made schemes.

4. Introducing a system of zoning which would allocate tracts of rural land for developers to build villages for people to live in.

5. Along the same positive lines, Sinclair advocates the revision of planning restrictions in areas as yet unspoilt by tourism so that houses specifically designed for weekenders and holiday-makers could be built in order to spread recreational and tourist demands over a wider area.

While Sinclair's ideas may sound idealistic, Croft's (1987) vision of the future is downright romantic, when he argues that the last decade of the 20th century offers a unique opportunity to replace mono-product mass-production in the countryside with multiactivity richness to provide employment for the flux of population returning from the cities. At the same time some functions which transport and economies of scale have lately concentrated in towns could be revived in rural areas and things which have not before taken place in country settings, for example, home working using modern communication techniques, and clean, light industry in relatively small workshops could become the norm.

6 Policy Proposals for Agriculture

The nature of the problem

Introduction

According to the agricultural economist Howarth (1985) the real nature of the 'farm problem' arises from a very slow growth in the demand for food and a rapid increase in technical productivity, which has only been partially offset by falling numbers of people working in agriculture. This has been exacerbated by a farm policy which has artificially raised prices and thus encouraged production to further exceed demand. The farm problem is essentially neither a price nor an income problem; fundamentally it is one of too many farmers, and too much production. Farmers have remained in agriculture because of the non-pecuniary advantages of the work, and although agricultural support has not prevented lower incomes generally, it has led to an increase in land values and rents and its effects on individual farmers have been extremely haphazard and regressive. Large and better-off farmers and long-time owners of land have benefited, while tenants and new entrants have lost out. In the meantime poorer households have had to reduce the quality of their diet (Moore, 1988).

Turning to the CAP, Howarth argues that it has added considerably to the existing wastefulness of agricultural support, imposed higher costs on consumers and taxpayers, encouraged farming practices with adverse environmental consequences and damaged the food exports of developing countries. In Europe the Economist Intelligence Unit (1989) has argued that current problems include: the cost of the CAP to the Community Budget, and thus the frustrated development of other EC policies; the limited finance available for structural adjustment; threats to the conservation of the rural environment; and the implications of the CAP for international trade. For the future the Unit only sees the problems of over-production becoming worse with further improvements in technology.

The rest of this chapter considers some of these background issues further, notably: productivity forecasts; guestimates of land surpluses; changing farm structures; and the nature of CAP decision making, and then examines future policy options for agriculture alone and then agriculture in a wider context.

Forecasts of productivity

Given a static population the key issue is the amount of food that may be produced from any given area. Estimates for this vary from the optimistic to the pessimistic. Starting with the optimistic, Girling (1990) a scientific journalist in a review of the rapid progress of genetic engineering, has noted that out of the 500,000 or so plants known to science, a mere 23 produce more than 90% of our food. This leaves a vast untapped storehouse of exploitable resources and for the plant geneticist, fields, hedgerows and jungles are a Pandora's box of literally limitless potential. For example, plants could be made to grow faster, develop their own pesticide and prevent themselves from rotting. Alternatively softwood trees could be re-engineered to produce hard wood. The potential for transforming agriculture is thus scientifically enormous.

A more cautious survey conducted within the Commission of the European Communities (1989a) has forecast that biotechnology by itself could increase yields by a further 10% or so by 2005. But taking into account the probability that only 50% of farmers will have taken advantage of the new techniques by then the likely increase in yield was put at 5%.

However, Brown (1988), director of the independent Worldwatch Institute, cautions that world food production, which faltered in the late 1980s could begin a serious decline in the 1990s leading to a major world crisis. Key positive factors will be attempts to halt soil erosion, the more efficient use of water and nutrients, the reform of farming in Eastern Europe and the Soviet Union and technological developments in biotechnology. Key negative factors will be the lack of any more land to crop, the growth of population in the Third World, and the increasing threat of drought in northern latitudes coupled with sea level flooding of Asian rice-producing areas as a result of the greenhouse effect. Brown concludes that food shortages may well increase in the 1990s.

Allaby and Bunyard (1980) two ecologists have also pointed out the unsustainability of modern petroleum-based agriculture, and the profligate use of energy by society. Instead they argue that the seeker of self-sufficiency, appalled at the trends of the 20th century, wants to eat his own food, and to visit a countryside peopled once again by families who are deeply involved with its cycles of sowing and reaping. To achieve these aims they argue for socialism, but based on the social democracy of the Kibbutz community.

In a similar vein the CPRE (1988b) argue against a common but mistaken perception that a surplus of land had become available in the 1980s. Instead the CPRE argues that the surplus will only exist as long as farmers are paid to produce food intensively and only if no account is taken of the landscape and wildlife habitats destroyed in the previous 40 years. The CPRE therefore proposed that the Government should turn its attention to encouraging farmers to produce food by farming less intensively rather than promoting the idea that there is excess land.

Finally, two social scientists, Fallows and Wheelock (1982), have mounted a formidable case for self-sufficiency. They have traced the long-term decline of Britain as a manufacturing economy and its decreased ability to purchase food with a balance of trade surplus from the manufacturing sector. (Between 1982 and 1990 the small surplus indeed became a large deficit.) This means that it is in Britain's economic interest to import as little food as possible, and also to safeguard the economy from any sudden rise in world food prices. Futhermore, Fallows and Wheelock argue that there is a need to maximize the resources already invested in agriculture and its research and development, and also to provide employment for the 18% of the work-force engaged in food-related activity.

However, the pessimists at least in UK and European terms have been largely outweighed by the optimists who have the physical evidence of current surpluses to hand, and so attention is now turned to different forecasts of the likely surplus of farmland in the 1990s.

Guestimates of land surpluses

The debate began in 1971 with a forecast by Edwards and Wibberley (two agricultural economists at Wye College) that continued growth in productivity would continue to provide enough land for all uses by the year 2001. However, five years later the CAS (Centre for Agricultural Strategy, 1976) argued that population and income growth, and a growing competition for rural land, notably by forestry, could lead to a position of land scarcity by the year 2000 unless a more centralized and integrated system of planning was set up to balance the claims for land between agriculture, forestry, urban growth and other uses. In their review of the CAS report, Wise and Fell (1978) argued (Table 6.1) that there is no case for restricting urban growth on self-sufficiency grounds since the productivity differences between rows (iii) and (iv) are negligible. In reply, Bowman and Doyle (1978) for the CAS countered that any further increase over and above the loss of 5–10% of the agricultural area forecast for the year 2000 might not be met by the expected

Table 6.1. Relationship between productivity growth in agriculture and land use (% growth per year).

Assumption	Edwards and Wibberley (1971)	Centre for Agricultural Strategy (1976)
i. 1970s level of self-sufficiency (68%) maintained	1.6	0.7
ii. Productivity growth expected to be achieved	2.6	1.25
iii. 100% self sufficiency by year 2000	4.2	2.9
iv. As (iii) but no loss to urban growth	3.8	2.8
v. As (iii) but no loss to afforestation	4.1	2.7
vi. As (iii) but zero growth in per capita demand	3.4	2.6
vii. As (iii) but 1% drop in per capita demand	1.8	1.2
As (iii) but zero population viii. growth	3.0	2.4

Source: Wise and Fell (1978, p. 6).

rate of increase in productivity of 1.25% a year. Wise and Fell (1978), however, countered that either eliminating or doubling the rate of farmland loss to other uses only changed the productivity increase needed from 1.6 to 2.0%. Instead the critical figure is not the rate of land loss but the rate of productivity increases which is likely to fluctuate far more widely than land transfers.

Bowman *et al.* (1978) reiterated their belief that the rate of productivity increases would slow in the 1980s, that land lost to urban uses was lost for ever, and that increasing pressure from recreation and other environmental considerations also reduce yield growth. Accordingly they argued for the country to be divided into two zones. In zone one all urban development would be prohibited on long-term agricultural strategic grounds, and in zone two planners would need to consult with the Ministry of Agriculture before releasing land.

In a concluding critique Whitby and Thompson (1979) argued that the year 2000 was far more likely to see food surpluses than shortages and that the narrowly conceived policies of Bowman *et al.* were antidemocratic, too costly too run and too slow to adapt to changes in the country's economic environment. Instead they suggested that thought should be given to alternative uses of agricultural land as pressure grows to deal with the forecast surpluses.

This view was confirmed seven years later when Edwards (1986) in a second attempt to forecast land surpluses combined three variables to

Table 6.2. Percentage of agricultural land area available for all other uses by the year 2000.

Annual rate of productivity growth	1.5		2.0		2.5	
Level of self-sufficiency	75	90	75	90	75	90
Demand						
1985 = 100						
103.0	22.7	7.2	28.4	14.1	33.4	20.1
104.0	22.0	6.4	27.8	13.3	32.7	19.3
105.0	21.2	5.5	27.0	12.5	32.1	18.6

Source: Edwards (1986).

produce the range of estimates for the percentage of the 18,168,000 hectares of farmland in the UK that may be surplus to requirements by the year 2000 as shown in Table 6.2. This table ignores any change of use into urban or forestry use, but even when these are included Edwards concludes, taking the EC context into account, that 3–4 million hectares (16–21%) of the total agricultural area could be surplus to requirements by the year 2000. Central to these assumptions are the gains to be made in agricultural productivity, and if farmers de-intensify production then the surpluses might be less, as shown in the 10% fall in stocking levels scenario shown in Table 6.3 (Edwards, 1987).

However, whichever figure is chosen the 3,600 million hectares or the 640 million hectares, Edwards and Wibberley (1971) many years ago pointed out that surplus land does not reduce the need to use land wisely, or to plan its use, since unplanned change can lead to *using the wrong land* or *using land the wrong way*. To a large extent whether this will happen or not will depend on farming structure, and so attention now turns to this topic.

Changing farm structures

There is little doubt that farming structures are changing, the real debate is about why they are changing and how they will continue to change. There are broadly two schools of thought: the classical economic view and the Marxist political economy view. Harrison and Tranter (1983), two classical agricultural economists, have shown how the financial structure of farming that developed in the expansion years from 1940 to 1980 has left the industry badly fitted to face the financial risks of the 1990s. In particular they point out how the massive substitution of capital for labour has turned the terms of trade against the industry, and driven down the rate of return on working capital to such an extent, that incomes per farm could be maintained only if

Table 6.3. Some possible land surpluses in the year 2000 (thousand hectares).

	Maximum surplus	Minimum surplus
Cereals	1509	1010
Oilseed rape	50	(+ 50)
Potatoes	35	20
Sugar beet	40	30
Horticultural crops	40	30
Alternative crops	–	(+ 100)
All tillage crops	1674	940
Grassland (at 1985 stocking levels)	1930	900
All 'surplus' land	3604	1840
Grassland allowing for a fall in stocking levels of (a) 4%	1500	425
All surplus land	3175	1840
(b) 10%	839	(+ 300)
All surplus land	2514	640

Source: Edwards (1986).

there were enormous reductions in the number of farmers. Because this did not happen net farm incomes fell by 21% between 1964 and 1978 and by 51% between 1978 and 1985. The result has been a massive financial crisis in the late 1980s as indebtedness has coincided with high interest rates and further cutbacks in farm price support.

In a survey of 1276 farmers, Harrison and Tranter found the following responses to this crisis: first, a perverse response of increased output (58%); second, a reduction in the amount of inputs used (40%); third, a reduction in machinery costs (34%); fourth, a reduction in labour costs (33%); fifth, cutting out an unprofitable enterprise (21%); sixth, taking advice on financial matters (21%); seventh, carrying on as before (13%); eighth, diversifying (8%); and ninth, paying off debts by selling land (6%). The overall impression gained was one of an over-optimistic industry with more than half the heavily indebted farmers continuing to erode their equity at rates which could not be sustained for long.

Similar findings have been found by Marsden *et al.* (1986a) a Marxist inspired team of geographers in a longitudinal study of farmers in the London Green Belt, Dorset and Bedfordshire between 1970 and 1985. Their data show to some extent the subsumption of farm business organizations by outside capital, with 20% experiencing subsumption but 64% of farms staying the same and 8% actually experiencing decreasing subsumption. The same team (Marsden *et al.*, 1986b) in a study of how farmers adapt to change found that this depended on whether they were full-time agriculturalists (34%), survivalists (32%), accumulators (26%) or hobby farmers (9%).

Whatmore *et al.* (1987a) have used these findings and Marxist theory to produce a typology of farms based on the degree to which their decision making processes and use of capital has been subsumed by outside organizations, or by increasingly complex internal business arrangements. The typology is fourfold, with at one extreme; the 'closed enterprise' where the family farmer owns and manages the business and land, through to the other extreme, where 'subsumed enterprises' are effectively run by outside interests, e.g. the growing of peas for contract freezing. The topology has been tested in the field (Whatmore *et al.*, 1987b) and it has been found to exist even though the process of transition is not as homogeneous as first thought either through time or over space. Nonetheless, the formulation of farm policy must clearly take account of the existence of this typology and the way in which each group will or will not be influenced by their position in the typology, as much as to the nominal enterprise type or regional location of the farm.

This theme is continued by a political economist and an environmental academic Goodman and Redclift (1985), who in a Marxist view of agricultural policy have pointed out that capital has eliminated not the family farm as such, but its central role in the food production process. Agricultural policy should therefore be directed at multinational corporations at the beginning and end of the food chain, not at the farmer – the 'pig in the middle'.

At the same time they acknowledge the very considerable achievement of farmers who have sought and in large measure achieved political legitimacy, and thus massive CAP support, by seeking to distance themselves from capitalism at the ideological level, while fully embracing it at the economic level. Thus they have used patriotic arguments for self-suffiency in food and the need to protect the countryside as ways to preserve farm support and their own way of life.

Ilbery (1988) a geographer in contrast has found from research in the West Midlands that the family farm continues to survive and even flourish in the restructuring of agriculture. It is thus still important to research the attitudes and motivations of farmers and how and why they react in different situations.

Turning to the future the National Economic Development Office (1989) has projected for the 1990s a decline in the number of full-time farmers, family workers, salaried managers and employees from 334,000 in 1988 to either 276,000 or 244,000 depending on the assumptions involved. A static forecast of around 330,000 is, however, made for the number of part-time farmers, employees, family workers and second or casual workers, as full-time work is replaced by part-time work.

Nature of agricultural policy decision making

From what has been said so far it is clear that the reform of agricultural policy must take into account many complex and interrelated variables. In addition the system of policy making itself poses a problem. Basic problems according to the Committee of Public Accounts (1986), and the Comptroller and Auditor General (1985) are the lack of precision in the agreed objectives of agricultural policy, and the fact that the objectives of the CAP are not expressed in terms of quantified criteria or targets.

Additional problems relate to the nature of bureaucracies which tend to be committed to the *status quo* (Tracy, 1989). Having been established to administer policy, they develop a vested interest in its continuation, so 'major reforms' are unlikely. In the absence of a crisis serious enough to threaten the survival of the organization, changes will be limited, each such step being constrained by past decisions (Collins *et al.*, 1990).

Overlaying the problem of bureaucracy is the problem of getting several nations to agree a policy change. For example, Petit *et al.* (1987), a group of six economists, in an international study of policy formation have highlighted four key aspects of the process. First, there is considerable inertia in the system as no one member state wishes to trade-in their own national interest in favour of supra-national European interests. Only when the cost of not making a decision becomes too great as in the case of the budgetary crisis leading up to the milk quotas is a decision actually taken. Second, such a crisis is often solved by a process of coalition building and the creation of package deals. Third, the process can best be explained by relating it to the individual behaviour of each Agriculture Minister. Fourth, the process often averts crisis by partial solutions which can only get worse as the CAP budget continues to face acute constraint while farm incomes also deteriorate.

In conclusion, Fearne (1989) an agricultural economist has developed a model of CAP decision makers as satisfiers rather than optimizers in four key areas.

1. Acceptable levels of production or costs are not optimized but simply have two values, good enough or not good enough (acceptable or unacceptable).
2. One issue is taken at a time and no attempt is made to achieve multiple goals.
3. Conflict is resolved by compromises.
4. Targets are flexible depending on the resources available and this has allowed farm support expenditure to rise.

This pragmatic and pessimistic view of policy making needs to be kept in mind as we now turn to the core of the chapter, proposals to reform the colossus of the CAP.

Policy options for the reform of agriculture in isolation

In spite of all criticism ranged at agricultural policy in the 1980s it is still easy to forget that there are still those who would continue with support policies rather than cut them back. Not surprisingly the National Farmers Union (1988a) remains an organization committed to farm support policies and although they recognize the problem of surpluses they have still been able to list nine reasons why farmers should be supported, albeit in a gradually modified form.

1. Farm support has a role to play in ensuring an adequate supply of food at stable prices.
2. Continuing major price reductions would dramatically reduce the viability of many farm businesses and large parts of the rural economy.
3. Surplus problems should be tackled directly via setaside not by reduced prices. Support should thus be transferred to products not in EC surplus while at the same time allowing a sharp reduction in public expenditure (although it is not clear how the NFU intended to square this circle).
4. Reducing farm gate costs would have little impact on inflation since processing and other costs now account for more than 60% of food prices.
5. Agriculture is the major rural industry, which directly supports 14% of rural employment and indirectly supports many other rural industries.
6. There is at present no possibility of creating sufficient alternative jobs in rural areas to absorb those forced out of farming if all support were to be removed.
7. Total reliance on market forces would concentrate production on large intensive farms. Rural dereliction would follow in some areas.
8. Farmers are the natural custodians of the countryside, the free market would not be capable of supporting farming's conservationist role.
9. The growing emphasis on land management and the environmental aspects of farming is a positive response to the problems of surplus production and greater interest in the countryside.

These themes were further modified throughout the winter of 1990/91 with a series of press releases from the NFU with more emphasis on: (i) achieving more financial return from the market than from the taxpayer, mainly by better marketing and quality production; and (ii) by strongly advocating supply management so as to keep as many farmers on the land as possible by de-intensifying production by setaside, limits on inputs, e.g. nitrogen, and extensifying via organic production.

Cox *et al.* (1988) in a commentary on the NFU's changing position argue that it has thus compromised its standpoint on 'agricultural fundamentalism' as an expedient act in the face of overwhelming odds. The NFU has, however, salvaged three features in its general retreat. First, it has ensured that as far as possible all the new controls will operate through the traditional administrative channels, and has thus retained its place in the decision making process. Second, it has ensured that the principle of compensation for foregoing production rights has remained predominant, and third, it has managed to attach values to some of the new controls, for example, milk quotas, even though initially the proposal was that these could not be owned or traded.

It is thus clear that even the NFU has had to abandon farm support as a good thing in itself. This was partly due to the demolition job carried out by Bowers and Cheshire (1983) in their book on agriculture and the countryside, in which they singled out two areas from which farm support policies were said to gain their credibility: first, the need to give agriculture a high level of protection as a special industry and second, the need to expand the industry. With regard to the protectionist argument, Bowers and Cheshire argue that the case for maintaining farm incomes the same as other workers is not a principle followed elsewhere in the economy. Similarly the need to keep farm workers on the land, has not been followed by a similar argument to keep coal miners down the pits or steel workers in the steel mills. However, there is a case for maintaining farming in remote rural areas.

Turning to the arguments for expansion, Bowers and Cheshire divide these into three categories. In category one, the balance or payments argument is dismissed since there are far more effective ways of reducing the balance by investing in industry for example. In category two, the self-sufficiency and strategic argument is dismissed as being out of date due to the rise of surpluses and nuclear weapons, and in category three, altruism to the Third World is dismissed as another way of subsidizing rich farmers and less effective than helping the Third World feed itself.

Having seen off the arguments against doing nothing it is now time to turn to the policy options available from a technical standpoint, before examining the policy options made by the various actors involved. The options can be divided into four broad groups: a return to the free market; price changes; controls on production; structural reform; and a fifth option a combination of options.

One of the fiercest critics of agricultural policy has been the Conservative MP Richard Body who in three books in the 1980s (1982, 1984 and 1987) evolved a set of free market options. In 1982 he advocated abandoning the CAP and protectionism in order that there would be fewer big arable farms but more small pastoral farms with corresponding livestock benefits. In 1984 he extended his theme and proposed the repatriation of agricultural policy with a new Agricultural Act which would create a free market for agricultural produce, compensate for profits foregone in favour of conservation, create free trade in food from abroad and cut grants and taxation aid to farming in order to achieve a lower input type of farming. In 1987 this theme was continued when Body proposed a move away from technological unsustainable farming towards biological cyclical organic farming, with the transition period being funded by the Government.

In a popular but hard-hitting polemic by another MP – this time for Europe – Cottrell (1987) has recommended a gradual but progressive evacuation from support; the abolition of the Milk Marketing Board; and opening up Europe to world market prices for farm products. This theme has also been advocated by Bowers and Cheshire (1983) who argue that the single most important change would be a reduction in the level of agricultural protection with a special reduction in cereal prices to redress the structural imbalance between horn and corn in the CAP. In order to stabilize support prices at a little above world market prices they propose the free entry of food at world market prices, and the replacement of intervention buying with the system of deficiency payments which operated in Britain between 1947 and 1973.

However, many of these proposals are politically improbable and returning to the pragmatic world the Agriculture Committee of the House of Commons has been and remains a strong advocate of price cuts and over the years it has called, for example, (1986) for a reduction of 10–15% in the price of cereals, backed up by the imposition of stricter quality controls.

Maillet (1987) a former general manager of the EC has also advocated a lowering of prices to the level needed to ensure the security of supply, and direct subsidies only to those farmers who need them, thus saving public funds both by lowering prices and by targeting income support.

Raymond (1985a) a former MAFF employee has, however, shown both empirically and theoretically how rises in farm productivity can offset real falls in farm prices, thus making the imposition of quotas of thresholds on production inevitable if overproduction is to be curbed. In a situation where a ceiling on output is imposed one option is to reduce inputs such as fertilizers, pesticides, machinery and labour. However, there are other options and Raymond (1985b) discusses the alternatives of taking marginal land in the uplands out of production altogether, or of reducing inputs in the rich farming areas with corresponding improvements to the ecology. A further option is to make a virtue out of reduced inputs by converting to organic farming and producing food with a premium price which more than offsets the lower output.

One of the most considered reviews about the various types of production controls remains the House of Lords Select Committee on the European Communities (1983) report on supply controls. This considered four methods of supply control: quotas, mixed price systems, acreage diversion schemes, and production thresholds. The report concluded the following.

1. A return to a free market situation and very low prices would be unacceptable on economic, social and political grounds, and is contrary to the concept of CAP.

2. Supply control via quotas related to area or output is unlikely to work where small farmers predominate and the produce is marketed through a large number of independent outlets.
3. Setaside and payment in kind programmes are unlikely to be successful in the EC.
4. Deficiency payments while appropriate are likely to cost too much and be difficult to administer.
5. Guarantee thresholds for cereals need stiff penalties if they are to contain excess production.
6. Guarantee thresholds for milk are a sensible mechanism as long as they are applied steadfastly, and are reinforced by penal levies above certain thresholds.
7. The adverse effect of such policies on disadvantaged farmers should be mitigated by direct income aids.

In conclusion the report could find no one method of supply control which offered an easy option. Perhaps this is why the only serious production control so far imposed has been milk quotas. According to a study carried out at the University of Exeter, for the Ministry of Agriculture (1988) the effects have neither been dramatic nor disastrous in England and Wales, at least for the 7400 producers who stayed in milk production between 1984 and 1986. No study was made of the 2700 (6.7% of the total) producers who left compared with 20.5% of the total who had left between 1976 and 1983.

Overall, as economic theory would predict, quotas focused the attention of producers on the control of inputs and restructuring the process of production. In the longer term the study recognized milk quotas as equivalent to an income earning asset which resulted in the creation of a market for quota. Indeed the sale of quota and the regular guaranteed income ensured by the quota system meant that by the end of the 1980s, quota was being re-evaluated as the best thing for dairy farmers since the advent of sliced bread. This mirrors the experience of Canada, where Bowler (1986) has demonstrated that the success of the Canadian system of milk quotas was due to three factors: a high rate of attrition in the number of milk producers; the expansion of the fluid market giving fewer producers a share of a bigger market; and tradeable quotas.

Another method of control is offered by limiting inputs. Controls on nitrogen have been a favourite option, largely due to the damaging effects of nitrogen if overused. For example, a study prepared for the Commission of the European Communities (1989b) has shown how the long-term use of nitrogen by intensive farming has led to nitrate levels in drinking water well in excess of advisable safety levels. Although accepting 'the polluter should pay principle' the study found that a tax on nitrogen would be an ineffective deterrent, and that quotas would be difficult to police. Instead they suggested that a policy on regulating land use, via land management schemes, allied to compensation payments over a transitional period, could be the best way forward since it could combine environmental gains in the countryside as well as reducing nitrate levels. These ideas have largely been implemented in the NSAs pilot scheme outlined in Chapter 3.

An alternative to production controls is provided by structural reform. However, although this has been a plank of EC policy since the mid 1970s, not only has it always been a beggar at the door of the support system, but it has increasingly been seen as a means of subsidizing labour, environmental programmes and diversification developments, rather than production. According to Baldock (1989) it is a policy which addresses symptoms rather than causes.

With regard to combinations of options, the House of Lords Select Committee on the European Communities has been a longstanding advocate of CAP reform via a mix of changes. For example, in (1980) it made the following proposals.

1. Extend and adapt the CAP to a Common Food and Agricultural Policy.
2. Initiate a five-year rolling programme aimed at reducing the number of producers, by using price support, structural reform and the temporary use of quotas on produce qualifying for support.
3. Initiate a progressive annual reduction in real terms for producer prices for surplus commodities, but not exceeding 2.5% per annum,
4. Use structural policy to encourage low-cost farming and become part of a comprehensive policy of diversification for rural areas involving food processing, forestry and tourism.

A mix of options has also been considered by Russell and Power (1989), two agricultural economists who have examined the budgetary costs of three different scenarios, A, B and C. Under A no change is assumed, at a budgetary cost of £269 per hectare; under B export subsidies are removed for beef and cereals, reducing the budgetary cost to £140 per hectare; while C is as for B but with intervention also removed, bringing down the cost to £65 per hectare.

A combination of options was also involved in the much hailed 1988 farm price settlement, namely, a decrease in intervention prices, the imposition of producer co-responsibility levies, linked to cuts in intervention prices for exceeding thresholds, and a modified form of production controls via setaside. Using econometric models, De Gorte and Meilke (1989) two agricultural economists concluded that cuts in prices were more efficient than co-responsibility levies, but that both were less efficient than quotas. However, none of the options chosen was the best policy in overall welfare terms, since they all assume EC prices being held above world prices. According to De Gorte and Meilke the only long-term option is to reduce EC prices below world market prices via export taxes and to compensate farmers via decoupled aids.

However, such a radical option is politically unlikely and Burrell (1987) using economic theory has concluded that a co-responsibility levy related to thresholds provides the least unpalatable political option but only if the size of the levy is far more restrictive, than the 1988 penalty.

In an alternative view Hill (1989) an agricultural economist has forecast three main changes: first, decoupling product price policy from income support; second, sieving out from support all those householders (perhaps one-third of the total) where agriculture is not the main source of income; and third, a reduction of support to 'agricultural' households and a shift of support to households who operate farms in a part-time capacity but with a broader concern for the environment and the countryside.

So far the discussion has centred on what policy makers want and believe to be achievable. An alternative dimension is provided by what farmers want. This is provided by the National Farmers Union (1988b) which has produced a shopping list of wants, divided into, what they wanted and why they wanted it. At the top of the list is the replacement of stabilizers and price cuts with supply management via quotas, since price cuts would lead to a devastation of the rural economy. In contrast milk quotas have cut supply and yet at the same time maintained profitability. Second, in the cereals sector the NFU wanted effective supply management either via a compulsory annual licensing scheme (e.g. potatoes) or a voluntary scheme with adequate compensation. It was recognized nonetheless that setaside by itself is inadequate to reduce production since it was merely acting as an outgoers scheme. Third, the NFU wanted milk quotas to continue beyond 1992. Fourth, the NFU wanted a European standard for organic production and financial support for farmers over the two-year conversion period. Fifth, the NFU wanted the definition of smaller farmers to be revised for the UK because of its larger farms and for all structural payments to be slanted in favour of the smaller farmer by paying a higher level for the first 'X' units per farm. Sixth, the NFU wanted a further expansion of LFAs even though these now cover over 50% of the UK. Seventh, the NFU wanted more aid for rural communities to be channelled to farming via a diversion of Social and Regional Development Funds from towns to rural areas, and eighth, the NFU wanted more help via advice and grants to encourage farmers further to adopt environmentally responsible farming methods.

Bradbury *et al.* (1990), in a survey of 102 farmers, confirmed some of the NFUs list when they found little support for co-responsibility levies. However, nitrogen use restrictions and setaside – current favourites with the NFU – found less favour with farmers on the ground who were particularly negative about schemes involving the withdrawal of land for agricultural use. Instead, the favoured option notably among cereal farmers, was production quotas rather than limits on land use.

If farmers are to achieve these aims they will need to convince politicians and not least the Labour Party (John *et al.*, 1987) who have been examining five negative and four positive approaches. On the negative side co-responsibility levies, setaside and limits on inputs have broadly been rejected in favour of quotas allied to price cuts for cereals, dairying and most live-stock. On the positive side expanding markets and alternatives uses for existing crops have broadly been rejected in favour of alternative land uses and less intensive farming. Notably favoured has been the option of planting around 1 million hectares of farm woodland over 20 years on grades 3 and 4 land and encouraging organic farming. Income support has also been advocated on social and economic grounds in the LFAs.

Throughout this section constant allusions have been made to actual and proposed changes to farm policy both by the European Commission and the UK Government. It is now time to discuss the possibly momentous discussions that have been taking place as this book was finally put together between September 1990 and March 1991, Four broad forces can be discerned in this process. First, external pressure to reform the CAP and completely abolish forum subsidies by 2000 coming from the USA and other major food exporters (the Cairns Group) as part of the Uruguay round of talks on the need to reform and update GATT. Second, internal pressure on the CAP to contain spending that once again had soared way over budget in 1990 due to the entry of the former East Germany into the CAP, extra expenditure on the unexpected beef surpluses arising from a fall in beef consumption following the 'mad cow' disease scare, and general further over-production. Third, ideological pressure from the UK Government to cut back farm support policies which it deemed to be unwelcome as a social subsidy, and fourth, division between the CLA and NFU as to how best to limit the damage caused by any change in farm policy.

The process began in November 1990 when the EC farm Ministers offered 30% cuts in farm support in contrast to the 75–90% cuts demanded by the US and Australians in the run up to the GATT talks in December. In a response to these proposals the NFU advocated supply management as a means of keeping all farmers in business. In contrast the CLA argued that the need was to take some farmers out of production and to pay them a reason-able level of redundancy payment. In March 1991, however, the new president of the NFU, David Naish, was said to be less enamoured with setaside and thought to be moving to nitrogen quotas. What the NFU cannot do, however, is to move to the CLA position on price pressure in order to remove inefficient farmers, since this would be unacceptable to the members.

In January 1991 the Commission debated proposals by the Irish Commis-sioner for Agriculture, Ray McSharry, which accepted the need for strong corrective measures, if serious crises were to be avoided. The proposals were centred on ten key points.

1. Maintaining the maximum number of farmers on the land.
2. Recognizing the dual role of farmers as producers and custodians of the

countryside.

3. Helping rural areas to develop other forms of economic activity.

4. Avoiding a build up of intervention stocks by controlling production.

5. Improving the competitive position of cereals.

6. Encouraging extensification and other environmentally friendly forms of farming.

7. Ensuring the EC recognizes its interdependence on the international scene.

8. Continuing the CAP on its fundamental principles involving a single market, Community preference, and common financing.

9. Ensuring the budget goes to those in greatest need.

10. Introducing measures whereby quotas and other restrictions are increased progressively with the size of farm.

In more detail the proposals contained cuts of 40% in cereal prices, 10–15% for dairy products, and 15% for beef. These cuts were not meant to fall evenly and a very controversial part of the proposals suggested that small producers would benefit at the expense of large producers, as shown below:

Cereals

Area of farm	Aid to offset cuts	% of land to be setaside
< 30 ha	100%	—
30–80 ha	75%	25% of land between 30 and 80 ha
> 80 ha	65%	35% of land above 80 ha

e.g. A farmer with 180 ha would have to setaside 0% of first 30 ha, 25% of next 50 ha, and 35% of remaining 120 ha.

Milk 4.5% overall cut in quota. No cut for producers < 200,000 kg, but 10% cut for producers > 200,000 kg per annum.

Beef 5% cut in intervention price. £28 per animal for three years but only for the first 90 animals.

The McSharry paper was agreed in early February 1991 by the Commission as a means of achieving fundamental reform of the main problems of the CAP, which were seen to be escalating budgets, out of balance markets, rapidly mounting stocks, growing environmental problems and declining farm incomes in spite of increased CAP budgets. However, the UK Minister for Agriculture, John Gummer, totally rejected the paper because: (i) it attempted to keep as many farmers on the land as possible by offsetting lower prices with higher direct payments; (ii) it thus involved a considerable increase in EC expenditure; and (iii) the modulation proposals for small farmers outlined above would hit the UK unfairly, with its large farm structure.

As an alternative the Minister set out a different way forward based on four criteria. The reformed CAP must be: (i) less costly; (ii) better directed to the farmer; (iii) better designed to improve the environment; and (iv) an economic, not a social policy. Accordingly, he proposed cuts in milk quotas, cuts in support prices for cereals, milk, beef and sheep across the board, a further use of setaside as an environmental as well as a production restraint and a further use of money for environmental schemes like ESA, as money is released from the 80% of the CAP budget consumed by support prices.

In an unprecedented move in February 1991 the NFU and CPRE joined forces in also rejecting the McSharry paper. In their alternative they proposed six points which included direct payments to farmers for any countryside management they undertake.

In parallel with this debate at the end of February 1991 the Commission put forward their proposals for the annual price review for 1991/92. This included price cuts but not those proposed by McSharry. However, the price cuts proposed would not have been big enough to stop CAP expenditure rising significantly by nearly £5 billion to £23 billion, even though they contained proposals to cut milk quotas by 2–3% and cereal support by 6–7%. The package was rejected by Ministers in March 1991, and so at the time of writing (16 April 1991) all three proposals: GATT, McSharry and the 1991/92 price review, were all still unresolved, thus continuing the chaos of previous years.

Policy options for the reform of agriculture in a wider context

Introductory comments

In a major review of agricultural policy McInerney (1986) has argued that a crossroads was reached in the 1980s as most of the traditional arguments for agriculture fell away. For example, three of the five classical reasons for any government to interfere with agriculture, namely, efficiency, stability, and growth, could no longer be sustained. First, the 'efficiency' argument is no longer tenable since agricultural policies have produced inefficient surpluses and sustained inefficient farm structures. Second, the 'stability' argument is no longer valid since stable supplies can be provided by an adequate futures market. Third, 'growth' is no longer needed because of surpluses and if new technologies are desired they can be provided by near market private research. Conversely, of the other two classic reasons for intervention, 'sustainability' may not be possible without government intervention if chemical farming proves too unsustainable and 'equity' is not achievable in a relatively declining sector of the economy except with the aid of government intervention.

Accordingly, McInerney concluded that all the arguments for agricultural policy reform point toward reducing support for farm products and redirecting policy to the direct support of farmers' incomes, possibly via the production of environmental or CARE goods (Conservation, Amenity and Rural Environment). Traditional agricultural policy always under-provides these because they do not have explicit market prices. This redirection, however, raises a number of issues. For example, can the free market approach work by itself, or does it need a system of planning controls, and should the policy have regional variations depending on land and/or land-scape quality.

McInerney's classical economic arguments have been complemented by Porritt (1987) a leading light in the green movement, who has produced a balance sheet comparing the costs and benefits of current agricultural policies as shown below.

Costs

Decay of rural communities
Elimination of small farmer
Unemployment of farm workers
Destruction of the countryside
Extensive loss of flora and
    fauna
Huge import bills for
    fertilizers and feedstuffs
Dependence on cheap oil
Dependence on pesticides and
    chemicals
Cruelty of factory farming
Decline of husbandry and
    farming skills
Misuse of the soil via
    monoculture farming
Wasteful surpluses and food
    mountains
Higher processing, packaging
    and transport costs
Misuse of subsidies and tax
    concessions
Concentration of power and
    wealth in fewer hands
Dearer food in the long term
Poorer quality of food and
    lower standards of nutrition

Benefits

Higher productivity
Greater efficiency
Cheaper food in short term

Porritt thus suggests a different use of grants and subsidies to reverse the balance sheet by creating a network of smallholdings on land purchased by local councils with the creation of over 1 million jobs in the EC as a whole. This would be based on a return to mixed low intensity farming capable of feeding most of the local community in a revived and repopulated country-side peopled by people freed from despised urban jobs.

However, Potter (1990), a geographer, has shown that current farm policies are in fact keeping existing farmers on the land through a series of schemes, such as setaside, which Potter dubs collectively a 'Farm Survival Plan' (FSP). Although there are some wider benefits from such an approach, for example, the potential to bring aggressive profit maximizers into the conservation fold via the back door of setaside, there are far more con-straints. First, the main aim of the FSP is the maintenance of farms, and rural incomes while at the same time cutting surpluses. Second, much spending on creative conservation comes about adventitiously at the time of major new investment (Potter, 1986a) and thus any cut in general support leads to a cut in specific spending on wider rural planning aims. Third, the FSP is vulner-able to political change, and fourth, the FSP keeps existing farm structures intact at the macro level and leaves any restructuring in the hands of indi-vidual farmers. It is not therefore targeted either at those farms or those areas where conservation aims could be maximized.

Continuing this theme of uncertainty and imprecision in present policies de Witt (1988) a Dutch agricultural economist has argued that increasing yields will lead to the disappearance of any form of intensive agriculture in the less-endowed regions of the EC. The question then arises as to whether to manage this land for some purpose or to let it run wild. It could be tempting, therefore, to adopt the latter course and thus allow the consumer to benefit via lower food prices and lower VAT charges, but de Witt argues that the windfall should be split between the consumer and the EC, thus allowing half the savings made on the CAP to be transferred to social and environmental spending in the rural areas.

However, it is almost certain that if the Thatcherite school were to continue to hold sway in the 1990s that money cut from the agricultural budget will not necessarily remain in the rural budget. For example, John MacGregor when he was Minister of Agriculture, has argued that:

> given the unsustainable scale to which the taxpayers'
> contribution has now grown, with all the misallocation of
> resources that it implies, it would be wrong to encourage the
> belief that as savings are made so the current subsidies can
> be automatically diverted to alternative support systems or
> indeed that alternative economic activity in the countryside
> must inevitably be grant aided (National Economic
> Development Office, 1987, p. 12).

These and other alternatives have been considered by the Centre for Agricultural Strategy (1986) who, in common with Newcastle University, have developed the so-called Newcastle model which has estimated the possible effects on employment, recreation and tourism, and landscape and wildlife of four possible changes in the CAP: first, the continuation of current trends; second, a free trade scenario; third, a quotas scenario and fourth, a prices policy scenario based on co-responsibility levies on surpluses. From this work it was concluded that removing the CAP would not by itself lead to environmental benefit, indeed, under some scenarios cereal farming profits might increase and lead to a further extension of arable farming. In contrast, a scenario that led to more lowland livestock farming at the expense of cereals could lead to environmental benefits. The study pointed out, however, that there is a very narrow financial boundary, with variations between regions, between keeping agriculture profitable enough to maintain rural environments without at the same time leading to over-production and damaging over-intensive production systems.

In a further analysis of the Newcastle model Bell (1987) has reported on work at ITE which estimated that three of the scenarios, quotas, price restrictions and free trade would lead to environmental gains overall, but not necessarily in all parts of the country, but that a continuation of existing trends would lead to environmental losses, but again not evenly spread over the country. In the area of employment, the current trends scenario would lead to a gain in jobs but the other three would lead to job losses, varying from 39,000 under the prices scenario to 170,000 under the free trade scenario. The process of change would not, however, be all one way and the CAS report also presented a list of opportunities and problems arising from their scenarios (Table 6.4).

Looking to the future Gilg (1991), in a review of possible options for the future of the CAP and the environment, has examined five possibilities.

1. *An overall cutback in CAP support.* If the cuts were hard enough to work then marginal land would fall out of production producing a poor conservation mix of intensively farmed land in one region and scrub vegetation of only common species elsewhere.

2. *Diversion of CAP support into other products.* The only real alternative is forestry which can use the mild wet climate of the marginal land to cut back the 90% of timber imported into the UK in the long term. Problems include acidification, farmer resistance and the need to subsidize the woods in their first 50 years of non-production.

3. *Diversion of CAP support to conservation.* An ideal but unlikely solution since other sectors will probably divert the CAP funds to their programmes.

4. *Diversion of CAP support to small farmers.* Small farmers tend to cause less environmental damage but cannot afford to invest in conservation, so a direct payment would be needed if this form of income supplementation were to be used for conservation, it could be a device to keep some of the funds that would otherwise be diverted in alternative **3** by justifying expenditure under social grounds but using it for conservation.

Table 6.4. Some planning issues arising from CAP change.

Issue	Opportunity	Problem
Declines in land values	Purchase of valued SSSI and Nature Reserve sites Forestry and woodland become viable options Recreational and other users can buy in	Land changing hands may lead to loss of features Development control of 'gardens' or 'fields'
Decline of returns	Management agreements become cheaper Less capital investment reduces countryside change	Less spare money for voluntary tree planting, habitat creation, or for general maintenance of the countryside Possible intensification on land so far left by choice
Farm diversification	New business, broader economic base, range of employment opportunities Utilization of farm buildings Integration of agriculture with local economy	Traffic, impact on open land policies Local 'amenity' objections Change to listed buildings
Shedding of farm labour	New business in contracting etc. Opportunities for part-time occupations, smoothing peaks and troughs in employment requirements	Unemployment Further decline of social fabric Vacant farm cottages Deprivation and call on services
Recreation	More land available for leisure use Permanent pasture for easy walking Farms seek to provide for tourists and visitors	Possible cereal expansion: poor walking Pressured farmers have little time for the non-paying public, or for input into local economy and society New, non-traditional owners may be unwilling to share use

Source: Centre for Agricultural Strategy (1986).

5. *Planning controls over agriculture.* CAP-inspired developments could be made subject to planning controls and could thus cut expenditure and prevent environmental damage. The experience of forestry and town planning has not, however, been very encouraging in this respect. Furthermore, planning control by themselves do not safeguard living environments.

Table 6.5. Possible land surplus by the year 2000 as devised by Brown (Hatfield, 1983), in thousand hectares.

	Lower estimate	Upper estimate
Cereals	900	1100
Forage	1400	1555
Potatoes	30	70
Sugar beet	15	30
Oilseed rape	(40) Gain	–
Horticulture	75	105
Totals	2380	2860

( ) Increase.

In reality these five options can be reduced to two broad themes: restructuring farmland to other productive uses or to overt conservation use.

Restructuring farmland to other productive uses

Once again the key issue is how much rural land will be surplus to current requirements. Various estimates have been made. For example, Brown (Hatfield, 1988) using trend projections has produced lower and upper estimates for the land surplus that might occur within each sector by the year 2000 as shown in Table 6.5.

Whichever figure is correct, Taylor (Hatfield, 1988) cautions, however, that there will be much more land available for forestry than there will be forestry available for land, unless a very positive and probably very expensive policy of subsidies is introduced.

This theme is taken up by North (1989) a land economist who has assumed continuing productivity increases for agriculture of the order of between 1 and 2% per year mainly based on advances in biotechnology. He then calculates how the surplus land generated might be used under two scenarios, market led or extensive subsidized farming as shown in Table 6.6.

North concludes that under the market-led scenario, agriculture would produce more as an efficient competitive industry requiring minimal taxpayer support and be more environmentally friendly due to biotechnology. Under the extensive scenario the industry would require substantial price support, be less competitive, operate in a smaller market and have little prospect of providing raw materials to the chemical industry. However, in either case none of the alternative uses is able to mop up the surplus land created, leaving at the very least 3.5 million hectares for conservation or wilderness.

In a more comprehensive forecast, the National Economic Development Council (1987) considered no less than six policy options.

Table 6.6. Potential use of surplus land under two scenarios, as devised by North (1989). (In million acres.)

	Market led	Extensive
Current area	17.65	17.65
Area needed for agriculture in 2015	11.27	12.46
Surplus	6.38	5.19
Other crops	0.08	0.08
Sheep, goats milk	0.06	0.06
Organic	0.10	0.10
Surplus	6.14	4.95
Industrial raw materials	1.00	–
Surplus	5.14	4.95
Formal recreation		
Horses	0.20	0.20
Sports	0.15	0.15
Parks	0.15	0.15
Surplus	4.64	4.45
Forestry and woodlands	1.00	1.00
Surplus	3.64	3.45

1. Price manipulation.
2. Physical limitations on output, e.g. quotas.
3. Physical limitations on inputs, e.g. controls on fertilizer.
4. Changing the costs of inputs, e.g. nitrogen taxes.
5. Taking resources out of agriculture, e.g. setaside, early retirement, alternative uses of land.
6. Discouraging substitutes, e.g. taxes on imported foods.

Out of these the council favoured prices for the long term and quotas for the short term, since none of the other offered significant enough cuts in production.

Whichever policy combination was chosen the Council argued that existing trends would have the following trends superimposed on them.

1. Some reduction in intensity of farming.
2. A reduction in the amount of land used.
3. Both of these reductions to occur on marginal land.
4. A shift from cereals and milk to livestock with a shunting effect down the intensive farming ladder with a subsequent impact on hill farmers at the bottom.
5. A reduction in net aggregate farm income.
6. A quickening of structural change in farming with fewer farmers and farm workers.
7. A need for farmers to earn more from alternative enterprises.
8. Regional variations in these trends.

Table 6.7. Possible changes in cereal area 1986–mid 1990 UK.

		Implied reduction in UK land ('000 ha)			
	Assumed once and for all impact on potential yield due to impact of controls %	Land leaving at average yield		Land leaving at 80% average yield	
Assumed potential growth in yields %		EC 150 mt quota	EC 160 mt quota	EC 150 mt quota	EC 160 mt quota
3	0	970	770	1210	860
	− 5.0	810	600	1010	750
1	0	400	160	500	200
	− 5.0	200	nil	250	nil

Source: National Economic Development Council (1987).

Using different assumptions about yield growth and EC production limits the Council then produced a range of permutations for the reduction in cereal area as shown in Table 6.7. From this table the Council then made a number of assumptions to come up with a figure of 700,000 hectares which was roughly in the centre of the wide range of possible outcomes. They then predicted the derived land use pattern shown in Table 6.8 based on the potential for novel crops and forestry.

In summary, the Council did not see a great potential for novel crops, and forecast that non-agricultural diversification would have no impact on land use but a partial role in supporting farm incomes, especially if payments for amenity management were increased in both scope and finance. With regard

Table 6.8. Derived land use for the 1990s, UK ('000 hectare).

	1986 Actual	1990s		
		Central estimate	Adjusted for novel crops	Adjusted for forestry
Cereal	4020	3300	3300	3300
Other tillage	1260	1230	1230	1230
Novel crops	−	−	200	200
Total tillage	5280	4530	4730	4730
Grass	6800	7370	7170	7020
Rough grazing	6070	5870	5870	5770
Other land	540	650	630	630
Total agricultural area	18,690	18,420	18,400	18,150

Source: National Economic Development Council (1987).

to forestry this was seen as being able to take up to 250,000 hectares, rising to 480,000 hectares, if land prices fell enough and financial incentives for both commercial foresters and for farm foresters were increased enough.

By the beginning of the decade even the farm lobby had recognized the magnitude of the problem and a panel of the NFU (1990) forecast a surplus of 1,400,000 hectares by the late 1990s. Examining how to deal with this surplus, the panel found that of the four main options *Urban Development* even if densities were halved would only take around 120,000 hectares during the decade. *Forestry* would probably only take 280,000 hectares, though there is a much greater margin for error here. *Diversification* which tends to re-use buildings rather than land would only take a few thousand hectares, for example, even if the demand for 600 golf courses, which is said to exist, could be economically proven this would only take 3100 hectares. Finally, the potential for *new crops* to take up the land is severely limited. Even under the most optimistic scenario all these alternatives would take up just over 400,000 hectares, leaving around 1,000,000 surplus hectares.

Accordingly, the Panel recommended the following.

1. An extension and improvement of the presently limited 'Environmentally Sensitive Areas' model in order to provide farmers with incentives to produce positive environmental benefits to the countryside.
2. Encouraging environmentally friendly farming methods and other alternative systems which satisfy consumer demand for such food production methods.
3. An examination of the pros and cons of extensification schemes.
4. A review but continuation of the incentives available for diversification.
5. A review of the incentives available for creating and managing woodland.
6. Increasing research into the potential for the new crops, livestock and their end products.
7. Increasing the flexibility of planning policies to allow small-scale developments which would meet socio-economic and environmental objectives.

With even the NFU clearly thinking of turning over at least one million hectares to conservation use or de-intensifying production on a wider scale it is now time to turn to proposals for restructuring farmland to conservation use.

Restructuring farmland to conservation

It might be thought that abandoning farmland would lead to land of high conservation value, but this is not so. For example Green (1989) (Fig. 6.1) has demonstrated that the most diverse ecosystems come from plagio-climaxes and that the creation and survival of such highly desirable environments, such as floristically rich hay meadows, depends on sustaining a finely

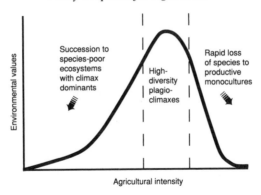

Fig. 6.1. The effect of agriculture in establishing and maintaining diverse ecosystems.

balanced intensity of agricultural use. According to Green a managed agriculture everywhere is to be preferred to agricultural monocultures in some areas and tumbledown farmland elsewhere.

In a similar model to Green's, Buckwell (1989) has shown how even primitive agriculture is an intervention in the ecosystem (Fig. 6.2). Modern agriculture could, however, achieve higher environmental outputs for a given food output than previous agricultures, which have developed as shown in positions A, B, C, D and E, with F representing the present position and 1, 2, 3, 4, 5 and 6 representing the different options now available.

Point 1 represents extra food output but a loss of environmental quality (the post-war scenario). Point 2 represents an environmentally neutral strategy in which food output growth is not achieved at the expense of the environment (by adopting clever science to work with nature rather than against it). Point 3 represents environmental gains and also food production growth (the view of the scientific optimist via biotechnology). Point 4 represents environmental gains with no loss of food production (the position

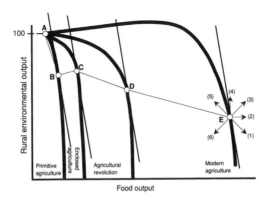

Fig. 6.2. The evolution of the agriculture–environment production possibility frontier.

claimed by the organic food lobby). Point 5 represents environmental gains with a loss of food production (the ESA scenario), and point 6 represents the worst possible scenario, a loss of environmental output and also food output (the doomwatch scenario in which the Earth bites back at its misuse).

Buckwell concludes that we have no overall policies to influence which of these courses is followed, since rural environmental failure is a result of market failure (exacerbated by government policies) since there is no mechanism for society to signal the socially optimal level of output of environmental goods. Therefore tinkering with agricultural policy will not be sufficient. To deal with environmental problems it is necessary to have an environmental policy.

Such a policy has been provided by Potter (1983), a geographer who in work for the World Wide Fund for Nature has proposed an 'Alternative Package of Agricultural Subsidies and Incentives' (APAS). His proposals remove the contradictory system of grant aid for agricultural production being offset by conservation compensation payments. Instead the two systems would be integrated but with three different systems for three different types of farmer as follows. In the first system (Special Assistance Areas) farmers who have tracts of land or sites of special conservation value would be eligible for 'special area' grants and subsidies aimed at protecting the income of the whole farm. In the second system, grants in LFAs should be paid to less favoured farmers rather than as at present to all and sundry, and the scope of the grants should be extended and modified to favour conservation of the landscape rather than increased production. In the third system (Intensively Farmed Land) the remaining farms would get grant aid only for whole farm schemes rather than one-off items and there would be a ceiling on the size of grant given. Although Potter's ideas were attacked by a special NFU conference (Korbey, 1984) for being too radical for their day, they have been taken up by other groups in the 1990s.

For example, the NCC (1991) has called for the ESAs regime to be offered to all farmers in order, to complement all the other schemes on offer. In a similar proposal the Royal Society for the Protection of Birds (1990) has used Manchester University costings to show how environmental cross-compliance in setaside schemes could provide environmental benefits on such land and also cut cereals production in the UK by 3.8%, thus saving CAP expenditure. Under the RSPB scheme farmers who wanted CAP support would have to register their farm and its land use. This would form the basis for claims either for traditional farm support or environmental support.

Finally, Jenkins (1990) an agricultural economist in a report for the CPRE and the World Wide Fund for Nature takes this series of proposals to their logical conclusion and proposes that food production should be rewarded by market mechanisms alone. Thus freeing consumers and taxpayers from the burden of supporting artificially inflated farm product prices. Overall farm incomes would in contrast be maintained by paying farmers for the

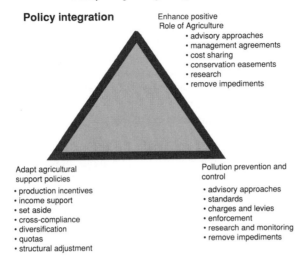

Policy integration

Enhance positive
Role of Agriculture
• advisory approaches
• management agreements
• cost sharing
• conservation easements
• research
• remove impediments

Adapt agricultural
support policies
• production incentives
• income support
• set aside
• cross-compliance
• diversification
• quotas
• structural adjustment

Pollution prevention and
control
• advisory approaches
• standards
• charges and levies
• enforcement
• research and monitoring
• remove impediments

Fig. 6.3. Opportunities for the successful integration of agricultural and environmental policies.

environmental goods they produce, via a system of Environmental Management Payments (EMPs) paid for the production of specific environmental goods on a voluntary basis, but within the framework of tighter statutory controls over farming practices. Because 30% of the EC budget is 'wasted' in inefficiency, the remaining 70% could be spent on EMPs giving a net saving to the budget, but still spending between £60 and £85 per hectare on farm support. According to Jenkins, the EMP system is capable of simultaneously reducing output, maintaining farm populations and incomes, reducing the cost of farm support, providing unequivocal environmental benefits, such as reduced pollution, improved habitats, and landscape, and improved food quality.

Six general proposals for restructuring agricultural support

Finally, six general proposals have been made in descending order of organizational size, by the OECD, the Countryside Commission, the CPRE, and three sets of individuals.

The OECD (1989) from a survey of all member countries has concluded that the 1990s offer opportunities for integrating agriculture with the environment by integrating the factors shown in Fig. 6.3. For the future, the OECD recommends that the principle of cross-compliance should be adhered to with farm funding being redirected towards conservation and management of land. However, cross-compliance can only work with direct support. Unfortunately, setaside does not offer an ideal opportunity although it does present a second best interim solution, especially if:

- Setaside is targeted at areas with environmental problems including key production areas.
- The time period is sufficiently long to induce farmers to diversify into environmentally favourable activities like certain types of forestry.
- Setaside land is selected by a tender type system in order to maximize budget savings.
- Short-term rotational setaside is extended.

The next proposal has been made by the Countryside Commission (1989b) who have proposed a 'comprehensive menu' of schemes which would cover everything from exclusively capital grants to payments which are of major benefit to conservation and recreation. Applicants would be encouraged to adopt an 'environmentally friendly' approach by qualifying for premium grants, either in certain areas or landscape types (grazing marshes, wet valley grassland, chalk grassland, limestone grassland, lowland heathland and moorland), or where an individual farm plan was implemented with a conservation and recreation orientation.

A third set of proposals, separate from the Jenkins' CPRE plan discussed above, have been provided by the CPRE (1990c) in which they recommend the following.

1. A steady reduction in farm product prices offset by direct income aids to farmers via environmental management payments (a less extreme form of the Jenkin's scheme).
2. The enthusiastic and imaginative introduction of extensification schemes to encourage less intensive farming.
3. Radical revision of the Hill Livestock Compensatory Allowance scheme with payments on an area not a headage basis so as to reduce overgrazing.
4. Greater policy inputs at the European and British level for environmental organizations.

Fourth, Baldock and Conder (1985) have proposed the nine reforms shown in Table 6.9.

More specifically Sinclair (1985) an environmental consultant has proposed how a scheme for transferring guaranteed funds to guidance funds, and to a new rural fund, over five years could actually save money as shown in Table 6.10.

Finally, Pye-Smith and North (1984), two freelance authors, in a polemical book have produced a new plan for a healthy agriculture based on a trilogy of criticisms of modern farming. First, it produces food for a diet that eats too much fat and little grains and vegetables. Second, it relies too much on factory farming, and third it relies too much on the chemical treadmill. The solution according to Pye-Smith and North is to change farming radically to a self-sufficient mixed type of farming reminiscent of the Norfolk four-course rotation.

Table 6.9. Baldock's options for reform of the CAP price policy.

Policy change	Comment
1. Reduce price levels of selected commodities	Large and sustained reduction needed to reduce production (severe impact on farming)
2. Increase price levels of selected commodities	Likely to increase production and intensification. May protect some marginal producers
3. Introduce multi-tier pricing	Higher prices for small farmers (Social rather than environmental)
4. Introduce selective pricing	Price premium for organic or environmentally friendly farming
5. Guarantee thresholds superlevies etc.	These reduce price incentives and could lead to lower imports
6. Quotas on production or imports	Scheme design crucial. May permit higher prices, more intensification, or lead to stagnation
7. Setaside of agricultural land	Temporary or permanent withdrawal of land. Could have environmental benefits. US experience relevant
8. Direct income payments for farmers	Not tied to output. May be used to compensate for lower prices. Could have an environmental component
9. Shift to structural policy	Change emphasis from prices to structural policies

Source: Baldock and Conder (1985, p. 73).

Table 6.10. A five-year programme for reforming UK farm support.

Year £m* Base	Guarantees	Guidance redirected to conservation and/ economic grants within agriculture	New Rural Fund for socio-economic support outside agriculture	Total
1	1228	322	–	1550
2	1105	363	41	1509
3	995	363	81	1439
4	895	363	146	1404
5	850	363	169	1382
6	808	363	190	1361

*1982–3 prices.
Source: Sinclair (1985).

In more detail the authors propose a period of 'de-escalation' in which the following methods would be employed. First, all subsidies would be phased out over five years but to protect UK farmers, import levies should be retained. Second, the beef and dairy industry would be radically restructured. In the dairy industry, the number of herds would be cut by 25%, and systems based on hormones and factory methods would be banned. At the same time the traditional system of raising beef cattle in the uplands for fattening in the lowlands should be reintroduced to provide an alternative mixed economy for the former dairy farms.

The third change would be an administrative one, devolving virtually all the budget and powers of MAFF to County Agricultural Committees of the type which worked so well in the war. These committees would dispense grants, determine local policy, ensure landscape conservation, and spearhead the de-escalation programme. At the heart of the system would be a new Domesday book of features needing permission if they were to be altered. Any farmer who wished to make a land use change registered under the book would need the approval of the Committee, perhaps informally by telephone. If approval was withheld, compensation could be paid on a once-and-for-all basis but only for all those who could prove financial need. Finally, de-escalation grants would be payable for any farmers who wanted to switch to a lower intensity system and needed financial support to do so.

Returning to the real world of incremental, inertia-laden politics this chapter will now conclude by examining two of the main policies being developed to deal with surpluses, namely, lower intensity farming and diversification.

Lower intensity farming

As shown in Chapter 3 there are a number of such schemes, but only those actually about to start operation are considered here, while those which involve forestry are considered in Chapter 7. In historical order the three schemes are ESAs, setaside and extensification. For a brief resume of the schemes see Chapter 3.

Environmentally Sensitive Areas

In an early review Potter (1988) concluded that ESAs do represent a radical step forward, since for the first time maintaining the 'particular character' of a farming area is now a legitimate policy aim funded by the agricultural budget. Much of their success as income support aids and methods of reducing surplus production will, however, depend on the level of uptake by farmers. So far this has been encouraging and the first annual report on ESAs by the Ministry of Agriculture (1989) recorded an 87% take up of land in the 10 ESAs designated in 1987/88. However Lobley (1989), an RSPB officer, concluded from evidence from the Broads ESA that the benefits are likely to be limited and short-lived since intensive farmers were not joining the scheme.

More fundamentally, Colman (1989), an agricultural economist, has used data from the Broads Grazing Marshes Conservation Scheme, the predecessor scheme used as a model for ESAs, to show that public purchase of land at a cost of £1276 per hectare over 30 years, with a leaseback to the farmer, is a cheaper option than fixed compensation payments of £1906 per hectare, and far cheaper than management agreements which cost £3898 per hectare. The advantages become even greater when: (i) the asset value of the land and (ii) the substantial benefit of collecting rent income from farmers instead of paying out compensation are taken into account.

Setaside

The operation of setaside raises a number of questions, in particular: which land; how much land; for how long; compulsorily or with inducements, whether positive or negative; what constraints should there be on the use of the land; and what limits should there be on individual participation (Buckwell, 1986). Because setaside like so much farm policy of the 1980s was an *ad hoc* panicky introduction few of these questions have been answered, and it is in essence a single purpose policy aimed at cutting production and saving money. Environmental gains might be made, however, if setaside policies were to contain conditions specifically related to the environment. Even if this does not happen there might still be some gain, for Burnham (1989) has argued that if setaside land were simply left to return to nature in its own way, it could in due course become valuable, citing the case of the Shenandoch National Park in the USA which had been farmed in the 19th century, before rapidly reverting to high forest in this century.

It would be preferable, however, to manage setaside land more positively and Burnham *et al.* (1986) have suggested that a future setaside policy which embraced environmental aims would need to fulfil three conditions: (i) long-term diversion of land rather than it's short-term retirement; (ii) be targeted at pieces of countryside rather than farmers; and (iii) must prescribe specific land use and management regimes which contribute most to realizing conservation potential. If these three conditions can be met Burnham *et al.* (1988) have also set out how conservation targets may be achieved via a variety of land use strategies, for example, creating forestry or shelter belts on head-lands, maintaining cover for game on headlands, and allowing whole areas to be re-created as wetlands or meadows.

These conservation benefits can only be achieved, however, if there is a significant take up. As Chapter 3 has already shown, take up in the first three years has been slow and is likely to continue to be so, for in a predictive survey of farmers' attitudes to land diversion, Potter and Gasson (1987, 1988) found that there would be low rates of participation with a majority choosing to divert relatively small and carefully selected parcels of land. While most farmers were prepared to envisage some form of short-term fallowing or even putting cereal land down to grass for a number of years, many were adamantly opposed to the permanent diversion of agricultural land to woodland. Brotherton (1989a) in a survey of two actual diversion schemes, 'setaside' and 'Environmentally Sensitive Areas' found that both the rate of participation and the area involved were quite close to the figures predicted by Potter and Gasson.

In order to improve the low conservation potential of present setaside arrangements Potter (1987) has suggested using a bid system for determining setaside prices. This idea has been examined further by Gasson and Potter (1988) who asked 145 farmers to consider three hypothetical land diversion schemes: (i) fallowing land for one or two years; (ii) converting cereal land to permanent pasture for five years with management restrictions to enhance conservation interests; and (iii) growing broadleaved trees on farmland. The average percentage of farm size offered, varied between 7.6% (for scheme 2 (pasture)), and 3.3% (for scheme 3 (woodland)), well below the 20% target of the setaside scheme. In addition the amount of money per hectare that farmers would need in compensation (bids) was far in excess of the £200/£180 offered by setaside varying from £336 (for scheme 1 (fallow)) to £437 (for scheme 3 (woodland)).

One solution to this poor response would be to target specific areas and so Burnham *et al.* (1987) used three indices to identify land that could be setaside. These are: (i) areas where crops are grown on poor land; (ii) areas where land is vulnerable to erosion or flooding; and (iii) areas where there is conservation potential. The resulting map shows widespread potential, but in particular, areas with chalk or sandstone outcrops, or sandy soil such as the Brecklands.

However, American experience going back to the 1930s tells us that it is an imperfect, blunt and expensive way (Ervin and Dicks, 1988) to control supply, and that it should be seen as an interim measure, while price restraint gradually squeezes production (Ervin, 1988a) and hopefully allows conservation and environmental gains to be made as agriculture goes through a difficult transition period (Ervin, 1988b).

In conclusion, Koester (1989) an agricultural economist has argued that setaside as constituted in 1989 will fail on several counts. First, it will not save money for the EC because the relationship between the premium paid for setaside and other inputs is too high (overcompensation effect). Second, the scheme will not reduce surpluses because only poor land will be setaside (structure effect) and a higher use of variable inputs on the remaining, better, land will increase output there (intensification effect). Third, and most crucially there is no financial incentive for member states to promote the scheme and it is clear that most EC countries are reluctant to implement the scheme efficiently.

Extensification

Setaside is an extreme form of extensification or lower-input farming. A policy which pays farmers for doing nothing, or to farm in a less-productive manner than they could, might of course be seen as politically unacceptable. Accordingly, this basic issue was addressed by the Agriculture Committee of the House of Commons (1985), as soon as the idea first surfaced as a realistic policy option in the mid 1980s. They noted that the British public would not tolerate agricultural over-production at the expense of other rural values indefinitely. The Committee thus went on to argue that if farmers were to lose profitability by the introduction of social values, such as an improved environment, public health, pollution control and animal welfare, into agri-cultural policy, then public funding would be justified for such purposes. If this is the case then clearly extensification can be justified on social grounds, and the debate can move on to the costs involved, and the social gains to be achieved.

The relationship here is not, however, always linear. For example, Laurence Gould Consultants (1989) in a study for the CPRE have shown that the reinstatement of hedges and the use of conservation headlands produce good environmental gains but only very small reductions in production of around 1.5%. In order to achieve the 20% level of reduction in output required, much more draconian changes in management are needed. For example, Laurence Gould have calculated that nitrogen applications would have to be heavily reduced, but that this would impose a severe cost on dairy farmers and a big cost on spring barley farmers. Turning to other options, switching from winter wheat to spring barley would bring big savings in production and costs but little environmental gain. Only two options offer substantial cost savings and environmental gains: first, winter wheat produced organically, and second, oilseed rape produced with reduced sprays and nitrogen. Big environmental gains can also be made by reducing hill sheep numbers but with only little economic gain.

Using the Laurence Gould work the CPRE (1988a) has proposed a scheme for less intensive farming to run alongside setaside. The scheme would be voluntary and its key element would be an agreement between a farmer and MAFF to cut the volume of production by a specified percentage using running averages over five years. In return the farmer would be paid an annual hectarage payment which could be weighted towards the end of the agreement as a spur to continued compliance. All agreements would carry positive environmental responsibilities like hedgerow maintenance. Proposed less-intensive regimes included: low nitrogen use; organic farming; extensive grazing; spring cereals; unsprayed game cover; reinstatement of landscape features, e.g. hedges, and the creation of wide headlands for recreational access.

In spite of some enthusiasm for extensification Harvey (1987) an agricultural economist using economic theory, has thrown considerable doubt on whether extensification schemes will actually work unless there are also substantial changes in support prices. The schemes also seem likely to involve considerable expense and a major risk of double-spending. For example, those 'who can afford to' will use the schemes to leave, or do things they would have done anyway, and thus cost the taxpayer money which need not have been spent, whereas those 'who cannot afford to' will be able to remain in the industry, since those 'who can afford to' will have left, or no longer be competing with them. According to Harvey the extensification schemes, will lead to inefficient farmers being retained and the scheme is thus seen as not only being inefficient but also a disguised form of welfare payment.

Harvey then goes on to argue that if the schemes are to be made attractive to farmers they will normally cost more than disposing of surpluses. Furthermore, the notion that surplus agricultural products can be simply translated into surplus land is subject to serious theoretical criticism. In addition schemes to transfer land out of farming are 'unnatural' and likely to fail.

There is, however, according to Harvey considerable scope for extensification via a sustained and substantial cost-price squeeze on the industry backed up with increases in the returns to be earned in non-agricultural activities. Given these conditions Harvey forecasts an extensified agriculture, employing fewer farm workers, but releasing capital and labour for other occupations.

If Harvey is correct then the lack of any but a token extensification scheme does not in fact matter. In a similar vein Curry (1988a) an economist suggests that extensification can more effectively be achieved by a different route, by decapitalizing agriculture. This would have the twin benefits of de-intensifying production and reintroducing labour into the countryside, more effectively than the current favourite, diversification.

Diversification

Changing agriculture support from farming to farmers is of course the main conceptual thrust of diversification. However, many farmers do not wish to change their way of life, although there is no clear pattern to this. For example, Potter (1986b) from a survey of 138 farmers' attitudes to the process of countryside change, has found that the pattern of change is related more to the processes of farm business growth and development than to typical farm or farmer characteristics such as size, type and tenure. In particular, Potter identified three types of investment style.

1. Programmers: expanding holdings with a profile of land improvement, often triggered by land purchase (about 30% of the sample).
2. Mixed: episodes of programmed land improvement preceded and/or followed by incremental investment, often triggered by new management or receipt of grants (about 20% of the sample).
3. Incrementalists: stable or declining holdings with investment carried out in *ad hoc* projects (about 50% of the sample).

From Potter's work it would be expected that one-third of all farmers would diversify. This has been confirmed by McInerney *et al.* (1989) who from a survey of 10,000 holdings in England and Wales found a diversification rate of 34.1%. Within this overall picture services which includes tourist accommodation and recreation are the most dominant enterprise. Contracting comes a close second, followed by the processing and sale of farm products. Diversification within agriculture is carried out by 28.30% of all farmers (with some double counting) and diversification outside agriculture (services and miscellaneous) is carried out by 20.1% of all farmers, with of course some overlap. For the future 7% definitely intend to diversify in the near future, to bring the overall percentage in England to around 50%. However, the future is closely linked to uncertainty over whether planning provision is needed for many of the new uses like farm shops and horticulture as shown in Table 6.11. Accordingly, Scrase (1988) an academic planner has called for a total rewrite of Class VI of the GDO. Under his utopian scheme a new Use Classes Order would be introduced exempting extensive agriculture and recreation from planning control but placing intensive agriculture under direct control thus simplifying and rationalizing the existing *ad hoc* and chaotic divisions.

Selman (1988b) an environmental scientist has endorsed and extended this view and argued that farm diversification poses a series of challenges for planners. First, planning must become more flexible and positive in rural areas and move towards a more managerial area-based approach. Second, planners must become knowledgeable about agriculture and be able to negotiate with farmers over diversification from all positions and not merely from the aesthetic one, and third, planners will need to challenge some long held shibboleths about the control of rural development, Selman concludes by suggesting that planners need to diversify just as much as farmers.

A diversification enterprise which also offers the advantages of extensification is provided by organic farming. Many of the arguments for organic farming do not, however, arise from short-term expediency, but from long-term concerns with the practices of modern farming. For example, Gibson (1987) an environmental scientist has argued that present agricultural practices will not be sustainable into the 21st century and that setaside is a

Table 6.11. Farm diversification and planning.

Diversification options with few or no planning implications	Diversification options involving 'non-planning' land use change	Diversification options with significant planning implications
Unconventional animal products: 　Sheep milk 　Rare breeds 　Deer and goats	Woodlands: 　Conventional timber 　Craft timber 　Fuel wood 　Game shooting	Tourism: 　B&B 　Farmhouse catering 　Caravans 　Activity holidays 　Camping 　Visitor centres
Unconventional crop products: 　Linseed 　Evening primrose 　Teasel	Wetlands: 　Fish 　Game In the case of freshwater fish farming which saw a 15-fold increase in the 1980s planning controls were introduced in Scotland in 1990 but have so far only been recommended for England (Agriculture Committee, 1990a)	Farm parks 　Riding 　Golfing 　Fishing 　Shooting
Organic farming Pick your own Direct sales		Adding value to produce: 　Meat (direct sales) 　Skins (hide/wool) 　Dairy (including goat and sheep) products and processing 　Milled cereals

Source: Selman (1988b).

short-term mistake. In contrast, he advocates a completely new emphasis for agricultural reform based on the building up of the natural fertility of soils, which while reducing output in the short term would in the long term develop the potential for increasing yields from sustainable practices. His organic farming policy would he claims have the added advantage of social, economic and environmental benefit while the alternative of setaside, paying farmers to do nothing is unlikely to be acceptable to the public. Likewise, paying farmers to engage in non-farming activities is also likely to be unacceptable.

The main advocates of organic farming, the British Organic Farmers, the Organic Growers Association and the Soil Association (1989), have used not only Gibson's arguments of environmental deterioration, but also market demand to argue for a conversion of up to 20% of British farmland to organic production by the year 2000. If spread across the country they estimate that this would lead to losses of 6% in cereal and 4% in milk production. The conversion could be achieved by the interim use of setaside but the group believes that the best way would be by way of: (i) five year conversion subsidies; (ii) a new category of ESAs management agreements;

(iii) research and development funding for organic farming; and (iv) grants for organic associations. The best land would be in the first instance, mixed farming areas, National Parks, ESAs and SSSIs which would make up the first 20%, leaving the remaining 80% to be converted as soon as possible in the next century.

Although organic farming is likely to become a main plank of EC extensification schemes in the 1990s, its ultimate success will depend on demand. An opinion poll of 2000 people (National Farmers Union, 1988c) concerning the image of farmers has thrown some useful light on this. For example, 51% were interested (28% definitely) in buying organic food, but only 4% were prepared to pay more than a 21% premium. However, if the premium fell to the 10% level then nearly half the sample would purchase organic food. Unfortunately at the time of the survey the premium stood at 33%, indicating a fairly small market. A further survey of 1418 people in September 1990 (*The Guardian*, 14 September 1990) found that 37% of people would pay up to 5% more for organic food, 32% between 6 and 10% more, and 22% between 10 and 20% more. A further boost to demand may have been given in March 1991 when Prince Charles, an organic farmer himself, recommended a move to organic farming as an alternative to current policies and proposals. Finally, there is a halfway house provided by the 'Conservation Grade' which designates food produced by a mix of organic and chemical farming, and only has a premium of between 10 and 15% (Porritt, 1990).

In the event that organic farming may not be attractive, off-farm diversification is an obvious alternative. Gasson (1986), has shown from a number of surveys that part-time farming accompanied by other gainful activities, both on or off the farm, is more widespread than often acknowledged, accounting for around one-third of all holdings. The motivation of these farmers may be owning land rather than farming it. Gasson thus recommends that farm policies should move away from discriminating against part-time farmers to actively encouraging them since they are a more effective way of maintaining the rural community than full-time farming.

This could actually cut the cost of farm support if as Robson *et al.* (1987) advocate, these other sources of income were used to calculate the amount of support that the CAP and the UK government should give to farmers, since official data underestimate the true income of farmers from all sources.

Unfortunately, as Shucksmith *et al.* (1989) research workers involved in a 12-country, five year research programme on farm pluriactivity have pointed out, the agricultural policy community, as only too patently shown by the McSharry proposals, is still fairly locked into agricultural fundamentalism and the merits of retaining the family farm, whereas academic theorists see the persistence of the family farm as anomalous. This has limited the policy debate to how best to redeploy the farm's capital and land resources instead of how best to redeploy the farmers in other employment, even if it leads to these farmers becoming ex-farmers in the true sense of the word, although a farmstead and a land holding will be where they live and derive some residual income.

Gasson (1988) in a critique of the Farm Diversification Grants Scheme concurs and notes that the scheme is too limited. Instead the goal of rural development would be better served by promoting a wide range of enterprises in rural areas, and she wonders why if the aim of the initiative is not *farm* development but *rural* development, why the aid needs to be channelled through farms at all. If, for example, it is acceptable to spend public money to encourage farmers to become part-time hoteliers or shopkeepers why not use the same assistance to encourage hotel keepers or retailers to become part-time farmers. She concludes that the absence of discussion on this point speaks volumes on the relative strengths of the agricultural and non-agricultural interests in the field of rural development.

Cloke and McLaughlin (1989) in a commentary on the diversification debate concur with Gasson and argue that the high level senior group of Conservatives who discussed the diversification package in 1987 made sure that it did not threaten to change established land use planning principles. This therefore suggests that radical policies for alternative land uses may be very difficult to achieve, and virtually rules out anything as truly radical as the land reforms suggested by Norton-Taylor (1982), a journalist. In a polemical book on the ills of Britain, notably the extreme divisions of wealth, with for example, 1% of the people owning 52% of the land, Norton-Taylor proposed abolishing:

> The automatic right to inherit estates. Large estates with
> parks and gardens and efficient agricultural enterprises
> would not however be broken up. Instead they would be
> handed over to trusts and cooperatives managed by local
> communities. In those few areas where it makes clear
> economic sense to maintain specialised farming – in parts of
> East Anglia, for instance, the present farming pattern
> (though not necessarily the system) should remain. In other
> areas, mixed farming must be the rule, not the exception.
> There should be a system of cooperatives, with no one
> occupying more than any other. In any case, no individual
> should own or occupy land above a certain agreed limit
> (varying with the quality of the land).

In conclusion, agricultural policy lost direction in the 1980s. It begins the 1990s not at all sure where to go. In all probability it will probably stagger from one *ad hoc* crisis to another with knee-jerk solutions in between. If this chapter seems to be a chaotic and repetitive set of policy prescriptions this is no more than the awful chaos of farm policy reflects. To have presented a logical, ordered account, would have been both misleading, and beyond my intellect. Indeed it is doubtful if anybody fully understands the Byzantine complexities of farm policy, in all its multilayered confusion. In this sense, farm policy represents a truly post-modern world!

7 Policy Proposals for Forestry

Introduction

There have been two major permanent changes of land use during the 20th century, afforestation and urban growth, with both roughly doubling in area. Within the forestry sector the main changes have been: first, a doubling of the woodland area; second, a movement of the wooded area northward and upward; third, a switch from broadleaved to coniferous; and fourth, the loss of ancient woods, either by clearance, or by transformation via different management practices, e.g. the cessation of coppicing (Peterken and Allison, 1989).

The first three of these changes remain as very live issues for the 1990s, namely, how much more to plant, where to plant, and with what types of trees. In addition some of the changes of the 1980s outlined in Chapter 3, will spill over into the 1990s, in particular: the effects of the 1988 changes in taxation and grant rates on planting in the private sector; the continuing disposal programme; and the possible evolution of EC forestry policy.

Taking these in turn the 1988 policy review set out a target rate of planting of 33,000 hectares a year, but Crabtree and Macmillan (1989) using economic costings have forecast a major shortfall in this 'target' planting rate since much planting on poorer land will cease to be economic, and planting will only transfer to better quality land if there is a substantial fall in the price of this land, mainly better sheep grazing and improved farmland, possibly as a result of decreases in agricultural support.

However, Spilsbury and Crockford (1989), two forestry economists, have cautioned against simplifying the expected returns for forestry after the changes of the 1988 budget, and the introductions of the Woodland Grant and Farm Woodland Schemes. For example, their multivariate computer model using seven main variables such as: choice of species; yield class; tax rates; grant aid; and discount rates produces widely different forecasts depending on the type of option available. In general, however, they forecast that the new farm woodland and setaside schemes offer greatly increased long-term profits from woodland, and that individuals now have a greater variety of forestry options than before. Nonetheless, in the short term private planting rates fell from 25,000 hectares in 1988/89 to around 16,000 in 1989/90.

Much will depend on the attraction of the post-1988 system to different groups of forestry investor, notably the personal investor, for as Mather (1988) has shown from a survey of 181 afforestation schemes, personal investors accounted for 53% of the planting by area (with an average block size of 145 hectares), corporate investors did 31% of the planting (average block size 183 hectares), but traditional estates planted only 15% of the total (average block size 94 hectares). The type of land planted, the type of tree planted and the motivation behind the schemes also varied with the type of investor.

Mather and Murray (1988) have also found that the amount of employment generated by new private sector afforestation varies with the type of forester (personal investor, 0.76 man years per hectare; corporate investor, 0.71; and traditional estate, 0.64) with a margin over agriculture of between 0.4 and 0.6 man years per 100 hectare. The net gains to employment are thus small.

A second hangover issue from the 1980s will be the disposal programme for Forestry Commission land, which has been given a further target of another 100,000 hectares, and £150 million for the 1990s. This may be optimistic for Mather and Murray (1986) have shown how the 1981 Act programme fell way behind it's target with only £13 million raised in the early years, against a target of £20 million.

The third spillover will be the gradual evolution of an EC forestry policy. During the 1980s the European Communities (1988) formulated for the first time a forestry policy comprising eight long-term strategy aims and an action programme for 1989–1992. The eight policy aims are as follows.

1. To participate fully in land use planning and encourage the development of rural life.
2. To ensure the security of supply of renewable raw materials.
3. To contribute to environmental improvement.
4. To give the forestry sector it's own dynamism.
5. To protect the Community's forests from damage.
6. To extend the role of the forest as a natural setting for recreation, relaxation and culture.
7. To participate in development in the most disadvantaged areas of the Community.

8. To give forests and the forestry sector their full place in the formulation and implementation of Community policies.

In the shorter term, the Commission also proposed a four-year action programme, 1989–1992, based on, afforestation of agricultural land and the optimal use of woodland in rural areas, and focused on priority regions: areas worst hit by the agricultural crisis; areas of conservation importance; areas where woodland can provide jobs; and areas where woodland provides an important recreation resource.

The development of EC policy provides an *aide memoire* for the key issues concerning forestry. In essence these are twofold, economic and environmental. In the economic field the key question is whether forestry is profitable or not, and whether it provides more or less jobs than the alternatives and at a greater or lesser cost. As we will see the answers to those questions depend on a number of variables, notably, the rate of inflation, the type of tree planted, and on what land. In the environmental field the key questions are the degree to which forestry disturbs existing land uses and habitats, and whether it should return land use to a climax vegetation, or continue to implant alien species to the British landscape, thus destroying well-loved and well-used recreational landscapes. A whole book could be filled by examining each of these very complex and interrelated issues one by one. In the small space available here, the approach adopted is to examine the arguments by the nature of the author and their viewpoint, or lack of it, under the following seven headings: Balanced Impartial Reviews; Balanced Partial Reviews; Balanced Economic Analyses; Pro-forestry-no reservations; Pro-forestry-with reservations; Anti-forestry-no reservations; Anti-forestry-with reservations.

Balanced impartial reviews

By and large the reviews of policy produced by the Select Committee system in the Houses of Parliament provide some of the most impartial one can find, at least in terms of the evidence which comes from all quarters, even though some of the members of the Committees may have too many forestry interests for them to be seen as impartial observers. A constant theme in these reviews has been the need to provide strategic advice on integrating forestry with other land uses in and at all levels of organization (House of Lords Select Committee on Science and Technology, 1980). This is a theme that has, however, been consistently rejected. For example, although the Government (House of Lords, 1982, 1983) has agreed that integrated land use is an important subject, it has nonetheless twice rejected the concept of a national land use strategy, in favour of the present system under which, problems of conflict between uses and the potential for land use integration are considered on a case-by-case basis against the background of broad policy objectives or guidelines.

In the absence of an integrated policy, overviews of forestry policy have to restrict themselves to existing policies, as set out by the Forestry Commission in its Annual Reports. Such a review is provided by the National Audit Office, (1986) an instrument of Thatcherism and its attachment to performance targets. In their rigorous review they concluded that the Commission has achieved its physical targets impressively and has operated with due regard to its other duties, including the social, recreational and environmental duties. However, the real rate of return at 3% per annum, or under some assumptions only 2.25%, was way below the target rate of 5% for other public sector operations. This rate could be reached, however, by more planting on better land. According to the National Audit Office, there is at present no financial case for forestry, either on the rate of return, or on employment, or balance of payments, or strategic grounds. Furthermore, the non-monetary benefits are unlikely to be enough to compensate for the low financial returns.

In the most up to date review the Agriculture Committee of the House of Commons (1990b) in their report on 'Land Use and Forestry', has argued that the Government has ducked the problem of surplus farmland. Leaving land to become derelict or paying farmers to keep it fallow is, according to the Committee, unsatisfactory. Forestry alternatively, has the potential to offer an attractive balance between commercial viability and environmental enhancement. Accordingly the Committee recommended the Government to review its simplistic policies of the last 70 years, so that the principles of multiple purpose forestry are combined with social and environmental objectives, timber production and rural development, in a new comprehensive statement of policy.

In more detail the Committee rejected planning controls in favour of planting licences for not just grant-aided, but all new forestry. They also proposed a reformed system of forestry grants with differential incentives as the main method of achieving objectives. Turning to organizations, the Committee proposed that the Forestry Commission should be split into its two components as two separate departments, thus removing the conflicts of interest in having regulation and promotion in the same organization. In the private sector the Committee recommended a far higher priority for farm woodlands, the promotion of community woods and allowing forestry on common grazing in crofting areas, for example, as proposed in the Crofters Forestry Scotland Bill (1990). Turning to wider issues the Committee also recommended rationalization of the present system of land use designations, and the establishment of a national land use inventory as a prerequisite to the development of concerted rural policies.

In their response, the Government (H.C. 402 (89–90), 1990) rejected most of the proposals, or noted that they would review some of them when current policies had had more time to take effect, notably the measures to reduce surplus farm production.

Balanced partial reviews

Balanced but partial views could also be expected in ascending order of partiality from the Countryside Commission, the NCC and the NFU. As the Government's key adviser in the countryside the Countryside Commission (1987b) has argued that the 1990s is the time for a major reassessment of what society needs and expects from forestry. They have advocated that forestry planning should be based on multiple objectives: to produce a national supply of timber as a raw material and as a source of energy; to offer an alternative to agricultural use of land; contribute to rural employment either in the timber industries or through associated recreation; to create attractive sites for public enjoyment; to enhance the natural beauty of the countryside; and to create wildlife habitats.

A good example of such a multiple policy is provided by farm forestry which the Commission argues could enhance the landscape, create new opportunities for recreation, reduce farm surpluses and sustain farm incomes, but only if substantial government support is provided in the short and medium term.

In more detail the Commission recommended an examination and revision of the tax incentive system in order to produce multipurpose forests and woods, a transformation of the Forestry Commission into a multi-purpose agency and modification of the present consultation scheme over forestry as follows.

1. Structure, Unitary and National Park Plans should contain forestry strategies indicating areas where afforestation would be acceptable.
2. Afforestation schemes over 0.25 hectares should be considered as 'development' under the 1971 Town and Country Planning Act.
3. The GDO should be amended to make afforestation schemes between 0.25 and 5.0 hectares permitted development.
4. All afforestation proposals over 5 hectares would need planning permission.
5. Plans of operations for all afforestation schemes under 0.25 hectares should be approved by the Forestry Commission after consultation.

For its own part the Countryside Commission planned to show the way be creating forests around some of the major conurbations, and by establishing a major new forest in the Midlands covering 150 square miles (Countryside Commission, 1990b).

The Nature Conservancy Council (1986) in their review of forestry, however, regard new commercial forestry as no better than modern agriculture as a destroyer of habitats, with forestry replacing one man-made semi-desert with another, instead of recreating Britain's natural vegetation, broadleaved woodland. Accordingly, the NCC reiterated the need to achieve a sensible land use balance, via a review of the rural estate, by the Government. In more detail the NCC called for a presumption against planting on SSSIs, and formal approval of all private schemes above 10 hectares by the Forestry Commission, linked to the removal of automatic tax relief on planting.

The National Farmers Union (1986) provides another example of a partial convert to forestry. For example, they point out that Britain has a favourable climate and soils for tree growth and that it is indeed the natural vegetation. They then make six classic points in favour of forestry.

1. We import 90% of our timber requirements, costing over £4.5 billion in 1985 (£7.0 billion in 1989, one-third of the trade deficit for that year).
2. World timber supplies are likely to diminish.
3. Only 9% of our land is under trees compared with 21% for the EC.
4. Rising agricultural productivity means some of the 150,000 hectares that could become surplus to agriculture each year could be planted with trees.
5. A growing farm forest industry would encourage new businesses and jobs.
6. More woodland would enhance landscapes, wildlife and amenities in most parts of Britain.

But the NFU point out forestry is a long-term investment and needs Government support in the initial period. As an example they cost out a possible planting programme which yields a total return of £10,002 after 50 years, but of which, as much as £7106 is produced only in the fiftieth year. If a reverse mortgage with a 5% final yield were taken out, a farmer could receive £34 per hectare per annum over the 50 years. Clearly this does not compete with the £200 per hectare being offered by setaside, especially when transferring farm land to timber would increase the pro rata costs of fixed capital on other farm enterprises.

Accordingly, the NFU argue that farm forestry can only be achieved via central government funding. They therefore propose a fourfold plan; annual payments; a favourable tax regime; only one scheme to be set up instead of the numerous schemes now available; and no planning controls to be imposed on afforestation.

In more detail the annual payment scheme envisages a farmer planting up a woodland in equal blocks each year over a 25-year period. If the annual payment for this planting was £150 per hectare, after 25 years the farmer would receive £3750 for 25 hectares. At this stage thinning would take place and the payment would begin to reduce, and after 50 years when clear felling and replanting commenced the payments would disappear as a commercial rotation developed. If 500,000 hectares were planted in this way, the maximum annual cost would be £50 million according to the NFU (but to my arithmetic £75 million). Against this, savings on support prices could be

£100 million giving a net saving of £50 million at some stage and at the end of 50 years a complete saving as the payment scheme is phased out.

The NFU's arguments are, however, based on an illustration of what might happen, they are not predictions or even assumptions. This is wise since Denne *et al.* (1986) in an exhaustive review of forestry policies and issues for the UK Centre for Economic and Environmental Development have argued that the economic case for forestry cannot be proven one way or another because of the unknown effects of inflation. As an alternative land use to unacceptable surpluses in agriculture, forestry does have many attractions. For example, there is a demand for planting by investors, and in due course a huge potential demand from the wider timber industry which imported £40–£60 billion worth of timber between 1975 and 1984 (at 1984 values) and employed 400,000 people in the mid 1980s.

Denne *et al.* therefore argue that further expansion of forestry industry is in the national interest and should be encouraged by.

1. Giving land managers the option of transferring from the current style of fiscal incentives to an annual maintenance grant, at no extra net cost to the exchequer, and subject to good silvicultural practice.
2. Controlling planting by a system of planting licences administered as at present, in order to encourage the rational growth of the industry.
3. In order to protect other interests rural land should be divided into three areas;
    (a) Heritage sites in which conservation and amenity would be paramount and there would be a strong presumption against afforestation;
    (b) Areas of natural beauty, to include National Parks and AONBs where forestry would be permitted subject to restrictions in the interests of landscape preservation, amenity, or nature conservation;
    (c) Remaining land areas where forestry would not be subject to restrictions but assistance could be given to encourage development sympathetic to amenity and nature conservation interests.

Balanced economic analyses

It should be clear that economic forecasting lies at the heart of the forestry debate. However, economists, although arguably providing a balanced impartial view cannot agree among themselves about which methods to employ for forecasting the future. There are two key writers, Kula and Price. Kula (1988) an agricultural economist, in a book on forestry economics has argued that there are three dominant factors in an economic analysis of forestry projects: the choice of discount rate; the choice of project evaluation method; and the future price of timber. Under the traditional method of ordinary discounting, forestry looks like bad economics, for example, at a

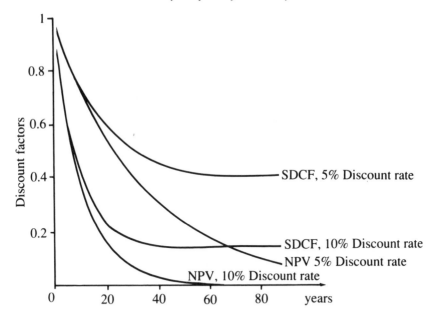

Fig. 7.1. Discount factor curves by means of the sum of discounted consumption flows (SDCF) and the net present value (NPV) criteria at 10 and 5% discount rates for forestry.

10% discount rate even a 2% real rise in timber prices a year produces a loss. Net benefits are only gained when the discount rate falls to around 3% and real timber prices rise by at least 1% per year. As a more favourable alternative Kula suggests the sum of discounted consumption flows method which looks ahead to the benefits that generations to come may derive from forestry rather than taking present values. Fig. 7.1 shows that this not only reduces the rate at which benefits disappear but also prevents the benefits curve from ever approaching zero. This method thus has the advantage that forestry does not have to be treated as a special case if it is to be funded, and can show a profit for forestry even with a 10% rate of inflation (Kula, 1986).

In the private sector Kula has also constructed a model which after empirical testing has forecast that a 1% increase in grant aid would generate a 1.4% increase in planting, and a 1% rise in timber prices would generate a 4.7% rise in plantings.

Price and Kula (1987) in a debate about the relative merits of using the Net Present Value (NPV) method or the Sum of Discounted Cash Flows (SDCF), both agree that future generations need to be treated in a just manner. Kula claims that the use of NPV is not only conceptually but morally wrong since it places all the weight on benefits today rather than tomorrow. In contrast Price claims that the use of SDCF would allow future generations to criticize us, not only for failing to create plantations for them, but also for placing an obligation on them to create the plantations for their own successors, which we had failed to provide for them. Price concludes that in fact neither the NPV or SDCF are without fault and suggests that there are better ways of allocating scarce physical resources and funds between forests, agriculture and other investments.

Indeed Price (1989) in a major book on forestry economics claims the best method to be shadow pricing under cost–benefit analysis. He then leaves it to the decision maker to choose between instinct or forecasting when he writes; 'The result (of quantitative forecasting) will not invariably favour traditional "sound forestry" or even forestry at all, because the analysis reaches beyond the objectives of forestry towards the purpose of existence' (p. 386).

Nonetheless, economic forecasting can provide indications for the future. For example, Price and Dale (1982) have shown how the area of potentially afforestable land is very sensitive to future prices for forestry. In a study of North Wales they examined rough grazings that fell between the limiting attributes for Sitka spruce and lodgepole pine and concluded that only between 19 and 5% was afforestable given no real increase in prices but that between 85 and 77% was afforestable given a 3.5% rise in prices.

However, other changes might have little effect. For example, Price (1987) has argued that the forecast recession in agriculture does not alter the economic equation for forestry, since land values have traditionally been put at a very low or even zero value in most forecasts. Price after a survey of the other economic factors, principally tax cuts, concludes that forestry will never be attractive to the average farmer, not least because the economies of scale in forestry do not fit well into small farming units. Price therefore concludes that farm forestry can only be achieved by a conservation programme aimed at upgrading existing woodlands and planting diverse woodland on better land. This can only be paid for by public subsidy and one way or another society has to pay for forestry whether it is for commercial extraction, for amenity, or for employment.

With regard to employment Johnson and Price (1987) have adapted a model developed in Scotland to the special conditions of Snowdonia to reach the following four conclusions. First, in the short term forestry cannot provide enough sustained work to compensate for the loss of agricultural employment, especially in the crucial 15–20-year period between establishment and first thinning/harvesting. Second, after 40 years forestry provides more jobs than agriculture if there are no productivity increases, but third, if productivity rises by 2% per annum forestry would never provide as much work as agriculture. However, fourth, if both forestry and agriculture achieve productivity gains of 2% per annum then forestry provides more employment after 60 years. Crucially, however, neither industry is able to retain enough employment in the area to sustain isolated communities.

In a further development of the agriculture–forestry debate Maxwell, *et al.* (1979) researchers at the Hill Farming Research Organisation have used a discount rate model to produce different economic forecasts for five per-mutations; all land to be afforested; some land to be afforested on an integrated basis with either improved or unimproved agriculture; and no afforestation with either improved or unimproved agriculture. Depending on the type of area, forestry performed better only at very low inflation rates, below 3–5%. Integrated systems performed better between 5 and 7% rates, and agriculture performed better at high inflation rates, above 7 or 8%.

Finally, an economic analysis of forestry has been provided by Planning, Economic and Development Consultants (1986, 1987) in two commissioned reports. In the first report an economic assessment for the National Audit Office, the consultants confirmed most the pessimistic findings of the 1972 Cost–Benefit Study, namely that forestry could not be expected to meet the target rate of return for public sector investment, the test discount rate. However, existing forests should be harvested since most of the costs have now been incurred.

Turning to the future, the consultants argued that the only method available for assessing the possible rate of return on new investments was the commission's planting models, even though these were highly dependent on the yield class assumptions made which had not been subjected to systematic review. These, however, give very low rates of internal return varying between 1.04% for new planting with Sitka Spruce in northern Scotland to 4.97% for restocking with Douglas Fir in north west England. Given these reservations the future event most likely to raise returns was thought to be an increase in the real price of timber. However, even very large increases would still not raise the rate above the test discount rate, and moreover such large increases in prices appeared unlikely.

The consultants also argued that the case for forestry on employment grounds was also weak, since the cost per job was extremely high both on the ground and in downstream processing industries. Turning to recreational arguments the consultants concluded they did not constitute a general argument for new planting, and neither did environmental, balance of payments or strategic considerations.

In conclusion the consultants stated that there appeared to be no clear rationale for setting a target for a rate of return on new forestry investment substantially lower than that required for other forms of public sector invest-ment, whether the forestry be in the public or the private sector.

In a second report, commissioned by the CPRE, the consultants this time under their acronym, PIEDA, again noted that forestry investment had provided a poor rate of economic return throughout the 20th century. Furthermore the consultants noted that the cost per job of £10,000 in forestry and £25,000 in processing was excessive, and that the import saving argument had to be looked at in the light of the returns available from investing resources elsewhere. In the light of this negative view of forestry, PIEDA recommended that the Forestry Commission should be expected to meet the

Test Discount Rate of 5% for new planting (compared with the current achievement of around 2.25%) except where it could demonstrate significant non-financial benefits, for example in areas of very high unemployment, or where environmental gain or recreational amenity could be achieved. Other recommendations included more grant aid to environmentally friendly broadleaved schemes and making proposals for all major new planting undergo an Environmental Impact Assessment.

The preceding summary of so-called Balanced Reviews of Forestry has already shown a considerable measure of disagreement, and so it is now time to turn to overt and explicit reviews which are either pro- or anti-forestry.

Pro-forestry arguments without reservations

Pro-forestry cases have been advanced from the purely instinctive to the highly technical. Beginning with the instinctive Fairgreive (1979) a Conservative MP has used seven main arguments in favour of afforestation.

1. The very small percentage of land under forests in the UK.
2. The need to import 90% of all timber used in the UK.
3. Future World shortages of timber.
4. The suitability of the physical environment for forestry, notably in Scotland.
5. The extra employment created.
6. The possibility of providing extra recreation resources.
7. The increasing amenity if sensible planting policies are followed.

To achieve these aims, Fairgreive suggested that an extra 1.8 million hectares should be planted, mainly in the private sector by increasing grant aid and by removing or lessening the tax burdens facing private foresters.

At the same time in a major technical forecasting exercise the Forestry Commission (1978) attempted to look forward well into the 21st century and predicted that current forests would only increase the home supply of timber from 8 to 14%. Dissatisfied with this they examined the three alternative options shown in Table 7.1. They then concluded together with Fairgreive that option 3, the creation of an extra 1.8 million hectares of forest between 1980 and 2025 was technically feasible and appeared to be a prudent investment of Britain's oil money.

Another expansionist case for forestry has been made by the Centre for Agricultural Strategy (1980) based at the University of Reading. Their case rests on a growth in demand for timber, the high potential for domestic timber production and the prospect of future world shortages leading to higher timber prices. They set out four alternative scenarios as shown in Table 7.2.

Table 7.1. Three options for forestry planting between 1980 and 2025.

	Year	Option 1. No more planting	Option 2. Planting a further 1.0 m ha 1980–2025	Option 3. Planting a further 1.8 m ha 1980–2025
Assumed demand in	2000	55–60	55–60	55–60
million m³	2025	70–90	70–90	70–90
Assumed conifer	2000	7.0	7.0	7.0
production in million m³	2025	9.2	12.8	14.1
	2050	10.3	16.8	20.4
Net jobs in rural areas	1985	14.8	16.8	17.7
including jobs lost from	2000	13.7	15.3	16.4
agriculture '000 man years	2025	9.7	13.2	15.1
Net jobs in wood	1975	4.0	4.0	4.0
processing '000 man years	2000	4.6	4.6	4.6
	2025	3.5	4.6	5.0

Source: Forestry Commission (1978).

Other pro-forestry arguments have centred on the poor use of so much of the uplands. For example, Coleman (1980), the doyen of land use mapping, has used data from her land utilization surveys to argue that the present wooded area could be doubled without any serious conflict with other interests because there is so much unproductive land: for example, 216,000 hectares of bracken, 187,000 hectares of mat grass, 178,000 hectares of molinia, 107,000 hectares of rushes, 106,000 hectares of waste land, 66,000

Table 7.2. Centre for Agricultural Strategy's four alternative planting programmes for forestry to 2025.

Extra area for each programme	Total timber production million m³	Self-sufficiency		Forestry and processing jobs	
		A	B	C	D
1.96 m ha	19.6	50%	26%	64,600	41,300
1.46 m ha	17.8	46%	24%	59,100	37,900
0.96 m ha	15.9	41%	21%	54,700	31,300
0.58 m ha	14.1	36%	19%	48,500	31,200

A: Assuming consumption remains constant at 39 million m³.
B: Assuming consumption rises to 75 million m³.
C: Assuming productivity rises by 1% anually.
D: Assuming producitivity rises by 2% annually.
Source: Centre for Agricultural Strategy (1980).

hectares of gorse and scrub, and smaller totals of either wasteland or other poor vegetation.

The better use of Britain's poorer land has also been advocated by Burnham (1985) who argued that most of the land in the grade four category (19.8% of England and Wales) should be afforested, since it would return the land to natural vegetation (pre-ice age spruce and fir for example) and would provide an alternative livelihood for marginal farmers. Indeed if timber prices were to rise by 2 or 4% by the end of the century farmers could expect a return of between 7 and 13%.

In an extension of these arguments Grainger and Hildyard (1981) argue that woodland is a renewable natural resource that cannot only sustain native wildlife but also replace the barren heaths and moors left by the deforestation of Britain. More controversially, they then proceed to argue that Britain will also have to deindustrialize and abandon consumerism. A natural consequence of this process will be a need to reforest at least a third, and ideally a half, of Britain.

It is, however, significant that nearly all of these unreserved arguments date from the 1978–1980 period. Since then pro-forestry arguments have more often than not been hedged with reservations or rejected altogether.

Pro-forestry arguments with reservations

Even before the 1978–1980 period, forestry policy had begun to be hedged around with reservations, and in the first serious reverse for forestry expansion since 1919 the early 1970s review of forestry policy (Agriculture, 1972) was able to justify a planting and replanting programme of 22,000 hectares a year, not on economic or strategic grounds, but as a means of retaining people in areas of depopulation. Since then pro-forestry arguments have often had to seek solace in a wider role for forestry. For example, the Council for the Protection of Rural England (1989a) has argued that since forestry is unlikely ever to be profitable, the only case for public subsidy is to establish, restore and maintain woods as a component of balanced and sustainable inhabited ecosystems, with timber as a useful by-product. The Council believes that this shift in policy would best be achieved by splitting the Forestry Commission into two parts, the Enterprise and the Authority, and placing both of them under MAFF rather than the rather unclear position at present where the Secretary of State for Scotland has overseen policy since 1980.

Another apologetic type of argument is provided by Nicholls (1985) a geographer who uses growth rates in existing forests to demonstrate that either by better management, or by planting in the warmer climates of the South and West of Britain greater forest productivity could be achieved. Under this argument the first plantations of the Forestry Commission can be regarded as experimental. The second rotation will thus see forestry begin in earnest, especially if it is allowed to expand into areas of better soils and climates and use more appropriate species for these habitats. This may well be true, for scientifically speaking forestry is still arguably at the neolithic stage of agricultural development.

Anti-forestry arguments with reservations

It is but one small step from a reserved pro-forestry position to an anti-forestry stance, albeit with reservations. Such a step has been taken by Stewart (1985) a lecturer in economics and, more importantly, a former member of the CAS team which advocated continuing afforestation in the early 1980s. In one passage he rejects the case for expansion by arguing:

> It should also be recognized that the existence of an asset does not necessarily mean that it must be used. Where neither farming or forestry can be carried on without subsidies or tax relief, it would be in the general interest for the land to be left unused. The effect of this in many cases would be a slow reversion to forest and this could be speeded by the planting in appropriate cases of seed-bearing trees and by the control of herbivores. Non-use is thus not bound to imply non-management and the provision of skilled management and research services could be an alternative source of livelihood for the population. (p. 28)

However, this does not preclude forestry everywhere and Stewart concedes that where exploitation of the land is viable without subsidy or grant aid, mixed estates of integrated farmland and woodland could be created.

Another argument for not foresting the uplands, is the problem of acidification of watercourses by conifers, and although the Forestry Commission (Nisbet, 1990) has argued that there is no evidence that trees by themselves cause surface water acidification in the absence of atmospheric pollution, it does concede that trees may scavenge more pollution from the air than other vegetation, thus leading to a rise in acidification.

Accordingly, the Environment Committee of the House of Commons (1987) has argued that any major expansion of coniferous forest should be carefully controlled and restricted to areas where there is no risk of damage to rivers and upland water sources.

In a similar type of argument which does not reject forestry entirely, but only in the wrong place, the Royal Society for the Protection of Birds (1987) from a study of the effects of afforestation on the Flow Country of Northern Scotland, one of Europe's last great wildernesses, has argued that:

1. The subsidy of afforestation produces a loss to the national economy and is thus a waste of taxpayers money.
2. Jobs are created but at a cost of £61,500 per job.
3. The subsidy does not benefit the local economy but a few rich individuals.

Accordingly the Society recommended: transferring the subsidies to crofters; designating the area as an ESA; and conducting research into what alternative use could be made of the public subsidy, for example, planting woodland on better land elsewhere where broadleaved woodland could improve wildlife rather than destroy it as in the Flow Country.

Anti-forestry arguments without reservations

Anti-forestry arguments range from the narrowly conceived to widespread holistic attacks. Starting with the narrowly conceived there have been a number of attacks based on the evils of state subsidy and controls. For example, Miller (1981) has argued, as a matter of belief, that the free market is better able to provide for timber needs in the future than the public sector. Miller also dismisses the arguments for state involvement in forestry as follows. The strategic argument is dismissed on the grounds that any future war would be short lived. The employment case is dismissed as being too expensive compared with other alternatives, whereas the amenity and recreation arguments are dismissed on the grounds that the loss of open countryside and water resources entailed imposes more social costs than the benefits. The balance of payments argument is dismissed not only on the grounds of being too far in the future, but also because Britain is at a natural disadvantage for afforestation, and it is thus a waste of resources for her to grow large plantations.

Accordingly, Miller makes some recommendations.

1. Selling the assets of the Forestry Commission to private investors who could charge for access to forests.
2. Transferring the regulatory functions of the Forestry Commission to the Ministry of Agriculture, and cutting most of its work thus saving £70 million at 1980 prices.
3. Abolishing felling licences.
4. Abolishing grants and tax concessions for forestry.
5. Bringing new plantations under planning control.

An updated free market critique by the Adam Smith Institute (1988a) has repeated Miller's call for a radical reconsideration of policy because of the absence of any economic or environmental justification for large-scale afforestation. They therefore propose: (i) abandoning support for any form of planting in either the public or private sector; (ii) the privatization of the

Forestry Commission as a single company; and (iii) the disposal of the Forestry Commission's regulatory functions to planning departments and the appropriate sections of other organizations.

In a quite different, but equally critical approach Whitby (1989) an agricultural economist has pointed out that an expansion of lowland forestry could have severe employment and thus social repercussions. First, it would employ far fewer people over the years, and second, because the peak labour requirement comes at the planting and felling ends of the forestry cycle, there would be no work for permanent village populations but only for itinerant workers based in far-away towns.

Turning to holistic arguments the Ramblers Association (1980), a long time severe critic of afforestation, has stressed the catastrophic damage to wildlife caused by afforestation, the dangers of monoculture, the loss of farmland, the effect of reduced run-off into reservoirs, the economic cost of forestry subsidies and the high cost of new forestry jobs.

In order to update and justify their case the Ramblers Association commissioned Tompkins (1986) a professional forester to produce a report on the three key issues of monoculture, landscape despoilation, and reduced access. In this report Tompkins proposes the following.

1. The introduction of planning controls over forestry including the use of public inquiries.
2. A drastic reduction in tax concessions, accompanied by a shift to a grant system which encourages a benign environmentally friendly forestry.
3. A substantial reduction in commercial conifer plantations in the uplands, accompanied by a growth in planting and regeneration of broadleaved and mixed woodlands in the lowlands.

McCluskey (1986), a landscape architect, in an endorsement of Tompkins' critique has produced his own four-point plan. First, the imposition of planning controls over forestry since it is absurd that a small extension to a cottage needs permission, but not a proposal to change whole hillsides and mountains. Second, the severe modification of tax concessions. Third, stopping all conifer planting in sensitive areas, and fourth, setting up an enquiry into how to rectify existing damage. Encouraged by this support Tompkins (1989a) in a thorough and severe critique of current forestry policies criticizes upland forests as no more than cellulose factories, blown over by winter gales and ravaged by insect pests which have had devastating consequences for the ecological balance of the uplands. In the meantime lowland woodland remains unmanaged and semi-derelict.

Most of the damage is now, however, being done by the private sector, with private planting in the 1980s rising from 4000 to 18,000 hectares per annum while Forestry Commission planting fell from 14,000 to 4000 hectares per annum.

Accordingly he proposes an eight-point plan to prevent the disaster of further afforestation in the uplands by updating and extending his 1986 proposals as follows.

1. Abolition of any target rate for planting.

2. Taper grant schemes to size of plantation with a maximum of 200 hectares being eligible for grant.

3. Use annual management payments attached to multipurpose management schemes to renew the emphasis on forestry as a multiple land use.

4. Ban planting on poorer land.

5. Introduce planning controls on new afforestation above 20 hectares.

6. Planning control should be guided by local planning authority zoning plans with three zones:

  (**a**) a heritage zone with no planting;

  (**b**) an intermediate zone with mixed land uses;

  (**c**) a forestry zone where forestry would be the main use.

7. Split the Forestry Commission into two, with the Forestry Authority becoming a Forest Service responsible for grant aid and advice.

8. Sell off most of the Forestry Enterprise's estate to the private sector, but keep the 10% of the estate with important environmental value within the public sector.

The introduction of planning controls is a core feature of both of Tompkins' considered reports. They are further justified in a personal polemic when he points out (Tompkins, 1989b) the absurdity of exempting forestry from planning permission but not extensions to a suburban house. In a purple passage he asks us to:

> . . . imagine a builders dream world. In this euphoric vision, housebuilders would apply to a Building Commission to be able to build an extension with at least 60% of their costs payable by grants from the same commission. It would only be natural for Building Commission Officers to think that virtually all extensions were a good idea, and the Commission itself would just happen to be the largest commercial building company in Britain. Because of public pressure and to retain a vestige of credibility, the Building Commission might consult selected outside interests about plans for extensions, but if agreement could not be reached it would refer the case to a Committee whose members it had chosen, and half of whom were builders or builders merchants. (p. 276)

This nightmare vision is, according to Tompkins, the way in which the Forestry Commission has force-fed Britain with 60 years of blanket afforestation and is the perfect reason for bringing forestry schemes over 10 hectares under planning control.

However, not everybody agrees with Tompkins' critique of the 'consultation process'. For example, Brotherton and Devall (1988) from a study of 250 afforestation proposals, in the 10 National Parks between 1974 and 1984, have concluded that the present consultation arrangements are not unfavourable to National Park interests, with planning committees getting almost all they request. Planning control they argue would make little difference to outcomes. If anything it might actually increase the amount of afforestation, since in some cases afforestation was approved by planning committees during the consultation period only for the proposals to be turned down later in the process.

Widening the case for voluntary controls Brotherton (1985) from a study of the advance notification system for agricultural grants which has operated in National Parks since 1980 found that 96–99.8% (Brotherton, 1988) of cases were concluded quite amicably, Brotherton thus recommends that the system should be extended beyond the Parks, partly because it leads to a dialogue between conservationists and farmers and thus a better understanding by each of the other's position. He does, however, admit that the system does break down in a very few cases where a voluntary agreement, or one based on financial compensation, cannot be reached.

Returning to his consideration of the case for retaining voluntary consultation procedures for afforestation in the National Parks, Brotherton (1987b) has found that 86% of cases considered by him resulted in the outcome requested by the National Park Authority. The issue at stake was often size, with foresters wanting big plantations of one species but conservationists wanting small plantations of different species (Brotherton and Devall, 1987). Accordingly Brotherton (1987b) recommends that conservationists work at making the consultation system more effective rather than advocating planning controls. Not only because the consultation system works, but because planning controls elsewhere do not have a marked effect on the amount of activity in the economy. The key to the control of forestry is thus not to be found in a system of locks and levers but in the mechanisms which map out the economic position of the industry.

Finally, in a review of his position Brotherton (1989c) argues that the system of consultation in National Parks and SSSIs is in fact far from voluntary. For example, there are significant penalties for non-compliance.

Mather and Murray (1988), from a study of private sector afforestation schemes in Scotland between 1975 and 1985, have also concluded that the 'consultation procedure system' has been a major influence in limiting the effects of afforestation on agriculture, which in fact have been relatively minor. However, they do not consider that this rebuts the case for planning controls over forestry by itself, but rather calls for a widening of the arguments to other considerations, namely, what are the objectives of afforestation, what is meant by 'good' land use, and what scope there is for discussing the possibility of achieving control over afforestation, not by the negative measures used at present, but by a better use of the positive incentives offered for new planting.

The future

Turning to the future, an example of the imaginative use of woodland by a private company using public money, as suggested by Mather and Murray (1988), is provided by the second version of the Central Scotland Woodland Project (Selman and Blackburn, 1986), announced by the Scottish Development Department in February 1989 (Stirrat, 1989). Under this scheme £2.5 million will be made available between 1989 and 2009 to establish three types of woodland; community woods; amenity woods; and productive woods. The aim of the private company, 'The Central Scotland Woodland Company', set up to run the project will be to improve the landscape of Central Scotland and thus provide planning gain by attracting investment from overcrowded parts of Europe to the less crowded but still well populated central belt of Scotland, in order to create a new type of *Ranstadt*.

Similar proposals have also been made for England in the Community Forest Programme as outlined in Chapter Three. In the wider English countryside, however, the success of private planting is increasingly going to depend on farmers planting up surplus farmland using grant aid.

Recent evidence on the use of such aid is not, however, encouraging. For example. Watkins (1984) in a survey of 72 Nottinghamshire estates found that 72% of all the woodland owners interviewed had never received a planting grant, partly due to a high level of ignorance about the aid available. Even when the details of schemes were revealed to owners only a third would seriously consider tree planting. The key variable being resistance to forestry as a concept.

Likewise in Scotland Scrambler (1989) from a survey of 36 Scottish farmers found a very low interest in forestry, with 86% not considering forestry to be a viable alternative land use. Most worryingly for farm-forestry advocates only 22 and 30%, respectively, stated the timelag involved or the lack of financial incentives as the greatest disincentives, whereas 50% stated their lack in interest in trees as the main disincentive. There is therefore a major attitudinal problem to overcome if farm-forestry is to become a significant land use. The only encouraging tendency for the future is that larger, younger farmers with their own farms expressed slightly more interest in farm-forestry.

In conclusion, forestry has been subjected to a mass of attacks, notably on its economic failure, and Wilson (1987) a political analyst has argued that the forestry lame duck has been able to break the rigid rules of Thatcherite monetarist policy only because it has powerful support not only in the House of Lords, via large landownership, but also in the Cabinet via directorships in forestry companies for past or future Ministers.

For the future, forestry can only expand if it mends its environmental fences and sells itself both as an environmental saviour, by moving towards an ecologically acceptable, sustainable and renewable form of production and as an alternative to surplus farmland.

8 Policy Proposals for Land Use Planning

Introduction

Before we can consider policy proposals for land use planning, we need to examine what it is and what has been happening to it. Government policy on planning is set out traditionally in White Papers, Ministerial Statements, Circulars and so on. In the late 1980s Planning Policy Guidance Notes were added to this list. These provide an excellent starting point for a review of extant policy. For example, in the note on 'General Policy and Principles' (Environment, 1988c) the Government advises that the system of planning is designed to regulate the development and use of land in the public interest, and to strike the right balance between development and the interests of conservation, but with a presumption in favour of allowing development. In the note on 'Rural Enterprise and Development' the Government advises that the planning system provides a mechanism for balancing the requirements of development and the continuing need to protect the countryside for the sake of it's beauty, it's diversity of landscape, the wealth of it's natural resources and for it's ecological, agricultural and recreational value. Exceptions to this policy could include infilling, but in the open countryside only the most exceptional need should lead to planning permission being granted for new housing. Within villages lower densities could, however, be allowed. In the note on 'Local Plans' the Government asks authorities to look ahead 10 years in providing enough land for new housing, and in the note on 'Land for Housing' the Government argues that in many villages modest development could be permitted without damaging the countryside and at the same time help to sustain smaller communities by helping to maintain local services, shops, pubs, schools and other features of community life, but without creating ribbon or isolated development.

The key feature of extant policy at the outset of the 1990s was therefore achieving a balance between development and conservation using four key measures: regulation; financial aid; positive developments; and the provision of information and guidance.

This official view of planning, however, masks a good deal of debate about what the planning system could and should be about. For example, Klosterman (1985), an urban studies academic, has divided the arguments for and against planning into four categories. First, the economic argument which accepts that even perfectly competitive markets require government action to correct market failures. Second, the pluralistic argument which argues that weaker sections of society are often excluded from bargaining and thus planners are needed to redress the balance. Third, the traditional argument that improving the environment is an independent function of government which is sustainable in the name of promoting the collective public interest. Fourth, the Marxist argument that only fundamental reform of capitalism in favour of state control can produce real planning. In conclusion, Klosterman argues that whichever view is taken, planning must recognize the tremendous gap between it's potential and performance, otherwise other groups will move in and claim the role that planners are failing to fulfil.

The fact that planners are only one set of actors in a complex struggle for power has been taken up by Rydin (1985) who has examined three typologies of the planning process from the view of power analysis. The first is the classical pluralist approach which looks for the exercise of power in observable overt conflicts. The second involves the analysis of covert conflicts as well as overt conflicts. These covert conflicts, e.g. gentrification, are recognized but not actually expressed in the political arena. The third relates to the perception of conflicts under which, either through ignorance or manipulation, the arena of conflict is set by the actor's perceptions of the issues.

From her examination of the residential planning process in the Essex Green Belt, Rydin rejects the pluralist view in which planners oppose developers or the local community as being misleading. Instead she argues that the covert and perceptionist view of planning is more useful in understanding planning, in that the decision to make no decisions about certain issues, or even to discuss some issues, is more significant than the issues that are discussed in the public arena. She concludes that the role of the planning system is thus fourfold.

1. The planning system has material economic effects on land values and the distribution of wealth. These indirect effects are more important than the direct and intended effects of planning.

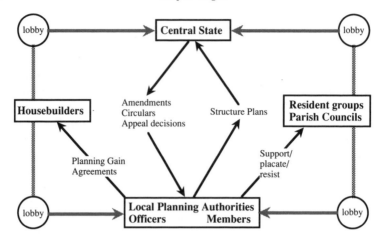

Fig. 8.1. Interactions between the four key groups in the land use planning process. Source: Short *et al.* (1986).

2. The beneficiaries of these effects are landowners and developers and the planning system therefore benefits certain sectional groups, mainly already powerful economic groups.
3. The professional ideology of planners, confused and limited as it is to mainly procedural discussions, obscures these distributional effects and legitimizes the benefits to powerful groups.
4. The internal ideological debate between planners often replaces the overt activities of local politics and keeps any resulting conflicts latent.

A similar model of the land use planning process from the political economy perspective has been produced by Short *et al.* (1986) as shown in Fig. 8.1.

Elsewhere, Short *et al.* (1987) from a study of residential development control processes in Berkshire using this model, have concluded that the state has been able to resolve the dual pressures of maintaining capital accumulation and ensuring social legitimation by: (i) overruling negative local decisions and thus allowing residential development to proceed in rural areas against the wishes of local residents; and (ii) by insisting, however, that planning gains are made via improved infrastructure so that the process is to some extent legitimized. However, Short *et al.* also note that the situation is fluid and that in some areas growing local opposition is already limiting the freedom for the state to allow macroscale growth even in vibrant areas like Berkshire. Indeed if too many pro-development decisions are made the Conservative Government is only too well aware of the strength of the opposition to widespread residential growth within its own political heartland.

In this sense Short *et al.* (1986) have to concede that the land use planning system is essentially a mechanism for balancing the demands of a host of competing interests, albeit with the scales weighted in favour of powerful groups.

Having examined what planning is, it is now time to turn briefly to some of its main effects. Its main purpose in 1947, when it was first introduced, was to contain the growth of urban development. It has by and large achieved this goal, since although as Anderson (1984) has shown 494,000 hectares were lost from agriculture in the 1948–1978 period this was necessary not only to accommodate an additional 5.6 million people but also to provide them with more space as living standards and expectations rose. Accordingly urban land provision standards rose from 28.8 hectares/1000 people in 1948 to 35.6 hectares/1000 people in 1978. If urban containment had been fully adhered to the space standard would instead have fallen to 25.6 hectares/1000 people. Nonetheless, the rate of land lost from agriculture has by and large continued to fall in the post-war years from an average of around 15,000 hectares a year to around 7300 hectares a year in the late 1980s (Environment, 1987, 1988). Current forecasts by Bibby and Shepherd (1991) for the DOE estimate that another 0.8% of England and Wales (105,000 hectares) will be lost to urban use between 1981 and 2001. However, the loss will not be even with the south east losing around 1.3% to take the urban percentage there to 13.5%.

In spite of restrictive planning policies counterurbanization has occurred (Champion, 1989). There is a debate about whether counterurbanization is a creature of the 1960s which faltered in the 1970s and collapsed in the early 1980s, or is in contrast a long-term restructuring of the British population. Champion (1987) has found evidence for both arguments. For example, although rural population growth continued into the 1980s the rate was halved from over 10 per 1000 to around 5 per 1000. Nonetheless during the decade Champion (1989) was also able to discern a slight revival in the rate of population deconcentration and a growing differential between the rates of growth in rural areas and elsewhere.

Explanations of the counterurbanization phenomenon are also open to debate. For example, in a survey of households in North Devon, Bolton and Chalkley (1989) dispel the myth that counterurbanization migrants are: elderly migrants, long-distance commuters, return migrants, refugees from decaying cities, commune drop-outs, hi-tech whizz kids, managers of branch factories and dole queue sun seekers. Instead, the majority of migrants were found to be conventional people in conventional jobs, who had relocated as part of the normal employment process, and did not depart from the norm in any significant way.

Bolton and Chalkley (1990) have also concluded that their data failed to fit any of the four main theories of migration: household-led, firm-led, state-induced, or the Marxist restructuring thesis. Instead the process was seen to be both eclectic and heterogeneous, and if so this must pose severe problems for rural policy formulation unless it too is eclectic and multi-headed.

In conclusion, the twin-headed issues of urban containment and counterurbanization lie at the heart of the land use planning issue. Urban containment continues to be the core of planning policy and yet at the same time rural areas continue to grow by infilling at the expense of the old metropolitan areas. The trend to decentralization is clear. The debate is about how much decentralization should be allowed and where. This central issue will surface several times throughout this chapter, but before going any further this section should be concluded by examining how Thatcherism has altered planning.

Thornley (1988) has outlined four key effects of Thatcherism. First, the consensus view of planning as a 'good thing' has all but vanished. Second, those limited opportunities to pursue social objectives that once existed have been withdrawn. Third, it is now impossible to view planning as an apolitical technical activity, and fourth, planning has been divided into a three-tier zoning system. At the top there is the system with strong planning controls, e.g. in National Parks or green belts, while at the bottom there are the new virtually planning free zones, e.g. Simplified Planning Zones. In the middle the so-called normal system still operates. For the future, Thornley does not see that a return to consensus is possible but that instead planners will have to decide with which political ideology they want to side. A social caring ideology or a free market enabling ideology.

Other commentators are less critical and indeed Burton (1990) the CPRE's planning officer has claimed that the reversals of policy made by Chris Patten, Secretary of State, in the winter of 1989/90 were not only a sea change but returned planning to the pre-Heseltine-Mark I era of 1979. To some extent this largely concurs with the view presented in Chapter 3 that planning in essence remained remarkably unchanged in the 1980s. This does not mean of course that it will remain so in the 1990s, and so it is now time to return to the main theme of this book, what planning could be in the 1990s, by examining three themes: first, holistic/political views of planning; second, proposals to alter the system in detail; and third, four key issues, housing demand forecasts, the case for new settlements, the future of green belts, and whether planning controls should be introduced over agriculture.

Holistic/party political policy proposals

This section takes a traditional left–right view of politics since the issues focus around the one central issue of how much control the state should exercise over the development process.

Right wing proposals

Starting at the extreme right, in the heady days of early Thatcherism when everything seemed possible, Jones (1982) a freeman of the City of London and a local councillor in the Chilterns, proposed radical reforms for planning: first, the complete scrapping of development control procedures and their replacement by low cost easy to use land use tribunals; second, the introduction of private covenants as a means of enforcing environmental conditions. At the same time historic and rural areas would be protected except from minor developments, but elsewhere planning consent would be generally assumed.

In a slightly less extreme view Mather (1988), the director of the right wing Institute of Economic Affairs, argued that planning like the other socialist creations of the 1940s, should be made to face the free market. Basing his arguments mainly on the inner cities he proposes extending and formalizing the principle of planning gain to a full-blown system of selling or auctioning planning consents.

In a similar vein Boyle (1988), the editor of *Town and Country Planning* has even suggested privatizing the planning process. He portrays a scenario in which a small group of local authority planners would commission consultants or local groups to prepare plans and make recommendations on planning applications. Actual decisions would still, however, be taken by local councillors. Boyle believes that this system would have a number of benefits, mainly, that development plans would have to be up-to-date and contain clear and precise sets of policies and standards, so that consultants could make their recommendations on planning applications, based on published policies, rather than on the *ad hoc* basis at present employed by councillors.

However, Ehrman (1988) a property developer in a pamphlet for the Centre for Policy Studies, rejects this role of planning as mapping out detailed land use. Instead he advocates a more limited role. Under his scheme, central government would draw up policies on planning matters which would be reviewed every two or three years. These would then be put into practice by strategic plans at the regional level prepared by County Councils which in simple terms would set out the future infrastructure and special development areas of the region. At the local level, district authorities would produce no plans at all, but merely respond to planning applications, including new farm buildings. The key factors would be social and environmental acceptability, and here Ehrmann suggests a form of bidding procedure where developers would seek to gain permission by offering low cost housing and/or better landscaping.

Continuing the low cost housing theme Evans (1988) an environmental economist in a pamphlet for the Institute of Economic Affairs has argued that planning has not only forced up house prices but has also imposed costs throughout the economy via higher prices and lost production. His solution is to loosen up planning control and to introduce the market mechanism into planning. He rejects the idea of bidding for planning permission as dealing with only one side of the system. Instead he stands the idea upside down and suggests a system whereby a developer agrees, with all those neighbours affected by the proposal, the compensation that they will be paid. This would mean that objectors would turn into supporters, more developments would thus be given permission and the net result would be cheaper houses built where people wanted to live at the expense of a slightly more built up countryside.

In a scheme to prevent more building in the countryside, however, Steen (1988) a Conservative MP has proposed a scheme to regenerate the inner cities and thus release some of the pressures for development in the countryside. The scheme known as PLUMS (Public Land Utilization Management Scheme) would involve the transfer of the ownership of all publicly held vacant land to a private body which would prepare, market and sell the land to developers. The profits realized would go to both the original owners and also the private body who had upgraded the land ready for the market.

Two Tory MPs, Baker and Wiggen (1987) and 13 other Tory MPs, have also linked increased hostility to green field development with the need to revitalize Britain's inner cities. They advocate setting up a land use survey and land register to determine land availability notably inside cities. Outside cities they propose the erection of permanent 'Strategic Development Boundaries' around conurbations to contain growth, surrounded by permanent 'Protected Green Belts' in which no significant development would be possible. Beyond these they propose the designation of either 'Housing Growth Areas' where large-scale housing could be allowed, or 'Housing Restraint Areas' where growth would be impossible.

At the end of the decade Lloyd (1989) a land economist in a review of the arguments of the free market planners, warned that they had been winning popularity for their radical proposals, by default, since few other alternatives had been proposed. Ideas like the auction of planning consents, were thus in danger of being automatically accepted as the planning system surrendered to the new realism of the market. Not everybody would agree with this view, and indeed the 1980s did in fact see a set of proposals from the planning establishment which proposed less extreme reforms.

Proposals from the planning establishment

A perfect example of such a proposal is provided by the 13-strong interdisciplinary committee of inquiry, drawn from all walks of professional life, but mainly the land based professions, which produced a report on planning for the Nuffield Foundation (1986) in the mid 1980s. The proposals they produced were based on both the general purposes of planning and also the characteristics that a planning system should have, which they argued, were as follows.

1. *The purposes of planning should be*:
   (**a**) to monitor and control the impact on the environment of present and future uses of land;
   (**b**) to anticipate and prevent the perpetuation of nuisances;
   (**c**) to provide a coherent and consistent framework for the operation of the land market in property and development land;
   (**d**) to reconcile conflicting demands for land as they arise from the development plans of private and public agencies;
   (**e**) to assist in the promotion of those developments, both public and private, that are considered desirable by the relevant public authority;
   (**f**) to provide the information necessary for the effective discharge of these functions.
2. *Characteristically a revised planning system should be*:
   (**a**) comprehensive;
   (**b**) transparent;
   (**c**) give discretion to local authorities;
   (**d**) be accessible to the public;
   (**e**) be modest about living with uncertainty and change.

In general, the Nuffield Committee made three proposals for the overall system: first, the role of central Government should be reduced and confined to only truly national issues; second, greater emphasis should be placed on the need for all bodies at all levels to coordinate their plans and be consistent in their decisions, mainly by introducing an Annual White Paper on land and the environment, regional reports and county strategies; third, local authority planning powers should be widened and local authorities should have the discretion to extend their powers to any social, economic, or environmental issues in their area which they would like to influence.

More specifically, the Nuffield Committee advocated the introduction of 'landscape control and management areas' where certain designated changes, such as hedge removal or major drainage works on agricultural land, would require approval, as well as other powers and resources for conserving the landscape. The Committee also advocated the right of appeal by the public against the grant of planning permission and public access to the services of professional planners.

The centre of the planning establishment is of course represented by the Royal Town Planning Institute. As such it has to steer a balance between the radical views of some of its members and the need to present a professional face to the Government. Sometimes these can coalesce as in the middle of the previous Labour administration when they (Royal Town Planning Institute, 1977) were able to propose an integrated system of planning not only for social, economic and environmental activities but also for the development of physical resources including food, water and minerals, via the development of Comprehensive Planning Strategies, produced at the community level, but guided at the national level by a newly created National Resource Planning Agency.

After ten years of Thatcherism and faced with a pragmatic Labour Party the equivalent document in the late 1980s (Royal Town Planning Institute, 1988) merely sought to improve rather than reform the planning system. The document in more detail contained 75 points which can be summarized as follows.

1. *National responsibility:*
    (a) the government should prepare national policy guidelines along the lines already developed by the Scottish Development Department;
    (b) a national policy should integrate all forms of transport.
2. *Regional action:*
    (a) there should be a revival and extension of effective government planning for the regions including Regional Development Agencies in England;
    (b) policies and guidelines should be prepared for each region following the example of the former Regional Economic Planning Councils;
    (c) there should be a review of the case for regional government with a consequent reassessment of the structure of local government, leading to the establishment of 11 regional authorities in England and Wales with a limited reform of regional councils in Scotland.
3. *Plan making:*
    (a) planning authorities should be required to prepare development plans for their entire area, and these should be regularly reviewed, perhaps every 5 years.
4. *Conserving heritage and the environment:*
    (a) agricultural buildings and roads should be subject to full planning control, but failing this the Town and Country Planning (Agricultural and Forestry Development in National Parks etc.) Special Development Order should be extended to all rural areas in England and Wales;
    (b) a statutory system of prior notification of intended landscape change should be established to reinforce the powers to enter into management agreements under the 1981 Wildlife and Countryside Act;
    (c) section 174 of the 1971 Town and Country Planning Act allowing for compensation when the felling of trees protected by a Tree Preservation Order is refused should be repealed;
    (d) environmental assessment should be made a statutory requirement for a wider range of development categories including many of those in Annex II of the European Directive.
5. *Democracy:*
    (a) there is a need for a major reform of public inquiry procedures, including a multistage approach involving an initial appraisal of the

project followed by detailed site analysis if the overall concept is
approved;

(b) applications which are clearly contrary to approved development
plan policies should always be subject to public inquiry;

(c) when the Secretary of State overrides an Inspector's recommendation
there should be scope for the decision to be subject to approval by
Parliament.

The Institute is, however, a coalition and increasingly its members work
in private practice and have free market rather than collective ideologies. For
example, Tibbalds (1988) a planning consultant, when he was president of the
RTPI, outlined a positive vision of the future of town and country planning,
in which he advocated a breaking down of the barriers between the development professions (which should be natural allies) since planning is necessarily
a collaborative process. In this view planning's role would be greater than
that of just a local authority regulatory function and would form an essential
part of the 'enterprise culture'. In this regard, planning gain and the sale of
planning permissions would be options but only if the emphasis was on
betterment within a plan-led environment. Bargaining and negotiating for a
price in isolation would in contrast lead to pretty rotten environments and
bring the system into disrepute, especially if it benefited only one section of
society at the expense of the less articulate and less powerful.

Proposals from establishment academics

The establishment planning academic has for over 20 years been Peter Hall
(1988a) a geographer of world renown. In recent years he has rounded on his
fellow academics and the current fashion for them and Marxist political
economists to write books on planning which claim that it is the handmaiden
of late capitalism struggling to ward off its terminal crisis. Hall counters by
arguing that planning is bound to be the handmaiden of capitalism since it
is the system we have and the only system we are likely to have.

Hall thus proposes a set of aims to deal with capitalism as it is rather than
how critics would like it to be. Given this position the main aim for the 1990s
is thus to create new types of settlement to deal with the new patterns of living
that emerged in the 1980s, namely new settlements in the countryside (Hall,
1988b). One way to achieve these would be by the creation of slimline
Regional Development Authorities which would identify zones of land for
development. These would then be given 'zoning rights' after a public inquiry
which could then be auctioned off to the highest bidder.

In spite of his ability to react to changing fashions in planning thought,
Hall is to some extent a lightweight academic lacking real substance in depth
and detail, an ideas man, able to chart broad patterns rather than the nitty
gritty. In contrast Patsy Healey in a series of publications in the late 1980s

has provided not only, an excellent review of the continuing evolution of planning thought, but also a comprehensive set of proposals for reform. Looking back over the 1980s Healey (1988) identifies it as a radical decade when the new left and the new right were joined by many other groups in an attack on the 'traditional' way of doing things which evolved in Britain's post-war consensus society. The key feature of this radicalism was the creation of a more pluralist society than before.

According to Healey this radical review by society of its own goals and aims will lead to the continued rejection of not only the blueprint model of planning (1945–1970) but also the rational model of planning based on alternative choices (1970–1990) as expressed in structure plans. It will instead lead to the creation of a new form of planning based on 'debate'.

This planning by debate in the 1990s will need to focus on the central issues of the 1990s which according to Healey will be: local development strategies; the quality of life; accommodating diversity and variety; promoting aesthetic quality; and developing the implications of widely shared values about environmental conservation and ecological balance. This will include: the polluter pays principle; the creation of more loosely knit urban regions with more development in the countryside; greater emphasis on the environment as inheritance; and a more active democracy.

Healey concludes that not only the context of planning but also the processes will also need to change. She concludes that planners will need to argue for the following.

1. An inclusionary approach, in which the notion of a single public interest disappears to be replaced by a broadly based approach which considers who gets access to the debate and how policies are made accountable.
2. An approach which fosters systematic identification of arguments, and the reasons behind them, and encourages social learning.
3. An approach which promotes the role of environment as collective inheritance, and is practical, fair and distributively just.

In essence, Healey's proposals for the 1990s are pluralist, democratic and rational, albeit tempered by pragmatism and value-laden considerations. Her key words for the 1900s are *citizen responsiveness* in a democratic society and *environment consciousness*.

In developments of these ideas (Healey, 1989; Healey *et al.*, 1988) four deficiencies in the planning system as practised in the 1980s are identified.

1. A lack of *accountability*;
2. *Institutional dispersal* with power fragmented between three levels of government; but at the same time
3. The *unfettered powers of Central Government* impede coordination and exacerbate conflicts; and
4. *Inequity* between individuals and groups in terms of their ability to challenge decisions and to influence policy formulation.

Healey then examines 18 various proposals for changing the planning system, made in the 1980s, and condenses them into the following four models.

1. A Market Criteria Dominant Model
(A bare minimum of ground rules for making planning decisions)

Instruments	Zoning schemes, pricing of planning permissions.
Institutional arrangements	Single-tier planning overseen by Secretary of State; planning staff appointed by Secretary of State.
Processes	Techno-rationality, advice from the business community.
Proponents	Adam Smith Institute (1983); British Property Federation (1986); Mather (1988) in part.
Commentary	Unlikely to be politically sustainable.

2. A Hierarchy, Coordination and Broadly Based Interest Mediation Model
(Market management via pluralism and hierarchical planning tiers)

Instruments	National policy statements, third party rights of appeal against public development projects otherwise as at present.
Institutional arrangements	Three levels of Government (central, regional, local) cooperating in partnership.
Processes	Techno-rationality, semi-judicial inquiry, pluralist politics or corporalist negotiation.
Proponents	Nuffield Foundation (1986), Royal Town Planning Institute (1986) in part, Social and Liberal Democrats (1988) in part.
Commentary	Embodies many of the current problems.

3. A Rights and Localism Model
(Locally based pluralism with high level of public participation)

Instruments	Strengthen role of local plans but offset power of these plans by the provision of widely based rights; to challenge decisions; demand information; debate policy and influence implementation. Site value rating and development land tax.

Institutional arrangements	Strong single-tier districts (counties abolished), regional authorities for strategic planning, role of community and parish councils strengthened.
Processes	Pluralist politics, open public debate, semi-judicial inquiry (to resolve disputes).
Proponents	Liberal Party (1984 and 1986), Labour Party (1985) in part, Royal Town Planning Institute (1986) in part, Social and Liberal Democrats (1988) in part.
Commentary	Difficulties in reconciling national, regional and local and community control and in reconciling conflicting demands.

4. A Maximize Distributive Justice Model
(Emphasis on positive development initiatives by the state)

Instruments	Public land banks, public action zones, third party rights to challenge planning decisions contrary to plans, positive discrimination in respect of gender, ethnicity and disability, site value rating.
Institutional arrangements	Firm democratic accountability, political rationality, open public debate, community groups to take control of policy making and implementation where possible.
Proponents	Labour Party (1986), Liberal Party (1984 and 1986) in part, Labour Party (1988) in part.
Commentary	A central problem rests on how the tension between strategic considerations and local control would be resolved.

Healey concludes that none of the four models meets anything like a majority of the four problems identified with 1980s planning systems. A new model therefore needs to be invented which will escape from both: (i) the centralist welfarist assumption which shaped the ideology of the system, from 1947 to 1979; and also (ii), the naive notions of 'privatization' that dominated the 1980s.

Accordingly, Healey (1990) proposes a radical revision of the planning system in which zoning plans would incorporate much of the British tradition of policy principles and performance criteria. Coupled wtih broadly based rights of challenge for all parties including third parties, this could not only be more efficient and democratic but also allow harmonization with European planning systems, which are nearly all based on zoning.

Proposals from the Centre Parties and the Labour Party

Healey's concern for the individual was also reflected a good deal in the thinking of the Centre Parties throughout the 1980s. In the mid 1980s for example the Liberal Party (1984b) criticized the existing system as being too ineffective, too undemocratic, too physical and too short term. It then set out 10 principles for a planning system including the following.

1. The right for an individual to do anything unless it is harmful to others.
2. The right of people to be told about all proposals likely to affect them.
3. The right of people to open and democratic government.
4. A fairer distribution of wealth and an emphasis on upgrading the quality of life for the worst off.
5. Conservation of resources and the environment to provide maximum freedom for future generations.
6. Integrating physical, economic and social planning into a coherent planning system.
7. Developing a hierarchy of plans at the local, regional and national levels.
8. Keeping planning as flexible and as positive as possible.

Using these principles a new plan-making system was proposed based at the lowest level, on local plans, to be prepared by and for enlarged district council areas in collaboration with parish/community councils. At the next level, regional plans would be prepared by elected regional councils, while at the national level a new Department of Regional Affairs would take over the much-reduced roles of the DOE, since most of the monitoring and control would be done at the lower levels.

In the area of development control the report proposed extending planning controls to agriculture and forestry. Appeals would be decided by the next tier up the hierarchy and appeals would only be allowed for proposals not contravening approved policies. At the level of major planning inquiries a two-stage process would consider the need for the proposal at stage 1 and if accepted stage 2 would examine the details of the proposal.

Five years later after the trauma of the Alliance the reformed Social and Liberal Democrats (1989b) in their White Paper on planning 'England's Green and Pleasant Land?' centred their proposals on three key themes; placing the prime responsibility at the local level; a long-term commitment to environmental protection; and integrating environmental issues into all decision making.

The prime objectives of the planning system thus should be:

• To use land in a way that is sustainable, protects diversity and minimizes environmental damage

- To ensure variety and choice in human activities
- To give precedence to long-term quality of life
- To reconcile land use issues in an open and democratic way.

Using these guidelines the document then made 25 main proposals, the most relevant and radical of these being the following:

1. Create a three-tier system of planning, National, Regional and Local, by devolving power from Whitehall to regional plans within the framework of:
2. National land use policies developed by a single government department and subjected to parliamentary approval; but
3. Give a key role to local plans which will provide the key guide to development control;
4. Give local planners the discretion to extend or relax planning controls in their areas but take away their power to grant themselves planning permission;
5. At the major public inquiry level the procedure will be split into two stages. Stage one to examine the need for the proposal, stage two to examine the suitability of the site;
6. All development in designated areas including green belts will be strongly resisted, existing powers will be strengthened and new green belts considered;
7. Planning controls will be extended to agricultural buildings, major afforestation schemes and significant developments within three miles of the coast;
8. Help should be given to first-time buyers and locals by the use of Section 52 agreements, and the creation of special Use Class Orders and Zones for social housing;
9. Optional powers should be available to extend planning permission to second or holiday homes.

Apart from the emphasis on individuals rather than groups these proposals are quite similar to those of the Labour Party which have already been considered in some detail in Chapters 4 and 5. In essence the Labour Party propose: (i) to strengthen and extend the scope of plan making to include social as well as land use issues; (ii) to introduce more equity into development control decisions by the use of environmental and social audits; (iii) to restore powers of land assembly; and (iv) to encourage the greater use of Public Action Zones to develop land ignored by the private sector. Nonetheless, Labour Party policy in its drive for electoral acceptability was still pretty much in the form of a skeletal framework by the late 1980s.

Accordingly, Coulson (1990) has attempted to put some flesh on the rather bare bones of the 1989 Labour Policy Review 'Meet the Challenge, Make the Change'. One of Coulson's main proposals is to abolish counties and to transfer their powers both upwards and downwards to Regional and District Councils. At the Regional level, ten English Regions would be created with Regional Assemblies elected by proportional representation in parallel with similar Assemblies for Scotland and Wales. The Assemblies would produce Regional Economic Plans. Coulson also considers the creation of Regional Development Agencies and the possible decentralization of: (i) the Rural Development Commission; (ii) English Estates; (iii) the Countryside Commission; (iv) the Nature Conservancy Council; (v) the National Rivers Authority; (vi) the Forestry Commission; (vii) the Sports Council; (viii) English Heritage; and (ix) the return of the Regional Water Companies to social ownership.

At the District level, Coulson finds the Policy Review flawed in that several of the existing Districts may be too small for strategic planning. He therefore recommends that Districts, could amalgamate for some of the higher level services such as education and planning.

The Labour Party's headlong flight to the right in the late 1980s, has to some extent left the hard left, rather high and dry. However, as Hall has already pointed out, academics have filled the gap with extraordinary vigour in adopting Marxist viewpoints of planning which may well be correct in their analysis, but are increasingly out on a limb as far as policy acceptance matters. For example Hague (1985), an academic planner, from a critical theory standpoint, has called first, for national and regional plans to be put into operation at the local level by local authorities publicly owning land. Second, the planning profession should undergo a radical transformation into a critical and independent institution producing and disseminating knowledge free from domination by either the interests of capital or the state. The radical planner must then confront realities with possibilities, oppose from within, while building dialogues outside, and must see his or her own frustrations as part of a much wider and more vicious repression.

In a second example, Reade (1987), in a major book on land use planning which has won widespread critical acclaim, claims that planning has failed on two major counts. First, by failing to recoup the increases in land values largely caused by planning controls it has not only legitimized these profits but also made itself socially unacceptable. Second, by trying to pretend that planning is a technical rather than a political activity it has perpetuated a fallacy without which planning control would and should collapse.

Turning to the future, Reade outlines the evolution of two likely scenarios, either, a different development of positive planning with planners aiding rather than abetting developers, or, the further growth of centralized corporate planning with local government being increasingly marginalized. However, it is a third scenario which Reade finds to be desirable if rather unlikely. In this scenario a really radical, if somewhat contradictory, future is portrayed.

First, the major aim of a reformed system should be the recoupment of all land value increases, on both the grounds of equity, and as the source of all the money needed to repair environmental damage. Second, the system should reject the holistic idea of planning in favour of specialized policies for different topics or sectors. Third, policy makers should base their policies on research into the effects of past policies not the forecasting of future trends.

Fourth, the system should be divided into intellectual policy making, and routine implementation. Fifth, the system should be based on the rule of law (zoning) and should reduce discretion to a minimum. Sixth, policies should be formulated at central government level and local authorities should not be able to make their own policies, and seventh, the system should be more highly politicized.

Finally, in a more realistic proposal Montgomery and Thornley (1988) argue that the immediate task is to prevent Thatcherism from undermining planning any further. In the future, planners should press for control over both land speculation, and compensation and betterment, via the creation of democratically accountable bodies. This is because the failure of planning can be traced to its almost complete lack of influence over the economy.

In view of the fact that development control has hardly changed since 1948, and plan making only once in the early 1970s, most of the more radical proposals discussed above have little chance of being implemented in the 1990s. It is now time to turn to more pragmatic proposals for gradually reforming the present system in detail rather than by root and branch.

Proposals for reforming the system in detail

Working from the centre of power outwards, this set of proposals can be divided into calls for regional planning, calls for local government reorganization, calls for the reform of plan making, and finally calls for minor reforms to development control.

Beginning with calls for regional planning Cameron (1985) has argued for the creation of a regional tier of economic planning for the English regions in order to build on the successes of the various Scottish and Welsh Development Agencies. He doubts, however, whether this by itself would bring greater equity to public expenditure, since the new regions would have to fight both central and local government, not only for funds, but for their very existence, especially local government which would feel threatened by a new bigger brother.

Nonetheless five years later, a report, approved by the Association of County Councils but prepared by the County Planning Officers Society (1990), gave full support to the more limited concept of regional plans. The plans would be prepared by groupings of local authorities in each region, dominated by the County Councils, and the draft would be subject to public scrutiny at a conference before being submitted to the Department of The Environment for approval. The plans would look at least 15 years ahead, and contain long-term predictions for population, housing, economic and travel change in a slim concise document. In many ways this proposal was similar to the *de facto* system which was coming into operation in the early 1990s with regional conferences preparing regional strategies, e.g. SERPLAN (see the 'housing demand' section later in this chapter) with national guidance for each region being set out in Planning Policy Guidance Notes from the DOE, at least for the Metropolitan regions and their immediate environs.

Turning to local government reorganization the Society of Local Authority Chief Executives (1986) have perhaps surprisingly made some radical proposals. Arguing that the great error of post-war governments has been the attempt to deal with local government in a series of uncoordinated developments, they instead propose the creation of totally new unitary authorities based on natural communities rather than size. The new authorities would be given adequate finances raised from a reformed rates system and a new local income tax. They would also have the power to carry out any functions which the community believed to be in its interests, within legitimate national constraints.

In the Scottish context Sewel (1987) has also concluded that the present two-tier system is fundamentally flawed. He concludes that if a Scottish assembly were to come about in the 1990s that the 17 single-tier unitary areas proposed by the Wheatley report in 1969 would provide the basis for a more effective system of local government in Scotland.

In contrast Wannop (1988) arguing from the position of both an academic and former local authority planner, has used the Scottish experience, to conclude that the present trend towards central government becoming more directly involved with local government, could be usefully reversed, by setting up a two-tier system, similar to say Strathclyde, where local and regional councils interact to reflect both community and strategic interests.

Finally, Barnett *et al.* (1989) in a report for the County Planning Officers Society, use 15 examples of the work of County Councils, such as, plan making, making things happen and helping people to work together, to argue for a continued role for the County in rural planning. Their argument has been continued by the Association of County Councils (1991) who point out that since the Counties provide some 80% of local government services they should continue to provide the unique base for strategic planning.

However, in the spring of 1991 the collapse of the Poll Tax panicked the Government into deciding that the fate of local government should be left to individual areas who would decide over one of three options: first, county councils only; second, district councils only; third the *status quo*.

Turning to the reform of plan making, the dawn of the 1990s saw proposals for the abolition of structure plans based on two White Papers in 1986 and 1989, still on the table. In spite of these proposals, the Department of the Environment (1990b) in Planning Policy Guidance 15, urged county planning authorities collectively to prepare regional planning guidance and individually to proceed with the revision and updating of county structure plans. In 1991 structure plans were reprieved, at least in advance of any Poll Tax induced local government reform, in the Planning and Compensation

Act 1991. In light of the continuing uncertainty over structure planning, the debate about the 1986 and 1989 proposals is still worth looking at.

Bruton and Nicholson (1987b), for example, criticize them as being too narrowly conceived, and would like to see national policy guidelines in addition to regional guidance prepared by bona fide regional authorities. In a further commentary Gwilliam (1989) a county planning officer notes that the proposals were tentative and evolutionary rather than revolutionary. In contrast Gwilliam argues for a system that would allow and encourage county and district councils to work together, and in particular one, that would place much more emphasis on environmental quality and planning values.

Shaw (1989) a County Planning Officer in a further commentary begins by arguing that current plan making already faces two main concerns. First, the weakened role of plans in making development control decisions, and second, the proliferation of *ad hoc* non-statutory plans in the face of out of date or non-existent statutory plans. If the proposals had been implemented Shaw forecast a two-tier system of over-weak plans instead of what was needed, one strong plan. He also foresaw an increasing centralization of planning powers. As an alternative Shaw proposed that any effective reform of the system should relate to the role of plans in managing change, and the extent to which planning authorities should be able to adapt plans to local circumstances.

Turning from the thoughts of two County Planning Officers, the County Planning Officers Society (1985) has proposed a three-tier system with a greater role for both the structure plan and County Councils. Under their proposals central government would set out a framework of national policies and endorse appropriate regional policies. These regional policies would be produced by intraregional standing conferences of local planning authorities. County Council structure plans would have to conform to these and the draft structure plan would have to be broadly approved by the Secretary of State. After this, however, the County Councils alone would set up the Examination in Public and give approval to the structure plan subject to reserve powers held by the Secretary of State. Local plans would be prepared where necessary, but Supplementary Planning Guidance should be used in preference to statutory local plans if possible.

In a review of the planning system from the other side of the negotiating fence, the British Property Federation (1986) has criticized the system for it's uncertainties and delays. Accordingly, the Federation make four recommendations.

1. Development plans should be more market-orientated and demand led.
2. Planning areas should be larger than existing areas in order to provide a strategic rather than a parochial approach.
3. Development plans should divide areas into three zones: stability zones,

activity zones and controlled activity zones. 'Conforming proposals' for development in these zones should have a virtual right to proceed.
4. Planning authorities should only have a broad power to designate the appearance of buildings.

In contrast to structure plans, local plans rule OK. For example Winter (1989) an academic planner, from a survey of over 150 local planning authorities, found that local plans were well regarded by both planners and councillors and had been an aid to local economies. He therefore advocates, not only their continuation, but also their extension to all parts of a local authority area. If this is to be done, however, extra resources will have to be provided.

The size of the problem has been highlighted by Coon (1988) who from a survey of local authorities has shown that only 20% of the population outside London is covered by an adopted local plan. If local plans are ever to have any comprehensive coverage and be kept up to date there will have to be a massive investment in planning staff, the output of graduates from the planning schools, and a greatly increased involvement by the DOE.

The final area for reform lies within development control, but not so much with the day to day processes, but with the public inquiry high profile, side of the work. Here some radical proposals have been made by the Environment Committee of the House of Commons (1986) including: a right for third parties to call in an application for appeal; a two-stage inquiry for major inquiries with stage one debating the national issues; and funding to be made available for third parties. These proposals were, however, rejected by the Government (Command 43, 1986).

Nonetheless, the principle of a two-stage inquiry was at the same time advocated by the Royal Institution of Chartered Surveyors (1986) who proposed that big issues, e.g. motorways, large coal mines, etc., should not be discussed in principle at a public inquiry but by Parliament. If Parliament decided to give the go-ahead then a local public inquiry would discuss the development in detail.

Turning to the future, Gilfoyle (1989) in a personal viewpoint has stated that strategic planning in the 1990s will be judged on how effectively it tackles the following six issues.

1. The ability to think strategically while remaining responsive to the accelerating rate of change.
2. Finding the route to real regional strategies based on a synthesis of elements for example, motorway corridors rather than topic-based strategies based on static areas.
3. Coping with the scale and distribution of residential development demands.
4. Resolving debates about major energy developments.

5. Meeting the growing demands for roads and transport in the face of environmental conflicts.

6. Achieving a 'greener' country by reducing pollution and improving the heritage from the past.

For rural planners the two most important issues listed by Gilfoyle are issues **2** and **3**, and indeed number **3** forms the thread linking three of the four key issues that conclude this chapter: the demand for housing; new settlements; green belts; and the case for the introduction of planning controls over agriculture.

Four key issues

KEY ISSUE **1: Forecasting and planning for housing demand (with special reference to the south east)**

Forecasting moral attitudes and family building is of course a hazardous exercise, but if the trends of the 1970s and 1980s continue, the 1990s will see the traditional nuclear family decline even further. If this happens the further growth of small households will surely lead to a demand for different types of housing unit away from the traditional three-bedroomed mortgaged house towards accommodation that can fit the more flexible lifestyle of the 1990s. Perhaps a return to leasehold accommodation in blocks as found in continental Europe. This could have the biggest single impact of any change in the 1990s if low rise surburbia were to be replaced by high density tenanted flats. Just as significant, however, could be the predicted fall in the number of additional households expected to be created each year, from 170,000 in 1990 to only 50,000 in 2001 (Ermisch, 1990).

These changes will not, however, be spread uniformly over the country, increases of over 15% may be expected in no less than eight rural counties, between 1985 and 2001 (Office of Population Censuses and Surveys, 1988). The forecasters note, however, that their projections may indicate that existing trends and policies are likely to lead to situations which are judged undesirable. If new policies are introduced which make the projections invalid, then one of the prime functions of such projections – warning of the consequences of demographic trends – will have been fulfilled.

Translating these projections, this time for 1991 to 2001, into, first household formation, and then the number of new houses needed, the Department of the Environment (1988d) has predicted that the south-eastern corner of England is under the greatest pressure. Indeed, 427,000 of the 1,180,000 houses needed to be built under this crude forecast would need to be built here if planners decide to accommodate the trend projection.

The biggest real rate of household growth is, however, forecast for East Anglia (over 12%), followed by the outer south east (10%), the south west (nearly 10%) and then the East Midlands (8%). All the other regions show much slower rates varying from 1.25% in the North to 4.83% in the West Midlands.

However, this rate of growth will not be spread evenly over the decade. For example, Kleinman and Whitehead (1989) have combined demographic forecasts, economic factors and government policy to forecast a rapid decline in housebuilding for the 1990s with expected demand falling from 189,000 dwellings in 1991 to 175,000 in 1996, and 137,000 in 2001.

In a third forecast the House Builders Federation (1989a) have examined occupancy rates (354 homes needed to house 1000 people in 1971, 420 in 2001), the numbers of unfit houses, the rate of housebuilding on recycled land (around 50%) and concluded that around 200,000 houses a year are likely to be built in the 1990s. Out this total they expect between 75,000 and 100,000 houses to be built in rural areas, leading to a rise in the built up area of between 1.0 and 1.5%. In order to provide a good environment for these homes the Federation proposes: a more positive use of planning powers by county and district councils; the release of more land; more voluntary agreements between landowners, planners and builders, notably to provide affordable housing; the preparation of regional strategic plans by the Government; and the introduction of new settlements in the countryside as an alternative to further additions to existing towns and villages.

These proposals introduce us nicely to the issues that these forecasts raise, namely: is there enough land allocated for immediate needs up to say 1995; will enough land be made available during the second half of the decade; where should this land be allocated – in the south east where the demand is or elsewhere; and if in the south east where within the region?

Beginning with the first of these questions, DOE Circulars in the 1980s asked local authorities to ensure at least a five-year supply of housing land in their areas. Recent surveys confirm that this is being done by the majority of authorities, and that there were planning permissions for 705,000 dwellings in March 1989, enough to satisfy the highest forecast demand for 3.5 years, and enough for more than five years if the building slump of the early 1990s continues (Environment, 1990a, b, c).

Not everybody agrees, however, with the techniques used to estimate the availability of housing land. For example Rydin (1988) from an analysis of 'housing land availability studies' has concluded that they do not provide a picture of land supply, but instead give a figure which totals the maximum possible development capacity of sites. But without knowing the financial situation of local builders, details of their landbanks, and their full range of options for development this figure could be extremely misleading.

In another critique the Council for the Protection of Rural England (1989b) point to the very significant fraction of new housing land which comes from so-called 'windfall sites'. They argue that if allowances were to be made for all windfall sites, regardless of size, in housing land availability studies, and not just for large windfall sites that this would significantly reduce the amount of land at present being unnecessarily released on green field sites.

However, Owens (1989) has concluded that green field sites have been better protected since the advent of Circular 16/87 and that this is not the developers charter it first seemed to be. This is because its substitution of 'protecting the countryside' for 'conserving agricultural land' has actually added more constraints to development by widening the issues to be considered. Returning to how to forecast the amount of land that might be developed Owens claims it is in fact impossible to estimate either how much land is needed or from where it should be taken. Instead a number of crucial factors need to be considered, for example, the willingness of landowners to sell, whether land is designated for conservation or not, whether land is next to existing development/infrastructure, and whether land is not grade 3a or better and is of no significance to the local economy.

In a similar view Blincoe (1987) an officer of the House Builders Federation concurs and argues that forecasts of housing needs and demand need to shift emphasis away from population forecasts towards an understanding of the *processes* that underpin the market. Releasing market demand, by showing how traditional methods can underestimate demand could have benefits for rural areas, by cross-subsidizing social needs housing, with the profits from upmarket housing development according to Blincoe.

This view returns us to the central issue, which according to Hooper *et al.* (1988) is the extent to which housing land should be made available in response to market demand or on planned assessments of future requirements. There is no doubt that if market demand were followed two consequences would occur, first, increased building in the south east, followed by a rapid widening of the so-called north–south divide. Accordingly, attention is now turned to the north–south divide, and then to the south east, the crux of the issue in microcosm.

One way of taking pressure away from the countryside in the south east would of course be to encourage development in the north, the aim of regional planning between the late 1930s and the early 1980s when it was largely abandoned. The reintroduction of such a policy has been advocated by the Town and Country Planning Association (1989) who have made 24 recommendations for weakening the growing north–south divide, including, attracting head offices to the north by providing better transport, notably via an expansion of regional airports.

Lock (1989) an academic, in a discussion paper graphically titled 'Riding the Tiger', for the Town and Country Planning Association has developed these ideas further. He begins by outlining four problems with the present planning system. First, the demand for housing exceeds supply; second, there is no relationship between plans for regional infrastructure and plans for housing; third, there is a mismatch between the housing provided and what people actually want; and fourth, SERPLAN is restricted to local authorities, it operates too slowly and its policies are too bland.

Lock considers three alternative plans for the south. At one extreme, a ring fence approach with virtually all new development being deflected to the north is rejected as undesirable and unworkable, whereas at the other extreme, a free market strategy of letting the tiger loose is seen as impracticable. Accordingly a planning strategy between the two extremes is inevitable.

Such a planning strategy would need to include: qualitative improvement of existing settlements; containment of existing settlements; creation of new settlements; improvement of the infrastructure; conservation and enhancement of natural resources and assets, including reafforestation; levering government defence and administrative functions out of the region; and identifying areas where cheap housing is needed.

The strategy would be prepared by a partnership organization drawn from the private and voluntary sectors, local authorities and central government.

This organization could then recommend some radical initiatives including the following.

1. New cities should be designated under the New Towns Act with private land appropriated at existing use value.
2. Land for new country towns should be acquired by District or County Councils, again at existing use value.
3. District Councils should assemble adequate development land at existing use value and dispose of it at market value, keeping the betterment for their own use.
4. Most existing settlements should have green belts, but existing green belts should be narrowed in width sufficient only to define the outer limits of a settlement.
5. Agricultural land should be subject to full planning control and any form of public payment to farmers should be conditional upon rights of public access or provision of recreational activity.

In summary, Lock proposes: the creation of a new regional planning organization; the stabilization of existing settlements; the creation of new ones, and the blurring of the traditional distinction between town and country.

Turning to one of Lock's criticisms, SERPLAN, or to give it its full title, the London and South East Regional Planning Conference (1988) has not been idle. For example, it has concurred with Lock that planning in the south east should mean more than resisting unwanted development, and that it should also include positive and coordinated action, notably, over new ways of providing low cost housing in rural areas, because there is a concealed and serious housing problem in many rural areas.

In a further development of their work, SERPLAN (London, 1990) issued a consultation paper in April 1990 which included the following two proposals for the countryside of the south east. First, for housing it accepted the advice of the DOE in PPG9 that 570,000 dwellings should be provided during the 1991–2001 period. In more detail, it predicted that the percentage built within existing urban areas would fall from 70% to 50% during the decade thus increasing pressure on the countryside. However, the review rejected the idea of any large new towns at least before 2006, and then only in areas of major employment growth, either where sporadic development from the 1930s could be restructured or where conservation controls prevented any further expansion of existing settlements in the area. In the 1990s, however, there might be a case for smaller new settlements in the 3000–15,000 population range. With regard to special local needs, for example, affordable housing, the review accepted the case in PPG3 for these houses to be extra to those provided for in statutory plans, but only as long as these exceptions were small scale and marginal in total.

Second, not withstanding agricultural surpluses the review argued that the long-term resource of the countryside must be conserved. Therefore, new developments like leisure facilities must not only be reversible but also enhance environmental quality. In addition the review called for the consideration of new areas to be designated for protection, the strengthening of presumptions against *ad hoc* development, and the creation of new habitats and wildlife corridors, possibly via the Countryside Commission's menu of environmental incentives or via whole farm management plans.

Both Lock and SERPLAN advocate a more relaxed approach to development control in the south east. King (1987) concurs and warns that the official forecast of 570,000 new dwellings could lead to a shortfall of between 190,000 and 340,000 dwellings in the region by the year 2001, thus posing serious planning problems for the 1990s. Finally, Chiddick and Dobson (1986) conclude that planning cannot stand, Canute-like, against the flood of development pressure in the south east but must respond positively to it, and give it shape and form.

Even if the flood were released, however, it need not be catastrophic. For example, Cheshire and Sheppard (1989) have estimated, just for the sake of argument (using hedonic equations of the housing markets in Darlington and Reading) that the effect of completely abandoning the planning system would be twofold. First, the mean size of plots in Reading would rise by 65%, and second, the urbanized area of the south east would rise from 19% to 28%, but much of this would be green garden space. It is very unlikely that such an extreme option would be tried, but a halfway house in which controls were substantially relaxed in both new settlements and green belts, is a live option. Attention is thus now directed to these key issues.

KEY ISSUE **2: The case for new settlements**
Lock has already outlined a case for new settlements in the preceeding section, and other proposals have been discussed in Chapter 5. The case has

also been advanced by Hall (1989) the director of the Town and Country Planning Association. He bases his case for new rural settlements on the need, not only to provide existing populations with a better environment, but also, and more importantly with respect to inward migration to Southern England, to provide well planned new developments. In order to oversee their development Hall has advocated: a regional development strategy showing the broad distribution of population and employment; approximate levels of housing demand; the location of new infrastructure; and the approximate location of the new settlements above say 15,000 population. Hall suggests that the developers could be conventional New Town Corporations, or that local authorities could be given the power to become Development Corporations and acquire land for new settlements for up to 15,000 people. This would be preferable to responding to the *ad hoc* proposals like Tillingham Hall, Stone Bassett and Foxley Wood.

In a survey of such developments Potter (1986) found that 12 private new towns were under construction between 1962 and 1985 and that 27 proposals had been made for new towns or large villages for the 1990s, the vast majority in the south east. Five years later Amos (1991) was able to identify a staggering growth to around 150 new settlement proposals.

Amos (1989) in an earlier review found that though there had been a number of proposals for quite large settlements, the majority of proposals were for large villages of between 1000 and 2000 dwellings. In terms of the criteria for judging the acceptability of new settlements, Amos then listed eight criteria.

1. There should be a shortage of housing land elsewhere in the area.
2. There should be an up-to-date plan referring to new settlements.
3. The proposals should be for a settlement below the size which would harm existing interests.
4. The proposal should be outside the south east.
5. The proposal should be well related to areas of housing demand, and close to major shopping and employment areas, and the strategic road network.
6. The proposal should avoid areas of good farmland and high landscape value.
7. The proposal should be far enough away from existing settlements to avoid coalescence.
8. The proposal should use a site which is underused or derelict in order to improve the environment.

Turning to the case of the main protagonists, Consortium Developments (1983–1991) were a grouping of some of the main volume builders who first tested the idea of new settlements, when they proposed a ring of 12–15 country towns around London in 1983. The first proposal was to build a new town of 10,000 people at Tillingham Hall in the Essex Green Belt. Consortium Developments if successful then intended to assemble the land and finance, construct the settlements and their infrastructure, and meet social and environmental costs, on a scale not seen since the Government's new town programme was closed down in the 1970s. Their case (Roche, 1986) was centred on the genuine and intense demand from people to move to the south east and notably the outer south east. Since this demand was not being met, by either SERPLAN or the local authorities in the region – both of whom, according to Roche, had an anti-growth attitude not only to planned growth areas, but even to the expansion of existing settlements – the net result has been a rapid rise in house prices, and thus housing problems for an increasing percentage of families. The solution according to Roche would be new country towns of at least 5000 homes covering between 300 and 400 hectares. This would not only bring down house prices generally by increasing supply, but also according to Lord Northfield (1989) the chairman of Consortium Developments the new settlements would also provide social housing by allowing for up to 10% of all the houses built to be cross-subsidized. However, Merrett (1984) estimated that Consortium Developments misled planners by underestimating the land they would need by up to 67%.

In the event Consortium Developments was disbanded in 1991 and the return of Michael Heseltine, Mark II, to the DOE in November 1990 appeared to signal the end of new settlements at least for the time being. The Town and Country Planning Association, however, remain a firm supporter as evidenced by the February 1991 edition of their journal, and the idea of new settlements will surely be a key issue in the 1990s.

KEY ISSUE 3: The future of green belts

Green belts covered 14% of England in 1988 and according to the Department of the Environment (Environment, 1988e) they have the following five purposes.

1. To check the unrestricted sprawl of large built-up areas.
2. To safeguard the surrounding countryside from urban encroachment.
3. To prevent neighbouring towns from merging into one another.
4. To preserve the special character of historic towns.
5. To assist in urban regeneration.

The essential characteristic of green belts is their permanence and thus the DOE advise in PPG2 that structure and local plans should give them a longer time scale than other policies. In terms of development control, planning permission for inappropriate development should only be given in very special circumstances. It would appear then that green belts have a very secure future with a very strong commitment to this continuity (Environment, 1988f).

However, there are a number of critics of the policy. For example, Willis and Whitby (1985) using economic valuation methods have argued that transferring green belt land out of agricultural use could lead to considerable savings in resources depending on whether it is amenity now that counts, or whether it is the value that future generations may place on green belt land. Willis and Whitby, in light of this uncertainty, concede that green belt land should not be transferred to other uses, unless the benefits from housing and industry substantially exceed the economic welfare value of green belt land. In the reverse case, however, the economic value of green belts (if any) does not justify any further extension of green belts.

Green belts are not as negative as many people suppose but have, according to Elson (1986), provided a very useful mediation device for land release. He supports this conclusion by noting that the population of the Green Belt Ring around London in the mid 1980s was 1.75 million, 1.3 million greater than in 1939. For the future Elson believes that green belts will continue to: (i) manage the process of decentralization; (ii) contain patterns of new development in the interests of economy and access to existing services; (iii) separate towns; (iv) retain valuable agricultural land and other space-extensive uses; (v) retain accessible land in pleasant surroundings; and (vi) assist urban regeneration. In conclusion, Elson argues that the green belt, like mortgage tax relief is politically unremoveable, but, like tax relief, may be subject to attrition. The policy will, however, survive since it offers something to everybody, and as part of planning's attempt to reconcile the irreconcilable forces in society it is one of the most successful all-purpose tools invented.

The importance of the green belt as more than apparently open countryside is also confirmed by Towse (1988) who notes that the London green belt contains a quarter of the south east region's manufacturing jobs, and that its 395,000 such jobs, represent more manufacturing jobs than the whole of the northern regions, and more than half as many again as Wales. The national dilemma is thus one of deciding whether these firms should continue to stay in or move out of the green belt. Because most of them are reluctant to leave the south east, Towse notes that most of them have overcome green belt restraints by redeveloping *in situ* or by finding *ad hoc* sites. Towse argues that a more positive planning response would be to assemble parcels of land that are either unused, wasteland or 'grey' land, rather than green belt land, and to develop such land with environmental improvements, in order both to tidy up the green belt and yet also maintain manufacturing jobs.

So far most of the critics have been guarded in their review of green belts, but there are also a number of more severe critics around. For example, a working party of the Regional Studies Association (1990) has concluded that green belts are outmoded and largely irrelevant. In particular they have restricted growth where development was needed, have been a weak instrument of regional strategic planning, have been instrumental in leading to too much growth beyond them, and have done little to improve the landscape or provide recreation.

Looking to the future the review predicts: (i) an even smaller role for agriculture in the green belt; (ii) a continuation of the rural housing crisis within them; (iii) a continued demand for major new settlements in or near the green belt; (iv) a continuation of the deep personal and political attachment to the belt based on the NIMBY syndrome; and (v) in light of these last two forecasts, an increased need for flexible planning policies.

The working party therefore called for a 'radical' rethink of green belt policy with the substitution of Green Areas, much larger areas in which planning policies would be formulated on a city–regional basis. Apart from expanding the size and function of green belts, the working party also proposed: (i) a shift in emphasis from control to management; (ii) regional freedom to allow more development especially in the more depressed areas of the North; (iii) the development of new types of open land policy with recreation, conservation and forestry being major land uses; but at the same time allowing (iv) significant development in appropriate areas. In essence the proposal is for a multiple nuclei spread city, in which there is enough land to plan for all land uses at a regional level, since the car has made cities not single but many centred (Ash, 1988).

In another critique Business Strategies Ltd (1989) in a report for ARC Properties Ltd estimate that the London green belt is costing a sum equivalent to 3% of Gross National Product in lost production, £9 a week more on mortgages over 25 years and £3617 extra on average house prices. The report does not, however, suggest dismantling the belt, but instead proposes the development of 5% of the 194,000 acres (40% of the green belt area) which are thought to be damaged in some way. The release of this land, it is argued would be enough to supply the extra housing needed in the south east and thus begin to reduce the land price spiral in the region.

The effects of releasing more land in the green belt are also considered in a multi-authored review of the London green belt for the Adam Smith Institute (1988b). This proposes that planning control for the green belt should be devolved to local parishes, since even though this could result in an additional 1 million people in the south east, it would only mean the loss of 2.8% of the green belt's area to housing.

KEY ISSUE 4: Planning controls over agriculture

This issue is considered in several other places in this book, but as an adjunct to other issues, and so for the sake of flogging the issue, two contrary viewpoints are presented here briefly before considering some proposals made by the DOE in the autumn of 1990.

McAuslan (1989) an academic lawyer has examined the arguments for excluding agriculture from development control and has found them all to be flawed. First, the argument that other industries have been deregulated in the 1980s is false since the vast majority of industry is still constrained. Second, the argument that most farmers care for the countryside is acceptable, but it can be assumed, similarly, that most house owners also care for their houses, but this does not exempt them from control over all but minor changes.

Third, the argument that the period of expansionary damage is over and being replaced by conservation incentives is partly acceptable but any system needs both sticks and carrots. Finally, the argument that agriculture has escaped control for so long, that it should continue to do so, ignores the fact that the law has one day to catch up with the changing world, McAuslan thus advocates the immediate imposition of planning controls over, for example, intensive agricultural buildings, grubbing up hedgerows and land reclamation.

In contrast, Brotherton (1989c) using the experience of prior notification in National Parks and SSSIs where the system offers *de facto* planning control has considered whether the so-called voluntary system should be extended to the wider countryside. He argues that this would depend on three factors: (i) the political party in power; (ii) the relative strengths of the agricultural and environmental lobbies; and (iii) the severity of the threat produced by agriculture. In light of the fact that the 1990s could see an increasingly benign agriculture, Brotherton argues that the environmental lobby would have little new evidence to impose further controls on agriculture, not even prior notification, let alone full planning control Brotherton therefore concludes that the environmental control of agriculture may have peaked in the late 1980s.

However, in October 1990 the DOE issued a consultation paper which would extend the discretionary powers which have been available to planners in all National Parks since 1986 (See Chapter 3) over the siting and design of farm and forest buildings, to all areas. Full planning control would be extended to farm buildings on units that fell below minimum agricultural thresholds, e.g. less than 5 hectares, involving less than 1100 man hours of farm work, or providing less than 50% of income.

The proposals thus stopped short of full planning control and did not extend to farm operations, although another consultation paper from the DOE (December 1990) did propose a positive order for local authorities to make hedgerow conservation orders, based on the payment of £300 per 100 metre length over 20 years, in order to provide funds for farmers to maintain hedgerows. In July 1991, a notification scheme was announced under which farmers would have to notify local authorities if they intend to remove a hedge.

Most reactions to these proposals were positive, but critical that they had not gone far enough. For example, the CPRE from a survey of the system in the National Parks (*Farmers Weekly*, 29 March 1991, p.24) noted that only 1% of notifications had been refused, and thus called for an extension to full planning control. Similar calls for an extension of the powers in various ways were made by the Countryside Commission, the Ramblers Association and the RTPI. The NFU, however, expressed concern about the costs and delays that the propsals would involve. In any event the proposals are only a halfway house, and it would seem certain that this issue will surface many times in the 1990s.

9 Policy Proposals for Socio-economic Issues

Introductory comments

According to Rural Voice (1987), an alliance of national organizations representing rural communities in England, rural areas in the 1980s continued to suffer from: (i) the damaging effects of a sustained and severe decline in rural services, (ii) a shortage of housing within the means of many lower-paid people; and (iii) a fragile local economy in many areas.

It may be thought that the counterurbanization trends discussed in Chapter 8 may have ameliorated the first and third of these problems, but Weekley (1988), from a study in the East Midlands, has shown that counterurbanization can actually lead to population decline. This is because the incomers tend to gentrify and geriatrify the area. The effect of this, on a static housing stock, is a decline in household size, via either, property amalgamation, demolition of several homes to make way for one new house, or the use of property as second homes. Only in those areas where new houses are built on estates will younger people with families tend to come in and lead to population growth.

The net result according to Harper (1987), from a study of three counties, is three types of settlement: (i) those still dominated by agricultural employment; (ii) those taken over by commuters or retired people; and (iii) those in transition. Harper concludes from an analysis of nine groups of people that settlements are also becoming polarized along class lines.

Other changes could be brought about by new technology. For example, Newby (1985) has outlined how fifth generation computers, and new communications technology (cable, satellite and video disk) could revolutionize the isolation of rural areas, both for employment, shopping and service provision, with fundamental implications for the future of settlements. However, this view of village life, dependent on electronic rather than physical contact, is not welcomed by Armstrong (1986) who argues that the computer is not as much fun as a real-life playmate.

But Black (1987) reflects the majority view that no longer do rural residents need to be consigned to 'second class' status in terms of access to education, business/commercial opportunities, information services or cultural activities. The net effect according to many forecasters will be an explosion of teleworking from home and a massive demand for rural homes with a consequent rise in house prices, especially in the south west and East Anglia.

These trends could further mask the other side of the prosperous rural coin, rural deprivation, which according to Midwinter *et al.* (1988) from a study in Scotland, is already understated. They also note that, although rural deprivation has distinctive aspects and a spatial dimension, there are no mechanisms of resource allocation which at present target resources for tackling it. Accordingly they recommend the creation of a £10 million Rural Aid Fund with a policy framework which could accommodate the diversity of rural deprivation, and would put a strong emphasis on specific projects meeting the needs of specific deprived groups in specific locations.

However, in the absence of such a scheme McLaughlin (1987) has shown how self-help has arisen as a philosophy: first, the Conservatives in the 1980s linked it to a mythical rural tradition of self-help; second, self-help saves government money; and third, self-help can fill the gaps left by declining public services. McLaughlin concludes, however, that the changing structure of rural society means that the deprived are now more isolated from affluent groups, and that there is little linkage between the two. Rural agencies cannot help since self-help is now part of their philosophy too and thus they cannot legitimately go to government for other sorts of funding.

In a further development of this policy inertia theme McLaughlin (1986) argues that the revival of popular images of the countryside, as the ideal environment, and the village, as the perfect model of social cohesion and integration, is a significant factor militating against the introduction of radical measures to alleviate deprivation in the countryside. What is needed instead is a recognition that deprivation is a result of structural divisions within rural society and the unequal allocations of wealth and power.

Griffiths (1989), however, from a questionnaire survey of 1044 Cornish people, has found a considerable degree of conservatism in regard to the form and function of rural areas. The overwhelming response was to keep Cornwall rural, and to prevent new building even for those who could be defined as being deprived.

Cloke (1988) in an analysis of the 'natural conservatism' said to exist in rural areas has made two points about its nature.

1. The majority of rural people have made a conscious decision to live in the countryside and have few complaints about their own lifestyle and welfare (Bentham, 1986). They are more interested in policies to conserve the landscape in which they live rather than policies to raise the standard of living for the minority of deprived or disadvantaged residents in rural areas.

2. Old-style Conservative politicians of the consensus school (often drawn from the farming and land-owning fraternities) are being replaced by the new 'Town Tories' of the Thatcherite philosophy drawn from the adventitious in migrant service class. This can produce a clash of interest between agriculture and conservation, and between landscape protection and new development, but at the end of the day these internal divisions are overridden by the need to show the traditional unity of the Conservative Party. In either case neither group is too bothered about solving rural deprivation in their areas, and in many cases wish to perpetuate it for their own ends.

In conclusion, the socio-economic issues of the 1990s will be those of the 1980s, but they will also be a mirror image of the issues of Chapter 8, namely not too much, but too little development, especially in the areas of housing (too few at too high a price), employment (too few jobs and too poorly paid), and services (too few and too expensive). Many commentators argue that it is a mistake to see these issues in isolation, since they are related, and thus argue that the only solution is a holistic one. Accordingly it is to holistic proposals that we now turn.

Holistic proposals

Although holistic proposals can overcome the dangers of sectoral and over-compartmentalized approaches, they can also fall into the trap of blandness, if they try and please all partners in the coalition. This is only too well illustrated in the consensus approach adopted by Rural Voice (1981) in their 'Rural Strategy'. In this document Rural Voice – which brings together the CPRE, CLA, NCVO, NFU, the National Association of Local Councils, the National Federation of Women's Institutes, the National Union of Agriculture and Allied Workers and the Standing Conference of Rural Community Councils – outlines an all-embracing, and well-intentioned, but meaningless set of policies, as for example reproduced below, which by the end of the paragraph is all things to all people:

> The rigour of 'key settlement' policies should in many areas
> be reexamined with a view to permitting the necessary
> organic growth of settlements and hence the survival of key
> services and of social balance within communities. Planning
> controls should be flexible enough to ensure that genuine
> local needs for housing or jobs can be met. Where

substantial growth is contemplated, on the other hand, the
scale of development must not be such as to swamp the
services or social structure of particular villages or to
damage significantly the visual amenity and wildlife interest
of the countryside. (p.3)

The 1981 'Strategy' was re-affirmed later (Rural Voice, 1987) but not surprisingly, given the eclectic nature of the ten-organization alliance, the proposals were once again, hardly radical, comprising instead, a shopping list of requests for each group. In more detail proposals were put forward in three areas, the Rural Economy, Rural Housing and Services, before being integrated in a final section. In the Rural Economy area the proposals included the need for agriculture to shift from a single to a multi-purpose industry and for existing help to small rural enterprises to be expanded. In the Rural Housing area, surveys of housing need were proposed, which would lead to the development of strategies for meeting this need via the provision of more houses by councils and housing associations. More radically, the organic growth of settlements was suggested in contrast to the rigour of key settlement policies. The Rural Services sector contained no new ideas, only a list of requests for the decline of services to be halted and if possible reversed.

In terms of integrated action the document proposed the creation of an integrated funding system for agriculture and encouraging the preparation of integrated farm plans. Along the same lines the Rural Development Programme should be extended and made more effective. Finally, parliament should be equipped with a means to review, both existing rural policies, and also the effects of proposed legislation and major spending programmes, on the countryside, possibly by setting up a House of Commons Select Committee for Rural Affairs.

Finally, many of these ideas found their way into a 'Manifesto for Rural England in the 1990s' (Rural Voice, 1991) with the additional idea of a two-tier housing land market to provide cheap housing land for the 300,000 rural households thought to be in need.

Not surprisingly Rural Voice has dominated holistic policy proposals, but the Association of District Councils (1989) has also taken a holistic view of rural planning and after examining rural housing, transport, planning, economic development, services, tourism, sport and recreation, and environmental management in turn, the Association argues that the experience of recent initiatives to deal with these issues provides the following important lessons.

1. Rural-based strategies need to follow the integrated approach and the benefits to be gained from partnerships between the public, private and voluntary sectors.
2. Districts should operate positive planning policies, promote integrated tourism development and formulate environmental policies.

3. Central Government should recognize the higher costs of providing services in rural areas and continue to support aid for rural housing and development via the Rural Development Commission and the European Structural Funds.

However, virtually all of these proposals are shopping lists rather than radical rethinks of underlying structures. This is not surprising given the nature of the coalitions making the proposals. It is now time to turn to sectoral issues to see if these have produced more adversarial and/or radical policies.

Policy proposals for housing

According to a discussion document from the Department of the Environment (1988g) rural housing policy although gradually evolving is still based on a firm framework designed to prevent sprawl and protect the countryside from haphazard scattered development. Within this framework there is, however, an expanded role for rural housing associations and they have thus been provided with greater sums of money and more flexibility. Limited measures have also been introduced to help them produce low cost rented housing. The DOE has also hinted that since key settlement policies have few supporters left, more positive policies should be put in place for all rural settlements, including the possibility that entire new villages would be allowed, if they offered a range of housing types in areas well away from sensitive or protected landscapes.

The key issue among these changes, however, is the supply of housing at an affordable cost. The supply of such housing has of course been much reduced by the virtual cessation of council house construction in the 1980s, accompanied by the sale of existing council houses. Dunn *et al.* (1987) who have mapped the sale of council houses have shown that sales have been heaviest in the South Midlands, and in parts of East Anglia. Even by the mid 1980s up to 27% of houses had been sold, and almost everywhere the figure was in excess of 8%. In spite of the 'Rural Area' provisions of the Housing Acts, sales have also been quite high in the more attractive parts of the country.

Estimates of housing need exacerbated by council house sales, however, vary widely. For example, David Clark speaking at a national conference in March 1990 (*Planning*, 23 March, 1990, p.34) claimed a figure of 370,000 households or ten times the Government's estimate, and the Rural Development Commission (1991) has estimated a need of between 116,000 and 198,000 homes between 1991 and 1996. In contrast most estimates range from 20,000 to 50,000 new houses (or three to six houses per village) (Winter and Rogers, 1988). Even this much smaller figure is vast, compared with the

Housing Corporation's grossly inadequate completion rate of 600 houses a year, and an estimated 34,300 'affordable homes' in the pipeline (Rural Development Commission, 1991). However, most commentators agree that relaxation of planning controls by itself would not be sufficient, although the creation of new planning classes for either 'social housing' or 'community need housing' would be some help. Another idea relates to formalizing the process whereby landowners donate land at cheap prices for the construction of 'social housing'.

One reason for the gap between the various estimates is that the largest estimates include everybody, including non-locals, who has 'expressed a need', whereas other estimates only include the more limited concept of 'local need'. This difference is, however, a hotly debated point. Rogers (1985) in an examination of the arguments for and against local needs policies has found five main arguments in favour of such policies. First, in the absence of reliable information on local incomes local needs policies can assume that local rural people are in general poorer and more deprived, and thus in need of positive discrimination. Second, pragmatically, a locals only policy reduces waiting lists by cutting out outsiders. Third, a local needs policy helps maintain local services and develop employment by keeping low wage earners in the area. Fourth, a local needs policy reflects the moral right of local people for housing over outsiders, and fifth, local needs policies are popular and help to politicize rural housing issues.

In contrast, arguments against local needs policies centre on their doubtful legality, and the problems of defining a local person or the local area. Other arguments state that the policies do not work and that if they do, they only elevate the notion of localness to that of a 'positional good' and are therefore regressive in putting up house prices in the area generally. In the long term this militates against low income households. Another problem is that local needs policies can lead to social atrophy as newcomers with new social and economic initiatives are prevented from entering the area, and that in the special case of, say, the Channel Islands this is both morally suspect and unjust. Rogers therefore concludes that there are sufficient doubts and uncertainties about the concept for it to be anything other than a very poor foundation on which to base a substantial element of welfare policy.

Some other general principles have thus to be found if a rural housing policy for affordable housing is to operate alongside the restraint policies discussed in Chapter 8 which inevitably lead to higher house prices. One such principle has been provided by the National Federation of Housing Associations (1986) who in the 1980s provided on average two to three times the number of new homes for rent provided by local authorities. These houses were built on the general principle that housing association houses should go to the genuine needy. If it is assumed for now that the difficulties of assessing genuine need can be overcome, a number of working principles can then be added. For example, Scottish Homes (1990), Scotland's national housing

Table 9.1. Possible land use planning options for social housing policy

	Aims	
Possible measure	To encourage more rented housing	To discriminate in favour of the local housing market
Use of local person condition	3	4
Use of a local person agreement or covenant	3	3
Condition on resale	1	4
Change of use control	5	4
Density policies	4	3
Less restrictive development control	0	0

Note: ratings out of 5. Least effective 0, most effective 5.
Source: National Council for Voluntary Organizations (1982).

agency, has proposed that rural housing policies should involve: working in partnership; tailoring plans to local circumstances; working with rural communities; ensuring affordability; and directing resources to where they are most needed and to who most needs them.

From the other side of the fence the House Builders Federation (1989b) has also proposed five principles for social housing provision. First, any housing provided must be additional to that provided by normal planning policies. Second, where necessary, a subsidy should be offered either via cheap land or via cross-subsidy from a mixed tenure scheme. But even this may not be enough for even a house built on virtually free land still needs an income of £11,500, which is at least £1500 too much, since two-thirds of those deemed to be in housing need have an income below £10,000 (Royal Institution of Chartered Surveyors, 1990). Third, 'local needs' policies should be replaced with a broader community need statement. Fourth, mechanisms are needed to ensure that social housing is provided in perpetuity, and fifth, the policy must be applied at the discretion of the local authority.

Turning from general principles to possible options a review of the wide range of possible land use planning options available for two policy areas and rated by their possible effectiveness has been provided by the National Council for Voluntary Organizations (1982) as shown in Table 9.1. From this review the Council concluded that most of the possible initiatives, lay with the local community, but that the Government could help by: (i) amending the right to buy provisions for council houses; (ii) clarifying planning powers to allow locally generated demand land releases to be tied to local occupancy; (iii) allowing local authorities to purchase existing houses on the open market; and (iv) introducing consistency in fiscal policies.

Turning to political parties, the housing policies of the two main parties have already been included in the holistic countryside section of Chapter 5. However, the Social and Liberal Democrats (1989c) have produced a separate White Paper on housing. This proposes new powers to enable local authorities to require the inclusion of housing at affordable rents in major developments. Powers are also proposed to protect the housing opportunities of locals where prices are bid up by the growth of second homes. The key to the housing problem is, however, seen as one of the inability to pay and so the paper's main proposal is for a new system of 'housing cost relief' targetted at those who most need support to either rent or pay off a mortgage in the difficult early years.

In addition to political proposals there have been a number of proposals made by various interested groups, organizations and individuals. For example, the Association of County Councils (1989) identified four problems in the field of rural housing: first, pressure on housing to be used as second homes, retirement homes and commuter homes; second, local people priced out of the market; third, a lack of sufficient accommodation to rent; and fourth, rural communities in decline. They argue: (i) for the provision of new mechanisms to allow for 'local need' to be included in structure and local plans; and (ii) for greater activity by the Housing Corporation and housing associations in areas where the gap between property values and earning levels is at its greatest.

Clark and Dunmore (1990) in a consultative document for Action with Communities in Rural Communities in Rural England, have proposed a more positive programme, given the need to provide for their estimate of 120,000–180,000 new social housing units needed between 1990 and 1995. Their programme proposes that rural community councils and district councils should establish district level 'Enabling Agencies' which would provide a catalytic role in helping parish councils to establish local needs. Once these were established the 'Enabling Agencies' would negotiate with planners over releasing extra land, prepare a development brief and finally attract finance either from public funds or via cross subsidy from mixed tenure schemes, in order to build the houses. The importance of finance is further stressed by the Royal Institution of Chartered Surveyors (1990) who argue that it is the only effective means of ensuring that all housing needs are met.

It is very unlikely that enough finance will ever be provided and most schemes will have to continue to be small scale in nature. For example, the National Agricultural Centre Trust (1987), a voluntary charity, has proposed an agenda for action which although mostly small scale in detail also includes the following more radical proposals.

1. To allow District Councils to use an additional 5% of receipts from council house sales to fund housing association developments up to six houses per village.

2. To allow local authorities to sell village sites at a discount to housing associations.

3. To allow local authorities to put 'local needs' statements in local plans.

4. To allow shared ownership schemes on a fixed equity percentage without the right to staircase, in other words to prevent tenants from increasing their share of equity.

Equity sharing schemes have also been examined by Greenwood (1989) who, after noting a tendency for builders to concentrate on upmarket low density housing, has proposed a more liberal interpretation of existing planning guidelines, in order to allow higher density development often on an equity-shared ownership basis. Not surprisingly this is an idea also taken up by Clark (1990) who, in a report commissioned by the House Builders Federation, has produced a guide showing how housebuilders can provide low cost housing, while at the same time producing profits. For example, by selling to a housing association, via cross-subsidy or by shared equity schemes. However, elsewhere Clark (1988) still maintains that the best means for producing 'village homes for village people' remains through charitable housing associations and shared ownership schemes.

In conclusion, MacGregor and Robertson (1987) caution that there can be no rural housing policy as such. Instead there can be a general housing policy which has rural dimensions, and takes account of particular localities. They pick out two ways in which a national housing policy could be modified. First, by providing more flexibility over giving permission for single houses in the open countryside, and second, by inserting a rural dimension, for cost and other standards, to reflect the loss of economies of scale in small schemes.

The real problem of course relates to the poor economy of many rural areas, and so attention is now turned to the issue of rural employment.

Policy proposals for employment

Any policies proposed for the rural economy must take account of the changing employment position in the UK as a whole. In the 1980s it is broadly accepted that these changes included a loss of employment in the cities, and the return of the north–south divide, with the north becoming increasingly deindustrialized with little new employment, while the south substituted industrial work for the joys of a post-industrial service economy staffed by Yuppies (Allen and Massey, 1988). Overlying all these trends, has been a move of employment to rural areas, as modern employers, both industrial and service based, became more footloose due to technological developments and the changing nature of work, and have thus been able to seek out cheaper, less unionized labour, and more pleasant surroundings, near to motorways and airports, in which to work. Nonetheless most employment growth has taken place either *in situ*, or within the immediate region of existing employment. The amount of truly mobile employment growth is still limited.

In contrast, in agriculture, there has not even been limited growth, but a steady decline of around 2–3% a year for decades. Classical economics explains the industrialization process behind this loss as one in which farmers employ ever more capital, to provide ever more productive systems, in order to offset falling prices. The neo-Marxist school, in contrast explains the process in terms of fractions of capital, restructuring themselves, in order to subsume farmers (Healey and Ilbery, 1986). Whichever explanation is correct the net result has been, according to Errington (1988) two significant changes. First, the replacement of full-time work with casual work, and second, a growing trend for family farm employment to be treated as a refuge from unemployment elsewhere. If this is the case it presages a situation in the 1990s where the farm labour force as a permanent feature of the rural economy may be more apparent than real.

Indeed this may already have occurred, for while the regular, whole time labour force in agriculture fell from 454,000 in 1956 to 135,000 in 1984, the numbers of seasonal or casual workers, in contrast, actually rose from 79,000 to 85,000. This could have important implications for the socio-economic viability of rural areas, with stable job opportunities being replaced by what Ball (1987) has called intermittent marginal jobs with limited incomes. These cannot in isolation support rural communities.

To some extent, however, farming jobs have been replaced by other rurally based employment. For example, Johnstone *et al.* (1990) have found a significant expansion of jobs in tourism, which account for between 35 and 40% of jobs in some areas, and also an expansion in a whole range of green or heritage industries, for example, the revival of wood- and stone-working industries. Nevertheless, as Armstrong and Taylor (1987) have shown, several unemployment black spots are to be found in rural Britain, most notably in the North Midlands, the south west, and throughout all of Wales and Scotland, except the north-east and the Borders. Armstrong and Taylor argue that the most effective way to reduce these regional disparities in unemployment is to improve the growth in the number of jobs nationally, and then adopt regional measures within this framework. Notably, by the creation of regional development agencies for all regions, and a substantial increase in regional policy expenditure both in the form of aid for firms, and also in improving the infrastructure.

This could happen anyway, for Cambridge Econometrics (1988) in their forecasts for economic prospects between 1986 and 2000, assume that the urban–rural shift in employment will continue throughout the 1990s, especially in the three fast-growing regions of East Anglia (+ 24.2%), the south west (24.2%) and the East Midlands (23.5%), as these areas continue to pick up growth from the congested south east. To some extent this urban–rural shift will more than compensate for the expected loss of 3.2 and 2.1% per annum in the agricultural labour force between 1987 and 1995, and 1995 and 2000 respectively, at least in the fast-growing regions. Elsewhere, however, in the slow-growing regions: the south east (8.1%); Yorkshire and Humberside (7.2%); the West Midlands (3.6%); Scotland (2.6%); and Wales (0.7%), employment growth may not be enough to offset farm job losses. Finally, in the declining regions, Northern Ireland (− 5.4%); the north (− 5.8%); and the north west (− 7.2%), redundant farm workers will be in the same queue as other workers.

Turning to proposed solutions, the Association of District Councils (ADC) (1986), in line with the regional differences highlighted above, has pointed out that possible solutions will vary enormously from place to place. This being so, it is argued not surprisingly, that district councils are best placed to coordinate policies at the local level. As a general rule these policies should include: more resources from central funds; the sti.nulation of the local economy by economic development through workshops and regional aid; measures to diversify agriculture; the encouragement of forestry; the expansion of tourism and leisure facilities; flexible planning policies; encouraging the use of redundant buildings; transferring development control powers in the National Parks to district councils; the provision of low cost housing; retaining the regulation and cross-subsidization of transport services; and the retention where possible of all other services even on a mobile or part-time basis. Financially, the ADC recommends the introduction of a Rural Aid Programme with an initial funding of at least £20 million. Similar proposals have been made in Scotland with a proposal for a £25 million Rural Development Fund made by the Scottish Affairs Committee (1985) although this was rejected by the Government (H.C. 352(85–86), 1986).

Armstrong and Fildes (1988) have also suggested a greater role for district councils, largely by transferring EC aid for industrial development purposes to district councils in the Assisted Areas, in order to preserve or increase existing spending differentials. However, Hayton (1989) has forecast, that the changes made by the 1989 Local Government and Housing Act, not only prevent Armstrong and Fildes' proposals from being implemented, but by giving central government greater control over local authority involvement in economic development, they may also force local government to withdraw from many areas of local economic development notably grants, subsidies, and the provision of equity finance.

In the light of this further withdrawal of employment aid added to the cuts outlined in Chapter 3, Rural Voice (1990) has called for a fully integrated rural employment policy embracing agriculture, forestry, the environment and social issues. This would include more extensive, low intensive farming, multi-purpose forestry, and green tourism. At the county level, policies for integrating these uses could be contained in countryside strategies and in extended structure plans which would expand to cover agriculture and forestry.

In Wales, the Development Board for Rural Wales (1989) in their strategy for the 1990s has accepted that their limited aid programme cannot be spread evenly, but instead has to be concentrated in six growth towns and areas, and 12 special towns. The strategy also recognized that agriculture will face severe pressures in the 1990s. Accordingly, although the strategy gave manufacturing industry the top priority it also looked for investment in tourism, craft and service industries, especially in those areas where 1 in 4 jobs depend on agriculture.

Finally, turning to area-based schemes Green (1986) has criticized the Rural Development Area scheme as being underfunded, overseen by too small a body, the Rural Development Commission, and too complex in relation to the limited resources available. There is thus a serious danger of the scheme losing credibility and disillusion setting in. This could indeed be the pattern throughout the whole employment policy scene, as the regional planning policies pursued since the 1930s, are finally abandoned, after their severe reappraisal in the 1980s. However, a counter view would be that 1992 will see a resurgence of regional policy, within a European context, and the multiplication of regional development agencies for not just parts of Scotland and Wales, but parts of England too.

Policy proposals for transport and other services

Although Clark and Woollett (1990) have found from a survey of rural services that the rate of loss slowed down in the 1980s, compared with the 1970s, losses had nonetheless still continued. Furthermore, they identified a number of threats for the 1990s. These included: for schools, the introduction of the National Curriculum and the possibility of opting out of local authority control; for medical services, the possibility of opting out and thus no longer providing a full range of services; for shops, the introduction of the uniform business rate at higher levels than rates; and in general the continued privatization of services, notably the possibility of removing social security and other payments from post offices. However, in spite of these policy changes the crucial point about poor rural service provision is the intractable nature of the problem, namely, the extra cost of providing services to a low density scattered population.

Accordingly, the National Association of Local Councils (1980) has argued that rural services should be seen as a special case, needing positive discrimination, and the payment of more money pro rata than for equivalent services elsewhere. In addition, self help can be employed by lifting some of the controls on providing services, and by decentralizing decision making to those most clearly involved, often parish councils. In the same vein Dean (1988) has shown that community spirit when allied to any increase in public spending on rural transport, which maintains rural communities, can provide a net benefit to the exchequer.

Turning, specifically to transport Moyes (1989) has shown from a comparison of transport need based on normative standards of provision, for health, school, work and shopping, and actual transport provision in mid-Wales, that, in spite of all the doom and gloom, nearly all these needs are met. The problem areas are other groups, notably, the elderly, and the non-car owner/driver.

However, according to White (1986), the problem of providing these people with transport is not one of scattered low density populations, but one of services being increasingly centralized, notably the education and medical services. Whatever the exact nature of the problem, no solution has as yet been found over and above the provision of basic needs, in spite of many attempts over the years. In the late 1970s the radical RUTEX scheme was, for example, tried in an attempt to provide unique services for unique circumstances. Although axiomatically no general solution emerged, pre-booked flexibly routed bus services were found to provide transport for a greater proportion of the population, than fixed route services, at virtually no extra cost (Transport and Road Research Laboratory, 1980). In a further survey of unconventional modes of transport Nutley (1988) noted that they had achieved low costs but at the expense of accessibility. In other words they were cheap to run because they did not really run, and could thus provide no adequate alternative to a proper scheduled service.

The current attempt to cure the incurable, relates to the deregulation of bus services. Unfortunately, there are few surveys of how this change has affected rural areas, and reliance has to be placed on work by the Transport and Road Research Laboratory (1988) who, from a general survey, has concluded that there had actually been a marginal increase in services after deregulation, with as many as 85% of vehicle miles being operated commercially, with a substantial saving in subsidies. At the same time fares had been unaffected except for price falls in areas of competition. In a study of bus deregulation in Scotland, Mackay and Farrington (1988) also found little change for rural services, since local authorities had 'bought back' those services which had not been registered commercially. Cross subsidy had also continued to be vital in maintaining rural services.

Turning from publicly or commercially run services Banister and Norton (1988), from a review and survey of the three principal kinds of voluntary transport in rural areas (social car schemes, dial-a-ride and community buses), have concluded that such services are not a replacement for statutory and commercial services, but they can be a complement to them. Given existing levels of support they will, however, continue to operate at the periphery.

In conclusion it is important to stress that much rural transport work concentrates not on really radical solutions but on making the existing limited provision work better, for example, attempts to match up existing data on rural people with observed public transport usage by using regression models (Coles, 1986). Really radical solutions seem as far away in realistic political terms as they did in 1981 when Stanley and Farrington (1981) suggested two fundamental ways in which accessibility deprivation could be alleviated in rural areas.

1. By improving the socio-economic conditions of the population.
2. By redesigning the provision of facilities required by the population.

In the meantime the 1989 White Paper on 'Roads to Prosperity' forecasts saturation car ownership by the year 2025, and a doubling of cars from 23 to 46 million. In a critique of this forecast Joseph (1990) argues that this implies a parking lot twice the size of Berkshire to park them. He also points out that the construction of the new roads proposed will: (i) cause much damage to the countryside; (ii) create urban sprawl; and (iii) add greatly to air pollution, at a faster rate than catalytic convertors will be reducing it. He therefore proposes a radical set of alternatives: first, greater subsidies for public transport; second, more traffic restraint measures; third, using the land use planning system to refuse any planning applications that would increase car usage; fourth, end tax concessions on car usage, notably company cars; and fifth increase taxes on car use.

These issues return us neatly to the central questions of Chapters 8 and 9, namely, what sort of countryside do we want: a protected one increasingly peopled by the service class; or an unprotected one in which housing and employment growth is allowed to expand in line with market forces. Whichever option is chosen, around 80% of us will continue to live in towns and cities for at least another decade and so use the countryside only for recreation and conservation. Accordingly, attention is now turned to these related issues.

10 Policy Proposals for Conservation and Recreation

Introductory comments

For most of this century conservation policies have been needed to fight a rearguard action against habitat loss and environmental damage caused by economic development. These trends show no signs of diminishing, and as shown in Fig. 10.1 (Pye-Smith and Rose, 1984) many threats are predicted over a large area for the rest of this century, largely centred on further intensification of agriculture and further afforestation. This and similar forecasts are often made using existing trends culled from various surveys of land use change. The latest of these began in May 1990. Organized by the Institute of Terrestrial Ecology it planned to cover 500 one kilometre squares at a cost of £1 million. Results were expected by 1992. Previous surveys by the same team (Bell and Bunce, 1987) have shown that the rate of land-use change has been increasing.

However, while surveys highlight the nature of the problems, they do not provide policy proposals, which in the field of conservation, according to Green (1988) face two formidable challenges: first, agreeing on what the objectives of countryside management should be, and second, setting up an advice programme that is as professional as the service already offered to farmers by existing organizations. Very few people have attempted to answer the first question directly, although a number of the policy proposals discussed later do take the question on implicitly, if not explicitly. Far more people have discussed the second question – especially the balance of power between rural planning organizations – because being procedural, rather than philosophical it presents a less demanding task.

For example, Roome (1986) has argued that the changes in the balance of power between conservation and agriculture, outlined in Chapter 3, have done little to alter the real situation. Mainly because, the development agencies, notably MAFF, have maintained total control over the new conservation functions, e.g. the designation of ESAs, and the type of conservation to be input via grant-aided schemes. In addition, Roome doubts whether MAFF will become conservation minded just because it has been given extra responsibilities for conservation among its many other goals and tasks.

In contrast to MAFF, the semi-independent status of the main conservation agencies, the Countryside Commission, the Nature Conservancy Council and the National Park Authorities gives them, in theory, great power to speak out for conservation, against government policies they disapprove of. Brotherton and Lowe (1984) have shown, however, how both Labour and Conservative Governments have used their powers of patronage to weaken the independent voice of these bodies, by nominating their own supporters to be members of these non-elected agencies, thus effectively drawing their political teeth. This lack of teeth is important because, in the absence of any national land use planning strategy, the Government lacks any basis for responding to conservation issues other than giving in to the strongest pressure group (Cox and Lowe, 1983).

Furthermore, the conservation lobby is further weakened by the peculiarly British system of nature conservation interests being represented by the NCC, and landscape interests being represented by the Countryside Commission. This division has been traced back to deep historical ideologies strongly influenced by the work of Constable, Wordsworth and Ruskin (Cox, 1988). In conclusion the conservation lobby has been hopelessly divided for most of this century, in contrast to the well-oiled machinery of agricultural fundamentalism. The first task therefore for the conservation lobby is to put forward a coherent view of conservation. Accordingly, attention is now turned to holistic proposals for conservation followed by specific sections on proposals for reforming the 1981 Act; proposals for landscape conservation; proposals for nature conservation; and finally a brief consideration of recreation policy.

Holistic and party political proposals

By the very nature of such policies, several holistic proposals for conservation have already been discussed in Chapters 4, 5 and 6. Most of these, however, began with a different premise, for example, the opportunity provided by the restructuring of agriculture. In this section proposals with an overt conservation component are discussed. For example, Rose (1984) writing on behalf of the Friends of the Earth has proposed a Natural Heritage Bill instead of other options. For instance, Rose rejects a land-use strategy since it would be hijacked by the existing power group of landowners and foresters leaving conservationists out in the cold. Persuasion is rejected since it promotes the myth that FWAG (Farming and Wildlife Advisory Group) type planting of field corners is creative conservation. The reduction of financial incentives to agriculture is accepted, but the reform of the CAP will take too long and in any case may not be targeted at conservation.

Instead, on the grounds of equity and democracy, and in order to give 99% of the people some control over the use of the countryside now taken by 1%, Rose proposes a Natural Heritage Bill containing the following main proposals.

1. SSSIs would be protected much as under the 1981 Act but a wider range of habitats would qualify.
2. Development control would be introduced over intensive agriculture, forestry, water authority and Internal Drainage Board operations.
3. Conservation Management Orders would be introduced which could prohibit damaging practices, stipulate management practices and would involve a once-and-for-all compensation.
4. Agricultural land would be bought into the rating system generating around 3000–6000 million at 1982/83 prices.
5. Agricultural grant aid would be limited to a ceiling of £10,000 and 50% would be allowable for conservation costs.
6. Grade I and II land would enjoy a greater presumption against development.
7. A publicly available register of land ownership would be established by the DOE.

In another holistic proposal, Adams (1986) begins by examining an incremental approach based on alterations to the 1981 Act and proposes the following.

1. Confining all obligatory payments for management agreements to a lump sum payment for loss of the capital value of land.

Fig. 10.1. Major threats to Britain's countryside and wildlife for the period 1985–2005. Source: Pye-Smith and Rose (1984).

✹ Most probable areas of oil pollution
▓ Threatened wetlands
▓ Major remaining areas threatened with agricultural intensification
▲ Major areas of remaining threatened heathland
▒ Areas most threatened by expansion of conifer plantations
▨ Main areas where semi-natural woodland will probably be converted to plantations
◆ Proposed Cairngorm ski development
◀ Westward spread of hedgerow destruction
▓ Threatened estuary of international ornothological significance
● Possible nuclear power sites
⬗ Likely offshore new gas/oil development

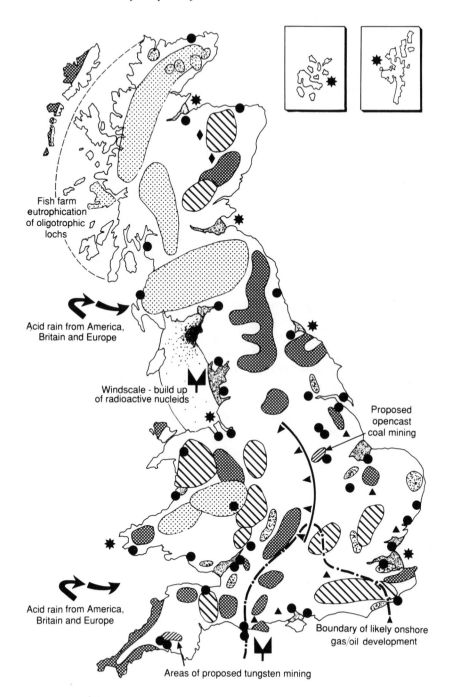

Fish farm
eutrophication
of oligotrophic
lochs

Acid rain from America,
Britain and Europe

Windscale - build up
of radioactive nucleids

Proposed
opencast
coal mining

Acid rain from America,
Britain and Europe

Boundary of likely onshore
gas/oil development

Areas of proposed tungsten mining

2. Expanding the use of voluntary management agreements.
3. Extending grant support and incentives for SSSI acquisition by voluntary bodies.
4. Introducing selective planning controls on agricultural and forestry land to cover the felling of ancient woodlands, the ploughing of moor, heath or herb-rich meadows, the planting of blocks of conifers and agricultural and forestry roads and buildings.
5. Reforming agricultural grant and support structures to promote conservation management directly, and indirectly to help less wealthy farmers.
6. Developing the concept of SSSIs.

However, Adams then queries whether reforming the 1981 Act approach is correct. For example, over 50 years, the amount of money spent on protecting SSSIs could well be enough to have bought them. More fundamentally, however, Adams rejects the accepted myth that conservation is compatible with intensive agriculture and forestry. It is not, he argues, and to seek compromise is to accept strategic withdrawal for the conservation case.

Instead, Adams argues for an holistic and integrated system of land management which develops both the themes of the Longor and Moynash experiments in the Peak District and ESA schemes, in such a way that totally new policies are developed. These would not merely be grafted additions to the Acts and measures of the last 60 years, but would totally re-examine policy making, organizations, controls and incentives from first principles.

If Adams' proposals are to make headway there has to be some indication that not all Tories are headed off down the free market route. There is no need to examine Liberal Democrat or Labour views here, since axiomatically they are committed to at least some form of conservation controls. In contrast, green Toryism seems a misnomer. However, Sullivan (1985), a freelance writer and leader writer for the *Daily Telegraph*, disagrees and reminds his Centre for Policy Studies readers, that the Conservative Party is the natural repository of the English 'green' tradition, with its themes of property, community, sense of history and love of rural beauty. He then argues that policies in the 1980s were merely tinkering with the issue, and did not tackle the need to reform the CAP and the unnecessary destruction of the countryside encouraged by its high prices and subsidies. Furthermore, the principle of compensation under the 1981 Wildlife and Countryside Act is not only wrong but also encourages farmers to propose damaging schemes. He advocates instead the use of Schedule A tax to encourage farmers to invest in conservation schemes, in return for tax concessions, and a system of notification for certain damaging operations.

Another Tory, Paterson (1984) a solicitor, writing for the Bow Group of Conservatives but not on their behalf, has also noted that the Conservative Party is the natural party of conservation since they are the party of thrift not profligacy. He advocates the appointment of a Conservation Minister with a seat in Cabinet and a staff within the DOE. Although the Minster would work under the Secretary of State for the Environment, the DOE would be given equal status with the Treasury, Home Office and Ministry of Defence. In more detail, Paterson argues that compensation paid under the 1981 Wildlife and Countryside Act should no longer include lost subsidies, and that drainage grants and Internal Drainage Boards should be abolished in order to protect wetlands.

Five years later Paterson (1989), by then a Conservative candidate at the 1987 General Election and an active green campaigner, produced a 209 page environmental manifesto for a radical new Conservative manifesto for the 1990s based on a better quality of life and a safer, cleaner environment. These policies he affirms can be based on traditional Tory values, for example, efficiency, thrift, and self-help. In more detail Paterson calls for the setting up of green units in all levels of government (an idea partially put into practice by the 1990 White Paper on the Environment) in order to integrate environmental considerations with policy making and to funnel these into an annual 'State of the Environment' speech. For the countryside, Paterson advocates: the withdrawal of compensation payments for profits foregone in SSSIs; introducing Landscape Conservation Orders for features such as hedges; replacing setaside with extensification; and introducing 'Care for the Countryside' grants covering a broad menu of good environmental practice.

All of these holistic and political party proposals have included a reference to the 1981 Act and so attention is now directed to specific proposals for its reform.

Proposals for reform of the 1981 Act

At the outset it is important to stress that only parts of the Act have been subject to calls for reform. For example, most commentators (Phillips, 1985) agree that Part One of the Act dealing with species protection is a step forward. It is in the area of habitat protection that the Act is said to have failed, with a 'no win' situation being created for farmers, since they can be cast as villains if they develop a habitat, and also if they fail to do so but claim compensation.

Continuing the conservation theme MacEwan and MacEwan (1982) have pointed out that the Act overturned some long-established planning principles, notably the non-payment of compensation for refusing permission to do something or imposing restrictions. In other words, the Act turned the polluter-pays principle into the polluter profits handsomely principle. Because of this, MacEwan and MacEwan dismiss the Act as being, quite literally, unprincipled, a dead end which leaves agriculture and conservation on a collision course, providing no way of regulating conflict except by pouring small amounts of money into a bottomless pit.

Rose and Secrett (1982) have also denounced the principles of compensation and voluntarism as unjust and dishevelled. They make ten recommendations, for its reform, two of which remain relevant to the 1990s. First, planning controls should be introduced to contain the worst excesses of agricultural and forestry operations. Second, automatic compensation payments should be replaced by discretionary ones.

In a commentary on the financial compensation guidelines Laurence Gould Consultants (1986) found the system to be too complex, and so recommended scrapping the annual payment method based on net profits foregone. In its place they proposed a simplified flat rate system for agricultural land, and for woodland, the introduction of a system based on the depreciation in capital value. The Friends of the Earth (1986a) have used the criticisms made by Laurence Gould to argue that farmers everywhere, should be eligible for payments for conservation purposes, since the whole countryside is environmentally sensitive. They also argue for the introduction of Conservation Orders and planning controls, an issue which, according to a survey of 41 County Planning Officers by Friends of the Earth (1986b) has a wide degree of support. For example, 68% supported planning controls over large-scale forestry; 73% supported controls over ploughing up moorland; and 61% supported controls over new field drainage.

Policy proposals for landscape conservation

Although landscape and nature conservation are linked, it is easier for the sake of discussion not only to divide them, but also to subdivide landscape conservation further into: landscape conservation in the lowlands; landscape conservation in the uplands; and landscape conservation in designated areas.

Landscape conservation in the lowlands

Policies for landscape conservation in the lowlands were first set out by the Countryside Commission in 1974 and then reviewed in 1977. These policies accepted the inevitability of landscape change and thus set out policies for creating new landscapes no less attractive than those destroyed. In the 1980s, however, as a result of several studies the policy was changed to the management and protection of those features that remained (Countryside Commission, 1984a). In more detail the 1984 strategy was twofold: first, to safeguard quality where it remained; and second to enhance it where deterioration and despoliation have occurred. This strategy was backed up by five elements; promoting conservation action on the farm; safeguarding key sites; advising government and public bodies; helping voluntary bodies; and acting as a watchdog.

Proposals to modify this policy have ranged from the procedural to the financial. Beginning with the procedural, Winter (1985) in a review of proposals to revive the wartime County Agricultural Committees, welcomes the idea of local self-regulation of agriculture and conservation, but argues that the details of their work would need to be considered very carefully. For example, if they operated like the Internal Drainage Boards or the Forestry Commission's consultative groups, then there could be considerable dissatisfaction. If they were to work it would have to be clear that a totally new policy bargain had been struck between the Government and farmers, in which farmers gave up the right to use land as freely as they do now, in return for continued financial support slanted towards conservation rather than production.

The theme of transferring support from farming to conservation has also been taken up by the Royal Society for the Protection of Birds (1988). Their detailed package of reforms for the CAP is based on a vision of the countryside which includes: a diversity of land uses; a viable mixed and sustainable agriculture dependent on low intensity systems and diversified sources of income outside farming; extensive areas of specialized farm habitats such as lowland wet grassland; extensive areas of non-farmed habitats; and many small features integrated into the broad pattern of use, such as copses and ponds.

If such a countryside is to be created the CAP has to be reformed to have four main objectives.

1. To protect existing habitats and farming systems which are in harmony with the environment.
2. To modify farming systems in order to improve farmland wildlife habitats.
3. To create new habitats on land withdrawn from intensive production.
4. To reduce environmental pollution.

In more detail these objectives would be achieved by: creating conservation headlands; fallowing arable land; switching to spring cereals; providing uncropped strips; reducing fertilizer use; switching from silage to hay; and creating grassland, scrub, wood and wetlands. In terms of policy measures the RSPB proposed three sets of linked measures.

1. Reforming price policy in order to reduce the incentive to intensive production, and prompt farmers to move towards less-intensive systems and new uses of land which bring environmental benefits.
2. Controlling production capacity by linking the payment of higher tier prices to participation in one of three production control options; environmentally sensitive farming; extensification; and setaside.
3. Optimizing environmental benefits by providing fine-tuning to the first two policy proposals, with, for example, schemes to convert land withdrawn

from intensive production to woodland or wetland, and measures to protect habitats, control pollution and allow environmental assessment of rural projects.

An alternative, or complementary measure, to the positive reuse of CAP support systems is the imposition of planning controls. Selman (1989) in a review of the issue, has argued however, that the arguments for bringing rural land-use under planning control are possibly outweighed by those against. In particular, the advantages of an open and publicly accountable decision-making process are offset by: (i) the loss of positive attitudes; (ii) the danger of bureaucratic delays hampering the farming calendar; and (iii) the creation of severe problems of enforcement. Instead Selman sees merit in a system of planning playing 'honest broker' between private, public and community interests. The success of such an approach is demonstrated by Selman, using four case studies from Scotland where some progress has been made in breaking down entrenched positions during the production of management and other plans.

In a further development of the positive agreement approach Waite (1988) an environmental solicitor has proposed the adoption of the Law Commission's idea of 'Land Obligations' which would be similar to American easements, a bundle of rights over a person's land, capable of binding successors to the land title. Another proposal involves the use of covenants on mortgages taken out by lenders, obliging them to manage the land for conservation purposes.

Turning to controls that could be imposed by planners one favourite option has been the introduction of Landscape Conservation Orders. Among others this was once a proposal made by the Government (Environment, 1986c). Under their proposals the system would have worked as follows. National Park Authorities would have designated certain areas of the wildest and most unspoilt parts of the Parks as areas where any proposal to under-take a list of operations which might be potentially harmful to the landscape could be prevented by the imposition of a Landscape Conservation Order. The Order would prohibit the operations from being carried out in return for compensation based on profits foregone, but this sum was not expected to be too high since only a few orders were expected to be made. The proposals were withdrawn later in the decade, largely as a result of many criticisms, for example, Denton-Thompson (1986) a local authority landscape architect argued that they would be costly to identify, and administer; would harm relations between conservationists and farmers and would be too negative. Instead he suggested their use as a back-up power only, complemented by a positive system based on the preparation of farm management plans which would integrate conservation and food production.

The idea of linking controls to payments has also been developed by Hodge (1989), a land economist, who argues that under current land use change rights, farmers have a claim for compensation if they are prevented from making land use changes on conservation grounds, but that no single level of compensation can provide appropriate incentives both to the farmer and the state. Accordingly, Hodge suggests taking land use change rights away from farmers, using the analogy of listed building control, and thus only paying compensation to land use changes not proscribed by such an extension of planning controls. More positively, compensation payments could then be paid for farming practices that actually improve conservation value but would not be financially sensible without compensation payments. The payments would be paid by two agencies, the conservation agency paying the opportunity cost involved and MAFF the remaining transfer payment.

The idea of creating special land use change categories has also been taken up by Denton-Thompson (1984). He has proposed an extension to the exemption from Capital Transfer Tax already operating for the protection of important landscapes. Under his proposal a Countryside Register would be opened which landowners could enter at their own request. In return for agreeing to manage the registered land in order to protect its landscape in perpetuity, the landholder would gain certain tax exemptions. The agreement would be binding on successors by being entered into the Land Charge Register as a form of Restrictive Covenant.

Landscape conservation in the uplands

In common with the lowlands the Countryside Commission has an uplands policy, but in contrast with the lowlands policy, this dates from the 1980s rather than the 1970s. The policy stems from 1983 when the Countryside Commission launched the so-called 'Great Uplands Debate' with a report on 'The Changing Uplands'. After a year of public meetings and consultations the resulting policy document 'A Better Future for the Uplands' (Countryside Commission, 1984a) made a series of recommendations under five headings.

1. A Clear Role for the Uplands
The Government should provide a clear statement on the Upland's role and adopt the complementary policy objectives of sustaining communities, encouraging sustainable economic development, and yet at the same time protect and enhance the environment and recreational access.

2. Strengthen the Upland Economy
By retraining, giving assistance to farming, increasing aid for development and tourism agencies, strengthening the socio-economic advice given by ADAS, helping small farmers by lowering eligibility for grant thresholds, but without allowing environmentally damaging projects unless there is an over-riding national need and no alternative site.

3. Conserving and Enjoying the Uplands

By not only extending Management Agreements but also increasing their funding, increasing the area to be considered for conservation under Section 43 of the 1981 Wildlife and Countryside Act, and modifying grant schemes to discourage land improvement, and encourage conservation, for example, by lowering stocking rates. Planning controls should also be introduced over farm buildings and all rural roads and, for afforestation of bare land over 50 hectares. A legal right of access should be given to common land and all public agencies encouraged to negotiate access to their land by agreement. Finally, the Upland Management Experiment should be extended to other areas.

4. Meeting the Needs of Upland Communities

By providing more low cost housing for local people.

5. Coordinate Policy

By extending LFA support for non-agricultural activities and by ensuring that all agencies attempt to seek the objectives set out in **1** above.

The Commission estimated that the extra cost of the proposals would be £5 million for the agricultural area, and another £5 million for the development and tourism area.

To this already long list of objectives Swanwick (1983) has added the maintenance of the distinct regional identity or 'landscape image' of each upland area. In order to achieve this methods should be encouraged which could classify and monitor landscapes and landscape change. There should be mandatory cooperation between the agencies involved and the system of financial incentives for conservation gains achieved rather than profits foregone which was pioneered in the Peak District should be extended both in area and in its scope.

In a fundamental critique, however, Roome (1984) argues that the report is procedurally flawed because: (i) it considers the problems of the uplands in isolation from the rest of the countryside; (ii) it accepts the existing distribution of property, wealth and power in and over land; and (iii) it only deals with changes in organizational structures within Government.

This theme is continued but from a different viewpoint by Brotherton (1984) who argues that the policy is too cautious given the radical nature of its analysis and the changing situation in agriculture. In more detail Brotherton argues that recommending planning controls over forestry is wrong. A preferable method for limiting or improving forestry is via the support system for forestry, because it is the economics of forestry which causes forestry change. Planning only deals with the resulting pressures rather than the root cause and so will always be reactive while controlling forestry via economics is proactive.

In contrast the Ramblers Association (1983) have proposed.

1. The introduction of planning controls over certain agricultural operations, afforestation, and the destruction of broadleaved woodland.
2. The encouragement of suitable forms of tourism by providing grants to conserve the landscape and encouraging craft industry by farmers.
3. Increasing public access for quiet recreation by creating a legal right of access to all open and common land, making increased use of access agreements and orders, and by creating new footpaths.

These proposals were to a large extent based on an alternative report to the Countryside Commission's produced by MacEwen and Sinclair (1983) from the work of an interdisciplinary group set up by the Council for National Parks. This produced a set of three discussion points not firm proposals for the uplands. These are based on the view that any support system must achieve an acceptable income level for all those who farm and use their land with reasonable efficiency and skill and do so in ways that are congenial to the needs of conservation and recreation.

The first proposal for consideration is a return to the free market which is thought to be realistic but 'thoroughly objectionable' (p.31) in that it would lead to dereliction of the landscape and indiscriminate afforestation. The second proposal is for a modified *status quo* in which help to farmers is tapered depending on the degree of difficulty.

The third, and favoured discussion point is for an integrated approach which combines reformed hill farming support with resource management incentives as follows.

1. A reformed headage payment system related to the severity of the handicap.
2. Modified capital grants for conservation compatible developments.
3. Comprehensive multi-purpose farm management plans to which some grants could be tied.
4. A range of resource management incentives including an Upland Management Grant to integrate land uses.
5. Comprehensive advisory services.
6. Planning controls over certain agricultural and forestry operations as an essential back-up.
7. Cut-off points and payments ceiling in order to target the aid where most needed.

Turning to individual proposals from National Park staff, Parker (1986) has demonstrated how a positive approach to landscape management can be employed. He describes how in the experimental Integrated Rural Development project in the Peak District three elements have been combined. Namely, the introduction of management grants to reward farmers the better their field walls and flower-rich fields have been managed; the voluntary giving up of some MAFF financial support; and the availability of free advice.

By paying for results achieved instead of profits foregone the scheme is not only overtly positive but provides a system parallel to the one of production incentives that farmers have grown to understand since 1947. Most importantly it continues to take pride in doing something, continues the competitive edge in farming, and thus provides a talking point in the pub about whose wild-flower meadows are doing well this year and why.

Statham (1986) a National Park Officer, however, has questioned the underlying assumption that the landscapes we have inherited must be the ones perpetuated, and queries whether this is any longer a valid platform from which to construct the future use of upland areas, since what people are trying to conserve is 'an impoverished and ecologically degraded landscape' (p.19). It is a strange irony according to Statham if society should continue to protect the product of bad management. Accordingly Statham proposes a fourfold zoning of land uses which would underpin rather than replace existing designations.

1. Heritage farm zones, inherited landscapes but with more conservation.
2. New farm landscape zones using the constraints imposed by the World Conservation Strategy.
3. Long-term investment in forestry zones to rebuild soil reserves after centuries of agricultural exploitation.
4. Pockets of semi-wilderness zones allowed to revert to true wilderness.

The designation of protected areas has of course been a key feature of British conservation and so attention is now directed to this topic.

Landscape conservation in designated areas

The British system of conservation designations has grown up haphazardly without any overall conceptual overview. This is not to say that such overviews do not exist, for example, Leonard (1982a), a Countryside Commission officer but speaking personally, has argued for a fourfold division of landscape protection areas.

1. Wild landscape, seminatural vegetation, e.g. High Dartmoor, to be strictly conserved thus placing severe constraints on farmers.
2. Traditional farming landscapes, e.g. White Peak, which can only be maintained by museum farming thus placing some economic constraints on farmers.
3. Farmed landscapes within designated areas where high design standards would be expected but at little economic cost to the farmer.
4. Agricultural areas, the remaining 75% of the countryside where farming objectives would dominate but with compatible landscape action.

Such a division presupposes, however, a common set of values, but these cannot be assumed, for as Leonard (1985) has pointed out there are several value systems involved in landscape conservation including ecological, scientific, aesthetic, historic and cultural. Since it is unlikely that any common agreement could be reached on a theoretical system of conservation areas acceptable to all value systems, most policy proposals have centred on the system we have, warts and all.

The centrepiece of the system is National Parks, and although they have their critics it is important to take a positive view of the Parks, not as places where nasty things are not allowed to happen, but as places where good things happen. It is a matter of saying (Redhead, 1988):

> 'Don't do that,
> Do this instead.
> It will be better!'

This of course begs the question of what the better things might be. According to Smith (1978) a left wing Labour activist this would include the creation of a three-tier system of Country Parks, Regional Parks and National Parks. National Parks would be run by independent planning boards and their primary purpose would be conservation. There would be a progressive policy of land acquisition by the National Park Authorities, and the introduction of planning control over forestry. National parks would be created for Scotland and further designation of parks in England and Wales would be as appropriate. An idea eventually endorsed by the Labour Party (1990) who put the New Forest and South Downs at the top of their list.

An extension of the National Park idea has also been advocated by Reynolds of the CPRE (Haynes, 1987). She has proposed creating new types of Park based on creating new landscapes for recreation using setaside money, for example in the Cotswolds and the New Forest.

More National Parks would of course be music to the ears of the Association of National Park Officers (1987) but only if a completely new policy aimed at rewarding conservation results achieved, rather than compensating for food production possibilities forfeited, were to be put in place. The policies of the 1980s merely added more knobs and levers to a machine designed for food production. It is folly therefore to hope that by adding more controls and by running the mechanism at half speed it will somehow move in a different direction. Instead, the Association call for a new system of incentives based on results, a principle already well understood by farmers. The proposed system rewards habitat management by, assessing the habitat created, by for example, a count of wild flowers in a meadow. In other words, the better the habitat or landscape, the greater the payment, and thus the substitution of one product, food, with another, environmental quality. Such schemes are already operating in the Peak District (see Parker above) and the North York Moors, where a pioneering scheme was so successful in 1990/91 that its budget was tripled to £140,000 for 1991/92 (*Planning*, 15 March 1991, p.5).

National Park Officers (Countryside Commission, 1990c) have also made radical proposals for charging for National Park usage, for example, charging for road space at peak periods, and introducing a tourist tax as a means of achieving sustainable development in the Parks.

Returning to 'Realpolitick' the Countryside Commission (1987c) have produced a manifesto for National Parks for the five years between 1987 and 1992. This seeks full recognition for National Parks in Government policies for agriculture, forestry and planning, and exceptional treatment for the Parks in the policies and plans for defence, roads, energy, water and minerals. As a power of last resort, the Commission also sought the introduction of Landscape Conservation Orders in order to block damaging agricultural or forestry developments. In addition the manifesto pressed for sufficient resources; sought National Park status for the New Forest; promised to defend the integrity of the Parks; and also sought to forge links between itself and the public.

As part of the attempt to forge these links the Countryside Commission (1987d) has secured the agreement of 26 organizations who own or manage land in the Parks: (i) to commit themselves to securing National Park goals; (ii) to consult with the National Park Authorities and the Countryside Commission over development proposals; (iii) identify programmes of joint action where appropriate; and (iv) to resolve conflicts of interest.

In spite of this achievement the Countryside Commission (1989c) still felt the need to set up a panel to review the future of the Parks, with the following terms of reference: (i) to identify the main factors likely to affect the future of National Parks; (ii) to assess in the light of (i) the ways in which National Park aims might be achieved, and (iii) to recommend how the ways identified in (ii) should be put into effect.

As Table 10.1 shows the panel was deluged with proposals, most notably concerning the need for greater powers over landscape change, greater autonomy of administration, and an increase in the family of Parks. The National Parks Review Panel (1991) in their report made 170 recommendations which would cost between £8 to £10 million a year to implement. The most   ɔrtant of these were as follows.

1. A new National Parks Act should redefine their purposes under two broad headings: environmental conservation, and quiet enjoyment and understanding.
2. Under the first purpose the Parks should produce an environmental inventory every five years, articulate long-term objectives via a vision statement, give nature conservation a higher priority via a nature conservation strategy, and seek to influence land management via new and existing systems rather than by ownership.
3. Under the second purpose, an effective rights of way network should be achieved by 1995, and access agreements over all open country should be negotiated by the end of the century.

Table 10.1. Responses to the Countryside Commission's review panel on National Parks.

Planning and managing the landscape

1 Strengthen planning controls over agricultural and other developments in order to manage change. Supported by RTPI, TCPA, CPRE and CNP
2 National Parks to be able to request an Environmental Assessment. Supported by CNP
3 Planning controls over forestry. Supported by TCPA, and CPRE
4 Veto over forestry grants which could damage the Parks. Supported by CNP
5 Positive/cash rewards for conservation instead of farming. Supported by ANPO, CPRE and CNP
6 Landscape Conservation Orders. Supported by ANPO, and CNP
7 Right of public appeal over planning permissions. Supported by CNP

Administration

1 Equalize representation of local and national representatives. Supported by ANPO, and CPRE
2 Increase funds. Supported by TCPA and CPRE who called for a quintupling to between £90 and £100 million.
3 Reserve fund for buying out inappropriate developments. Supported by CNP
4 Adding socio-economic well-being to the list of 1949 Act aims and objectives. Supported by ANPO and RTPI
5 National Parks Agency to replace Countryside Commission. Supported by ANPO, and RTPI

New National Parks

1 New Forest and South Downs. Supported by CPRE, and TCPA
2 North Pennines, Cambrian Hills, Scottish Highlands, Southern Uplands, and Mourne Mountains. Supported by CPA
3 North Pennines and Cambrian Mountains. Supported by CNP

ANPO: Association of National Park Officers; CNP: Council for National Parks; CPRE; Council for the Protection of Rural England; RTPI: Royal Town Planning Institute; TCPA: Town and Country Planning Association.
Sources: Council for the Protection of Rural England (1990c); Council for National Parks (1990), *The Planner* 18 May 1990 p. 6; *The Planner* 8 June 1990 p. 6; *Planning* 6 April 1990 p. 8; and *Planning* 8 June 1990 p. 38.

4. Farm grants should be modified to provide incentives for farmers to take positive measures to improve the environment and improve access, at the same time as supporting incomes, some areas conversely might be encouraged to revert to the wild.
5. In forestry, no further major coniferous afforestation should be allowed, indicative forestry strategies should be prepared, and all proposals over 10 hectares should require an EA and a licence to plant.
6. Military training in the Parks should be removed as a long-term objective.
7. Park-wide local plans should be prepared by the Parks. The Parks should be responsible for all development control, be given a last resort power to impose Landscape Conservation Orders. Greater control should be exerted

over major developments, and farm/forestry buildings and roads should be brought under planning control.

8. The Parks should be run by independent Boards.

9. The New Forest should become a National Park, but with a tailor-made constitution.

Turning to Scotland, the absence of National Parks in Scotland has been reviewed from time to time, in 1974, for example, the Countryside Commission for Scotland produced a proposal for a four-tier system of urban parks, country parks, regional parks, and special parks. The special parks would have been areas of substantial recreational pressure and scenic character which would have justified the involvement of some national input in decision making, but this proposal along with the other tiers was not supported by the Scottish local authorities. Nonetheless, the Countryside Commission for Scotland (1982) continued to press the idea of special parks in the 1980s. They did recognize, however, that these could not be National Parks in the international sense, where conservation must always take precedence, since this would reject Scotland's traditional land use history and lead to Scotland being managed as though it were a museum.

Garner (1989) has also pointed out two further difficulties in the Scottish context. First, there is a feeling that they would be too limited in area to tackle the main issues which are extensive in character, and second, a feeling that further new bodies would get no nearer curing the root cause of problems, and merely divert resources into an extra level of administration. A further fear is that National Parks would fare no better than the National Park Scenic Areas which though a fundamentally sound idea have not been executed very well.

These problems were confirmed again in March 1991 when the Government rejected a third call for National Parks in Scotland made by the Commission in September 1990, and instead proposed a system of natural heritage areas to include the Cairngorms, the Flow Country and parts of north west and central Scotland.

In conclusion this section has confirmed once again that policies in the UK are developed incrementally. However, a group of students on the University College London Conservation Course (Micklewright, 1988), using SSSIs as an example, have shown how this *ad hoc* pattern of designations is a minefield. For example, SSSI controls are assessed as being bureaucratic, insensitive to day to day needs, costly, voluntary, and not binding on successors. In sum they are 'wholly inadequate' (p.19). The group therefore proposes the integration of current designations into a single system of protection. Under this strategy, a new Ministry would be conflated from the NCC, the Countryside Commission, and parts of the DOE. It would be given the task of assessing and protecting all sections of the cultural and natural heritage, including National Parks, Nature Reserves, SSSIs and

Listed Buildings. Each potential site would be assessed for its value in terms of wildlife, landscape, archaeology, historical/cultural significance, recreational potential/use and educational potential/use, and then graded 1, 2 or 3.

The sites would be called Heritage Areas, and be purchased by the nation with the posibility of lease back to the former owners. The Areas would thus eventually become self-financing as rent over the years paid back the capital outlaid in the first case.

Policy proposals for nature conservation

Turning from landscape to nature conservation, opinion polls have revealed a strong and growing concern for wildlife. For example, in a poll for the NCC (MORI, 1988), 14% were extremely interested in nature conservation, 45% very interested, 38% interested and only 15% not interested. A total of 65% would support an increase of 1p in the pound on Income Tax to aid conservation, with 85% supporting wildlife for the sake of the future and 69% for wildlife itself. No other reason for conserving nature scored over 20%.

However, public opinion by itself will not necessarily lead to policy changes and although Ratcliffe (1981), a former chief scientist at the NCC, concurs with the general public's unassailable philosophical viewpoint that mankind has a duty to nature, he argues, in order to convince decision makers, that the hard nosed pragmatic view that nature can offer something to man in terms of aesthetic enjoyment, recreation and economic benefits has to be used. In the longer term, however, Ratcliffe hopes that the civilizing nature of nature conservation will lead to a self-sustainable society where consumption is gradually replaced by contemplation.

In a reflection of changing attitudes to nature conservation Perring *et al.* (1987) noted that the negative attitudes of the 20th century engendered by agricultural expansion should now come to an end. Instead as never before, conservationists should come out of their reserves and concentrate on replacing the wildlife which has been sacrificed on the altar of cheap plentiful food. This could be done, either by creating new landscapes, or recreating old ones.

This positive view has been endorsed by the Nature Conservancy Council (1984) who in a mid 1980s review concluded that its overall programme had until then been hopelessly inadequate. It therefore decided that it was time to go on the offensive and argue for conservation as a land use in its own right. Such a strategy would still need measures to prevent any more destruction but would also include new measures to recreate some habitats. The basic strategy (Fig. 10.2) recognized political realities and the need to protect the most important sites at the top of the pyramid. This approach has since been adopted by the NCC in their rolling five-year corporate plans (Nature Conservancy Council, 1987) in spite of the fact that in essence it still follows the approach of the 1970s in emphasizing site and species safeguard at the

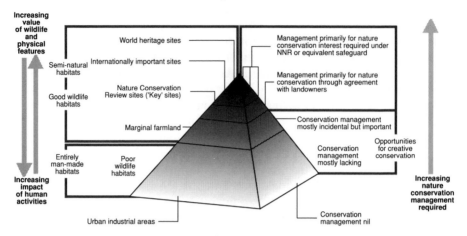

Fig. 10.2. Nature conservation management strategy for terrestrial wildlife. Source: Nature Conservancy Council (1984).

expense of more radical measures for protecting wildlife at large. This emphasis on rarity was reaffirmed three years later when the Nature Conservancy Council (1990) outlined a plan for restoring the habitats of all 181 rare species of flora and fauna at a cost of £12 million.

Cost is of course a major factor in the current main plank of nature conservation, the management agreement, but not the only one. For example, Leonard (1982b) from practical experience with management agreements has concluded that they have three considerable disadvantages: first, they are not in perpetuity; second, they require considerable resources of professional expertise; and third, where they are based on opportunity cost they are expensive and few authorities are willing to pay the cost.

The theme of cost has also been taken up by Adams (1984) who has argued that the NCC's estimate of £20 million (in mid 1980s money) as the cost of management agreements for SSSIs might be unrealistic and suggested that a figure of £42.8 million would be needed if all SSSIs were to be protected by management agreements.

Willis and Benson (1988) from a study of management agreements in SSSIs have also concluded that there is a high cost to be paid in conserving these sites both in social and financial terms, with opportunity costs varying from £64 to £181 per hectare. These costs are made much bigger by the CAP which raises both farm output prices and land prices, and so although the cost of conservation seems expensive, it is in fact the cost of agricultural support that is excessive.

Developing this theme further, Willis *et al.* (1988) have calculated that the cost of protecting SSSIs via management agreements varies considerably depending on whether CAP prices or world prices, for the agriculture production foregone, are used, for example, using CAP prices costs around

£120,000 per site but using world prices costs only around £80,000 per site. If it is then assumed that the extra production that has been prevented, would only have been stored or destroyed, then there would be a net social cost in expanding agriculture, and thus nature conservation can be seen actually to save money.

Carrying the argument to its logical conclusion Benson and Willis (1988) point out that especially high costs may be encountered with a management agreement if agricultural use of a SSSI is abandoned in the face of falling support prices. In this case the full cost of 'farming' the land to keep its farm-related habitat will then have to be paid for by the land conservation body, again with the imposition of further costs. This is clearly a crazy and unacceptable principle, but there is a far better alternative, namely, taking over the land and managing it purely for conservation, even if this means carrying on 'farming' it to preserve a unique habitat.

Already some conservation groups are already doing this, notably the RSPB, the National Trust, the Woodland Trust and the County Nature Conservation Trusts. These groups provide major environmental improvements by purchasing or leasing land. Accordingly, Hodge (1988) has concluded that some form of public intervention appears to be warranted to encourage land ownership by these groups. However, there are problems, including how to manage the land, especially when in the case of the 250,000 hectares owned by the National Trust there are competing claims over the use of the land (Hearn, 1988).

One surprisingly desirable management of land may in fact be for field sports. For example, a survey of shooting in Scotland (British Association, 1990) revealed over 2100 jobs directly related to shooting and another 5100 indirectly related, providing a useful source of extra income for rural areas. As an alternative use of rural land it was thought to provide a negative return compared to farming, albeit a better return than other uses. Crucially, however, field sports provide a more conservation minded use with active management or creation of woodland and wetland. However, to some extent this is offset by the killing of predators, in some cases even protected birds of prey.

In conclusion this section has shown that rural planning for conservation remains an ineffective muddle, and that we are still unable to answer the five key questions posed by Phillips (1985).

1. How can the systems of protected areas for landscape and nature conservation be more closely integrated?
2. How can the systems operating in different parts of the UK be harmonized?
3. How can the systems be simplified so that the many types of existing protected areas are replaced by fewer categories with clearer objectives?
4. How can social and economic policies be integrated with conservation?

5. How can improvements be made in the protected areas system without neglecting the wider countryside?

These questions thus pose a considerable agenda for conservation in the 1990s.

Recreation

In contrast to other rural planning issues, the debate over rural recreation policies rather went to sleep in the 1980s. Whether this will continue into the 1990s depends to a large extent on which of Veal's (1987) visions of the future comes true. First, is the view of the Conservative Party which sees leisure as an enterprise and an industry with exceptional growth prospects. Second, there is the 'Athens without slaves' perspective of the free enterprise system in which a move to science-based employment offers material prosperity and leisure to all. Third, in the centre ground of politics, is the view that there will continue to be a shortage of work and that work should thus be shared out with obvious implications for greater leisure time. Fourth, is the green perspective which sees the end of the technological economy as a way of moving to a more environmentally acceptable self-service economy with increased leisure hardly featuring at all. This is because the new life-style will be more satisfying and thus not need the artificial forms of leisure needed by a high technology economy. Finally, in complete contrast, there is the liberation from work perspective of Gorz (1976) who portrays technology as the means by which workers can finally free themselves from dependency on wage labour and capitalism, and self-determine their activities.

Veal's own view is that the three forties – a 40-hour week; for 48 weeks; and for 45 years – is a virility symbol that no party or government is willing to abandon, however hopeless the task. In contrast most employers are forecasting a severe shortage of labour in the 1990s as the number of young people entering the labour market rapidly declines.

Turning from general forecasts of leisure to specific forecasts of rural recreational demand, Phillips and Ashcroft (1987) believe that the most significant changes will be a 15% increase in the 30–44 year age group, the most frequent countryside users, offset to some extent by a rise in small or single person households, the least frequent visitors.

Locationally more people will live in the suburbs and will have greater mobility. The key factor, however, is the attraction of the house and garden *vis à vis* the countryside. Phillips and Ashcroft believe that the growth of home entertainment, and better gardens, though important, will not prevent a further growth of interest in the countryside not only as a place to visit but also to care about.

In contrast Leisure Consultants (Martin and Mason, 1982) in their forecasts for new patterns of leisure in 1991 and 2001, did not pick out rural recreation as a specific activity, but instead picked out home electronic entertainment, creative and productive leisure and non-family based leisure as the main areas of growing interest in the 1990s.

Tourism is another dimension to be considered, not least because it offers one alternative to the 70,000–150,000 jobs expected to be lost in rural areas by the end of the century as agriculture and other rural industries, such as mining, decline. Accordingly the English Tourist Board (1988) in a development strategy for rural tourism has forecast a 60% rise in expenditure by rural tourists from £1054 million in 1986 to £1600 in 2000. However, the Board believes this figure, which is based on existing trends, can be exceeded and that other areas can reach the 35% of jobs already accounted for by tourism in Restormel and the Isle of Wight. The Board recommends that this growth can be achieved by: (i) enhancing and conserving the countryside as a tourism resource; (ii) providing for and enhancing the visitor's enjoyment of the countryside; (iii) raising the profile of the countryside as a place to visit; and (iv) by providing more opportunities for people to spend a longer time in the countryside. In particular the Board advocate the promotion of 'Areas of Developing Identity', namely, the Borders, North Pennines, South Pennines, Lincolnshire Wolds, English Marches, and the Mendips.

Returning to recreation, two issues currently stand out. First, the whole problem of access to the countryside, and second, the related issue of whether to charge for recreation or not. The first issue, access, has already been made the centrepiece of the Countryside Commission's policy for the 1990s. Following the release of consultation papers (Countryside Commission 1987e; Curry *et al.* 1987) it published two statements. The first 'Policies for Enjoying the Countryside' (Countryside Commission 1987f) justified a policy review because of the longstanding nature of access problems, and the changing nature of the demand. Its overall objective was to improve and extend opportunities for the public to enjoy the countryside. To this end it set out its key policies as: (i) opening up rights of way (the prime task); (ii) creating a well-informed public; (iii) providing countryside management in areas of conflict; and (iv) creating a new climate of opinion in which providing for countryside recreation is an essential component of any strategy for land management.

In a second statement 'Enjoying the Countryside: Priorities for Action' the Commission (1987f) set out specific targets as follows:

- By the year 2000 the provision of countryside information services in the major cities using all sorts of media and networks
- By the year 1990 local authorities to be aware of their powers; by the year 1992 all farmers and landowners to be aware of their rights and responsibilities; and by the year 2000 all people to be aware of their rights and responsibilities

- By the year 2000 public transport systems to be in place which provide effective countryside recreation opportunities for non-car owners
- By the year 2000 the entire rights of way network to be legally defined, properly maintained and well publicized
- Recreation forests to be started in the early 1990s.

In a further development of these Recreation 2000 papers the Commission in a discussion paper (1988b) set out a number of options including powers for farmers and ramblers to act on their own behalf in diverting or improving rights of way, and the possibility of stronger enforcement powers. The discussion paper was followed by a survey of rights of way which revealed that 18% of the 140,000-mile network was unusable and that at best walkers and other land users had only a one-in-three chance of completing a two-mile walk, a one-in-ten chance of completing a five-mile walk, and horseriders, only a one-in-50 chance of completing a 10-mile ride.

These findings were used to justify an agenda for action (Countryside Commission, 1989d) which urged highway authorities to increase spending from £14 to £21 million (compared with £1000 million on other sport and recreation) in order to get the rights of way network fully operational by the year 2000. Under these proposals the net cost of each long walk would be 9 pence compared with 50 pence for a visit to a Country Park (Countryside Commission 1989e).

As an expression of commitment to the network the Commission announced an increase in its expenditure on providing access from £2.9 million in 1988/1989 to £5.08 million in 1991/1992.

At the same time the Commission (1988c) was also examining the specific issue of paths, routes and trails, and in particular the long-distance footpaths, via the publication of a consultation paper. The resulting document (Countryside Commission, 1989f) set out policies and priorities and reaffirmed three key critera: (i) ease of use; (ii) accessibility; and (iii) range of choice. It reiterated the contribution that a good network can make to both local and international tourism. It also set out four categories of path; parish paths and community paths; local walks and rides; regional routes; and national trails. Although most work needs to be done at the local level the document also proposes the creation of two long distance routes: Glyndwr's Way in Central Wales and a Cotswold Way from Bath to Chipping Campden.

Finally, the Countryside Commission (1989g), following on from the Operation Gateway project of the mid 1980s, has sought to expand countryside recreation use to the 'disadvantaged'. Namely, those with low incomes and/or low physical and mental ability. It has thus targeted poor-quality older terraced housing; the poorest council estates; multiracial areas; and the less well-off council estates as key areas where local authorities should seek to increase participation rates.

In a critique of the proposals, Kay (1989) has argued that more attention should have ben paid to short distance paths, near urban areas, and less attention to long distance routes and the whole network of rights of way.

In a more wide-ranging review of countryside recreation policy, Curry (1985) has argued that policies have so far been based on market demand rather than on social need, and on the notion of 'free access'. This notion is socially regressive since it only provides free access for the mobile and the relatively affluent. Curry then poses some challenging questions. For example, should provision be based on people's preferences rather than assumptions about them, and would it be a legitimate function of public policy, if the philanthropic notion of providing healthy recreation like bird-watching was overturned by popular demand in favour of bingo.

Indeed the growth of noisy new rural pursuits like war games, clay pigeon shooting and other activities often related to farm diversification has prompted both the Government (Environment, 1990c) and the Sports Council (1990) to propose hierarchical policies for rural recreation, based on different levels of recreational activity between areas, in a tacit acceptance that quiet enjoyment of the countryside is not the only legitimate form of rural recreation, and that market demand will increasingly have to be taken into account.

If recreation and tourism are to be judged by their market value, then we need to know something about charging. According to Bovaird *et al.* (1984) charging for recreation provides substantial scope for increasing revenue through price increases at the gate. The corollary of this is that any attempt to restrain visits at heavily used sites would necessitate very large overall price increases. Similarly, in order to even out demand away from peak times, there would have to be high differentials in prices. However, low income groups are more likely to be deterred by increased prices, and so pricing policy may have serious implications for equality of access across social groups.

In spite of this last finding, McCallum and Adams (1980) have argued that the advantages of charging for countryside recreation are weighty, and that charging should be normal practice except where convincing counter-arguments can be advanced. In essence the arguments for charging include the possibility of raising revenue, and allocating demand by consumer prefer-ence, by the willingness to pay, for example, for golf *vis à vis* visiting stately homes. In other words the market plays its classic role of allocating resources efficiently. Arguments against include the public good nature of recreation, e.g. health, the idea that everybody should have access to recreation, that recreational landscapes are handed down across the generations as a free good, and not least the administrative difficulties involved. In the short term there would also be the problem of working out the exact price to charge since the income elasticities are not well enough known.

However, evidence for elasticities is provided from North America. For example, Stevens *et al.* (1989), Americans employed by the US Forest Service in a country where charging for public recreation has a long tradition, have concluded from both an empirical and theoretical standpoint the following.

1. User fees account for less than 30% of operating costs.
2. Attendance at recreational sites is relatively responsive to price, and so price increases may not result in complete recovery of costs.
3. This relationship can be used to protect ecologically fragile sites from overuse.

In conclusion they found that recreation produces positive net economic benefits and therefore conclude that public recreation sites should be supported from public funds.

Not surprisingly this view of recreational access as a public good has been endorsed by the Labour Party (1990c) who have proposed a legal right of access to common land, mountains, moors and heaths and all other uncultivated land. In conclusion restricted access to the countryside has been allowed to continue by a duality of interests. On the one hand, there are planners and conservationists who are happy to see day-trippers flock to honey-pots thus leaving more fragile sites protected and the wide open spaces unsullied by the common herd. On the other hand, landowners are only too happy to use the environmental arguments of the planners to keep their land free from 'rash assault' and yet charge for access when they can make a profit. How long this situation will continue depends on how quickly the general public wake up to the confidence trick that has been perpetrated on them.

11 Appraisal

This book has been about one simple issue. How much land is needed for agriculture? Everything else in the countryside is consequent to this. However, while the question is simple, the answers are not. They are complex, interrelated, and highly political, as the 1990/91 debate over the reform of world-wide farm policies, outlined in Chapter 6 has already shown. If, and it must be a very big if, given 20 years of failure, fundamental reforms can be made to the CAP during the early 1990s, then really radical changes will have to be made to the way in which we use our countryside. It is, however, far more likely that compromises will be struck as many times before, and that the CAP will continue to evolve incrementally. If this is the case, then all the CAP-related rural policies in the UK – effectively every rural policy – will also continue to evolve incrementally.

The choice is thus between revolutionary or evolutionary policies, with of course historical inertia, favouring evolution. Accordingly, the first section of this Chapter divides the policy proposals most often advocated into evolutionary and revolutionary. This section is then followed by a review of possible political developments in the 1990s, then by two forecasts for the 1990s, and the Chapter then closes with a revolutionary manifesto by the author.

Policy proposals most often advocated

If all the policies discussed in this book are added together an indicative list of the most common can be prepared as shown in Table 11.1. Popularity may not of course be a guide to political acceptability, rather a measure of persistence or beating one's head against a brick wall. In spite of this in an allegedly pluralist society popularity should have something to tell us.

Table 11.1. Policy proposals most often advocated.

Agricultural proposals	
Restructuring via prices	
Evolutionary	Revolutionary
16 Continued to cut back price support 12 Further encourage less intensive/organic farming	4 Remove price support 3 Move to world prices
Restructuring via controls	
9 Introduce further quotas 9 Introduce Landscape Conservation Orders 5 Restrict aid to certain upper limits 5 Impose controls on inputs including taxes 3 Relax planning controls on reuse of farm buildings	18 Introduce planning controls over farm buildings and/or farming operations 5 Make any form of aid dependent on approved farm plan 3 Compulsory move to smallholdings
Restructuring via grant aid	
11 Reform of Management Agreements and compensation provisions 8 More environmental use of extensification 6 Support farmers/workers not farming 4 More use of Premium Conservation Grants 4 More Structural Aid 3 More ESAs 3 Increase size and extent of LFA Aid	17 Scrap farm grants for production and replace them with conservation grants 4 Move to payment by results, e.g. number of wild flowers 3 Grant aid for creating 'New Countryside' 3 Tax concessions/impositions for good/bad land use
Proposals for forestry	
6 More help for farm woodland 6 More emphasis on multiple purpose forestry 5 Reform the consultation process 3 Increase the disposal of Forestry Commission Land 3 Grade all areas by suitability for forestry	19 Introduce planning controls 5 Abolish all subsidies 4 Abolish all tax concessions 3 Ban planting on poor or sensitive sites 3 Create Community Forests

Table 11.1. Continued.

Organizational and administrative proposals	
Restructuring organizations or areas	
Evolutionary	Revolutionary
5 Implement Common Land Reforms 4 Create more Designated Areas 4 Review system of Designated Areas 4 Modify Forestry Commission 3 Merge Countryside Commission and NCC 3 Modify Ministry of Agriculture 3 Combine Counties and/or Districts	13 Set up Regional Planning Authorities 10 Create new Ministry/Committee for Rural Affairs/Countryside 7 Set up a different system of Designated Areas 3 Create Environmental Agency 3 Reform democracy by devolution
Restructuring guidance and integration	
5 Further develop national planning guidelines 4 Improve existing arrangements for integration	13 Set up regional plans/strategies 5 Set up a system of countryside audits 5 Create a new type of plan for integrating socio-economic and/or land use issues
Land development proposals	
Restructuring via planning controls	
8 Increase range of uses allowed or reduce size of green belts 5 Relax planning controls a little 5 Introduce two-stage public inquiries	9 Allow new settlements 6 Introduce zoning 5 Release a lot of land for growth 3 Introduce 3rd party right of appeal
Restructuring via positive development	
6 More use of land for recreation 5 Greater use of land assembly powers	6 Reintroduce social ownership of land
Restructuring via social policies	
5 Greater use of cross subsidy in housing 5 Greater use of shared ownership in housing	7 Make houses for locals a legal planning condition 5 Allow planning permissions to be traded for social gains

Note: The numbers are only indicative, and there could be an error factor of at least plus or minus two, because of double counting and/or the same policy being given a different name.

Thus starting with agriculture, there have been 18 proposals to introduce planning controls over farm buildings and/or farm operations, and nine proposals to introduce a less draconian system of Landscape Conservation Orders. It is very likely that some increased form of planning control will be needed in the 1990s. The main debate will be over the range of operations that controls are extended to, and how they will avoid the Listed Building Syndrome of benign or deliberate neglect. They should be seen as a stick of last resort for day to day farm operations, but should be introduced immediately for all buildings and non-farming operations.

The positive contrast to negative control is provided by grant aid. In this case 17 proposals have been made to scrap farm grants and replace them with conservation/land management grants. This proposal is subject to two problems. First, will politicians allow the funds now being used for grant aid to remain in the countryside, instead of being diverted to other spending areas? Second, are farmers with their abysmal record of landscape destruction the right people to administer such aid? A more radical proposal would be to allow farmers to go to the wall and give small grants for conservation agencies like the RSPB to purchase the land at knockdown prices.

A fall in land prices would of course be a consequence of a further cut in CAP support prices as advocated by 16 proposals. However, these price cuts can only work if they are big enough to offset productivity gains. Price cuts by themselves are, however, messy and unpredictable, and although essential they should not be used in isolation.

Accordingly there is much merit in the next most popular proposal, less intensive/organic farming, which has 12 advocates. A return to tasty regional food may be romantic but it is a practical possibility. The real difficulty is how to make policy proposals that will bring it about. The best offer at the moment seems to be extensification, which has eight advocates. If a whole host of environmental and food quality standards could be added to this scheme then a genuine return to the mythical past of 'Trumpton' may be achievable.

An almost equally popular reform is the reform of Management Agreements and the related provisions for compensation. The problem with this approach like ESAs is that they are too limited in extent and would be very costly to implement nationwide. A more fundamental problem is that they perpetuate the *status quo* of the countryside we have, rather than the countryside we could have.

This is the same problem with quotas (advocated by nine proposees) especially if as with milk quotas the quotas are set well in excess of demand. Quotas are also difficult to police except for milk, and for minor crops like potatoes and hops. Nonetheless they have worked well for farmers by providing them with stability, but for the long term they can lead to fossilization of the patterns of production. They should thus be seen as a short-term or fall-back measure.

Turning to alternative land uses, forestry is the most favoured option. However, because of its chequered landscape past, it is also the subject of the most common proposal, namely, the introduction of planning controls on various aspects of the forestry industry. In contrast only five proposals have been made for a reform of the consultation process, which for most people is discredited, simply because it is undemocratic. It is hard to see any reason why planning controls over forestry should not be introduced in six months by an amendment to the GDO.

However, it is much harder to see another popular recommendation, the introduction of Regional Planning both in the form of Authorities and Plan/Strategies. In spite of the fact that both proposals have 13 advocates a whole host of practical problems emerge. Not least would existing organizations allow such a creation to upset their own power base. The only way for regions to be anything other than tokens is for them to be democratically elected bodies with real budgets and powers.

Turning to Central Government, another popular proposal is for a Ministry/Committee for Rural Affairs. There is, however, much debate about the form of such an organization. Once again if it is to be more than a token it would need a radical reform of all forms of Government.

Similarly, the seven proposals for a total reform of Designated Areas while logically appealing ignores the sheer inertia existing in an *ad hoc* system which has grown just like Topsy. It is far more likely that the various proposals for modest reforms outlined in Table 11.1 above will be the model for the 1990s.

Finally, popular proposals in the area of land development have been the creation of 'New Settlements', and modifying the green belt. Behind these proposals are two forces. What to do with land released from agriculture, and how to meet the desire for rural living. However, energy considerations by themselves will not let any Government allow scattered development in the countryside. The only way to repopulate the countryside, as employment continues to seek dispersal, is in purpose-built villages, towns, or cities linked by a modern transport network, and guided by a firm set of Regional Plans. In this regard the Regional Studies and Town and Country Planning Association's plans to spread multi-nuclei cities in green areas rather than green belts has much to commend it.

Political scenarios for the 1990s

There are five broad political scenarios for the decade, but of course they are not mutually exclusive and they may occur in any sequence. Taking them in turn from right to left they are as follows.

A rebirth of Thatcherite conservatism. Thatcherism was in fact relatively muted, but as this book has often shown there has also been a group of people calling for really radical reforms and the cutting back of all forms of Government control. If this group managed to regain the initiative from the Major moderates, and more problematically managed to get elected then there would eventually be a return to a free market in agriculture with a host of unforeseen and largely unforecastable effects. Most likely, however, would be a division of the countryside into areas of high-tech farming and abandoned land, with all shades of variation in between. Geographically this would be on an east–west split with the lowlands winning out over the uplands. With huge amounts of land becoming derelict, but with no aid to support other uses, the pressure to abandon planning controls would become irresistable.

It is much more likely that muted Thatcherism, as remodelled by John Major, will continue, both within the Party and in the electorate. If this is the case then muddling through will continue, and farm support will gradually be replaced by support for alternative employment or land uses, in order to let agriculture run down more gently than other industries, like coal and steel. Planning controls if anything will get a little tighter as the Green imperative impinges on the free market. As urban-based employment continues to devolve, the countryside will gradually evolve into the most prosperous and successful part of the nation. Protected by planning from unpleasant uses it will become even more desirable to relocate there and thus a vicious circle will develop exacerbating the urbal–rural divide.

Moving to the centre, the Liberal Democrats with large numbers of votes cast in local and by-elections can still cling to the hope of a coalition. Ironically a coalition could be the most radical option of all. This is because the Liberal Democrats will make it a condition of any coalition that proportional representation and a devolution of real power to the grass roots takes place. Axiomatically a move to such a system will lead to a drastic reform of present structures and be irreversible since minority Governments, the norm so far, could no longer make major changes. The system of planning would thus rapidly evolve to the bottom-up Swiss model (Gilg, 1985c).

While a coalition remains a pleasant mirage for Liberals, the Labour Party, after all the turmoil and policy reviews of the 1980s are desperate to please the electorate and return to power. Their current policies are thus not very radical. They would almost certainly introduce planning controls over agriculture and forestry, but would retain support for rural areas, notably the uplands. They would also introduce regional planning, but how effective this would be would depend on the Scottish factor which undermined and effectively ended not only the previous devolution proposals in 1978/79, but also brought the Labour Government to an end in March 1979. In terms of development the Labour Party would also probably introduce a social element into planning and seek to build cheaper rural houses.

Finally, the real Labour Party is alive but not well. Its addiction to central controls, corporate powers, and national ownership have been discredited by the collapse of Communism, and ridiculed by Thatcherism. Nonetheless if the 1990/91 recession were to continue on and beyond 1992, with the revised EC, then centralized controls might once again seem appropriate as a crisis measure. In such a scenario a 1947-style set of reforms would include the imposition of controls over most land uses, quotas and powers to assemble land for the purpose of development. The driving force behind these controls would be the long-standing chimera of a National Land Use Plan based on the rational exploitation of resources as identified by surveys. For planners this would be truly the promised land, but more probably as unrealistic as the Holy Grail.

Two forecasts

In contrast to the hundreds of people forecasting policies, only a few have risked their reputations by forecasting the 1990s in detail. A rare example is provided by Adams (1986) who has forecast that the effects of quotas, price restraint and setaside policies will not be uniform, and that there will be major differences either side of the Severn–Tyne line of pastoral farming to the west, and arable farming to the east. Quotas will favour larger and intensive farms east of this line and in this area farms will become larger and more mechanized. Price control would lead to more industrialized and intensive farming in the east, and uneconomic farms in the west. Setaside would be the only policy to hit farmers in the east where the grain surpluses are produced, whereas in the west much land might go to forestry.

As farm profitability falls, money for environmental conservation will become an economic lifeline. Therefore, in the west farming could become a low input–low output conservation-orientated system which exists primarily to maintain wildlife habitats and landscape beauty, and where farm tourism and craft products dominate the economy. To the east there could be an area, albeit decreasing, of intensive profitable agriculture.

In another forecast Brown and Taylor (1988), two planning consultants in a report for the NCC, have assessed the changes likely to take place in the use of rural land by the year 2000. Using a qualitative evaluation of policy, prices and behaviour they forecast, that by the year 2000, visible changes in the majority of Britain's rural land are likely to be relatively small. In the uplands we are likely to see increased or at least maintained income support, and thus the continuation of traditional systems largely because of public demand, and the creation of limited tourist and leisure facilities. In the lowlands, farming is likely to continue in much the same form as at present, but with trends towards larger farms, more environmentally friendly husbandry techniques, and continued technical improvements to maintain profitability.

Only in the marginal lowlands is the rate of change likely to be fast. Indeed Brown and Taylor forecast it will be greater than at any time since World War II since here the pressures are greatest. They define the marginal lowlands as chalk downland, river valleys, urban fringe, heavy and wet lowlands and sloping arable land prone to erosion. The pressure for change will come from reduced prices and the lack of any extra support available as in the uplands. These pressures could well lead to land going out of agriculture to other uses, such as sport, recreation, conservation and forestry. There will also be the growth of both old and new 'cottage' industries and housing conversions as redundant buildings are redeveloped.

Manifesto for the 1990s

The so-called new world order that potentially began with the fall of the Berlin Wall offers a unique opportunity for the environment. If the world is not to head into the abyss of overpopulation and environmental pollution so graphically portrayed in Streiber and Kunetka's (1986) novel *Natures End* then the newly resurgent United Nations, revived by Saddam Hussein, must begin to implement radical reforms throughout the world, based on draconian birth control measures and making self-sustaining development mandatory. This will mean an immediate end to policies based on the continuing technological development of agriculture. This does not mean that research into biotechnology and other sustainable agricultures should cease. Indeed it means the reverse, research should redouble to find a modern form of organic farming that is as productive as the unsustainable chemical farming it needs to replace.

These changes cannot take place in isolation, at no time before in our history has it been truer that 'no man is an island'. If the world is to survive it must move fast to a world government dedicated to greater equality. As a consequence the UK will have to surrender not only sovereignty but also her standard of life. But not – repeat not – the quality of life.

Ironically the loss of sovereignty will mean not less democracy but more. This is because in a Federal World there will have to be proportional representation for all levels of democracy at the World, Continental, Nation State, Region and Local levels.

Given self-sustainability and a democratic world order how would rural planning in the UK evolve? First of all there would not be a UK but instead a four federal states: England; Ireland; Scotland and Wales. Within these states a level of self-sufficiency in food supplies would be set, related to the physical ability of the land to produce and the need to trade non-indigenous food supplies. In order to reduce world food shortages and to encourage better diets the meat content of diets would be encouraged to fall as far as possible. Meat would be supplied from animals kept for other purposes such as egg production or to utilize otherwise unusable land, e.g. deer on steep uplands.

Given the amount of land released from agriculture by cutting out the grossly inefficient meat production process, and progress made by biotechnology aided organic farming there should be a large surplus of land left for other purposes. After satisfying the need for immediate uses this would still leave millions of acres.

Using the following principles a land-use planning system could be created by the end of the decade to oversee the right and proper reuse of this land.

Principle One: The need for a self-sustaining and ultimately more satisfying life-style.

Principle Two: The need to move to a less mobile society with a massive reduction in car usage.

Principle Three: Most food as now to be produced by large enterprises and traded through large corporations. Fun/weekend food would, however, be produced by smallholdings in a traditional way and through small outlets. In time, as self-sustaining communities grew, the percentage of food produced this way would increase, and even supermarkets would return to regional supplies where possible.

Principle Four: Similarly work would gradually be decentralized as it already is into smaller units based on the original New Town concept of self-sufficient communities, but with trading links for those products that can still only be produced in large plants.

The underlying ideology for all these principles is a two-tier society in which as many needs as possible are provided by the local community, but that the wider world provides for those that cannot be so produced.

In four words this becomes, Think Globally, Act Locally.

How would these ideas pan out in practice? Politically there would be a three-tier system of Government on the Swiss model. In essence this would involve most power being set at the local level where most laws and taxes would be set. In order to coordinate the local level, a regional tier would provide guidance and some redistribution of funds for the purposes of equity, and for projects beyond the scope of local councils. At the national level politics would only involve representing the wishes of local councils to the rest of the world. At all levels from the Chairman down, every position of responsibility (not power since this would reside with the people) would be electable and for a maximum or rotating term. Mrs Thatcher could not have existed under such a system nor indeed does any leader in Switzerland for more than one year.

Turning to detailed policies. Agriculture would become markedly less intensive, and return to the principles of good husbandry related to the need to reuse so called wastes like straw, and to grow crops best suited to each habitat.

There would be a massive expansion of multiple purpose, basically native broadleaved, forestry, again related to habitat, and hopefully a full development of food-producing trees, an idea still in its infancy.

There could not be an overnight change in settlements largely because of the huge investment existing in the cities. Instead of rebuilding/infilling, however, as old buildings came to the end of their lives the land should be reclaimed – not half as expensive as people think, especially if land value can be stripped out – and the cities should gradually be allowed to become villages with increasingly large interstices of green land. In the countryside to aid this process people rehoused from redundant city buildings would be allowed to move to purpose-built new self-sustaining communities with populations in the ranges of 500–1000, 5000–10,000, and even 50,000–100,000. Conversely the big cities should be encouraged to reduce their populations to 250,000 at the most.

In conclusion if these three key factors of farming, forestry, and settlement are well planned then the rest will fall into place. What are the chances of this manifesto coming into place?

Realistically none, but so too have very few of the hundreds of proposals outlined in this book. One can but dream. Otherwise we wouldn't be planners and you wouldn't have read this book.

References

Abercrombie, N., Warde, A., Soothill, K., Urry, J. and Walby, S. (1988) *Contemporary British Society*. Basil Blackwell, Oxford.

ACRE (1989) *Rates Reform – Rural Impact*. Acre, Cirencester.

Adam Smith Institute (1988a) *Pining for Profit*. The Institute, London.

——(1988b) *The Green Quadratic*. The Institute, London.

Adams, W. M. (1984) Sites of Special Scientific Interest and habitat protection. Implications for the Wildlife and Countryside Act 1981. *Area* 16, 273–80.

——(1986) *Nature's Place. Conservation Sites and Countryside Change*. Allen and Unwin, London.

Agriculture and Food Research Council (1987) *Science, Agriculture and the Environment*. The Council, London.

Agriculture Committee of the House of Commons (1982) *Financial Policy of EEC with Particular Reference to Less Favoured Areas*. HMSO, London, H.C. 41-I and -II (81–82).

——(1985) *UK Government Agricultural Development and Advisory Services Including Lower Input Farming*. HMSO, London, H.C. 502 -I and -II (84–85).

——(1986) *The Storage and Disposal of Cereal Surpluses*. HMSO, London, H.C. 23-I, -II and -III (85–86).

——(1990a) *Fish Farming in the UK*. HMSO, London, H.C. 141-I and -II (89–90).

——(1990b) *Land Use and Forestry*. HMSO, London, H.C. 16-I and -II (89–90).

Agriculture, Fisheries and Food, Ministry of (1972) *Forestry Policy*. HMSO, London.

——(1988) *Milk Production Before and After Quotas*. HMSO, London.

——(1989) *Environmentally Sensitive Areas*. HMSO, London.

Allaby, M. and Bunyard, P. (1980) *The Politics of Self Sufficiency*. Oxford University Press, Oxford.

Allen, J. and Massey, D. (eds) (1988) *The Economy in Question*. Sage, London.

Ambrose, P. (1987) *Whatever Happened to Planning*. Methuen, London.

Amos, C. (1989) A testing time for new settlements. *Town and Country Planning* 58, 314–19.

——(1991) Directory of new settlements proposals. *Town and Country Planning* 60, 53–6.

Anderson, M. A. (1984) Complete urban containment. A responsible proposition. *Area* 16, 25–31.

Armstrong, H. and Taylor, J. (1987) *Regional Policy: The Way Forward*. Employment Institute, London.

Armstrong, H. W. and Fildes, J. (1988) Industrial development initiatives in England and Wales: The role of district councils. *Progress in Planning* 30, 87–156.

Armstrong, J. (1986) Too much of an idyll for country people. *Town and Country Planning* 55, 8–9.

Anon. (1983) *The Conservation and Development Programme for the UK. A Response to the World Conservation Strategy*. Kogan Page, London.

Ash, M. (1988) Plus ca change. *Town and Country Planning* 57, 162–3.

Association of County Councils (1989) *Homes We Can Afford*. The Association, London.

——(1991) *Counties: A Unique Base for Strategic Planning*. The Association, London.

Association of District Councils (1986) *The Rural Economy at the Crossroads*. The Association, London.

——(1989) *The Future of Rural Communities: The District Council View*. The Association, London.

Association of National Park Officers (1987) *National Parks at Risk: The Case for a New Integrated Agricultural and Environmental Policy*. Yorkshire Dales National Park, Leyburn, North Yorkshire.

Attfield, T. and Dell, K. (eds) (1989) *Values, Conflict and the Environment*. Ian Ramsey Centre, St Cross College, Oxford.

Baker, N. and Wiggen, J. (1987) *This Pleasant Land. A New Strategy for Planning*. Conservative Political Centre, London.

Baldock, D. (1989) *The Common Agricultural Policy and the Environment: The CAP Structures Policy*. World Wide Fund for Nature, Godalming.

Baldock, D. and Conder, D. (eds) (1985) *Can the CAP Fit the Environment?* World Wildlife Fund, London.

Baldock, D., Cox, G., Lowe, P. and Winter, M. (1990) Environmentally sensitive areas: incrementalism or reform? *Journal of Rural Studies* 6, 143–62.

Ball, R. M. (1987) Intermittent labour forms in UK agriculture. Some implications for rural areas. *Journal of Rural Studies* 3, 133–50.

Banister, D. and Norton, F. (1988) The role of the voluntary sector in the provision of rural services – the case of transport. *Journal of Rural Studies* 4, 57–71.

Barker, A. (1984) Planning inquiries. A role for Parliament. *Journal of the Rural Society of Arts* 132, 619–32.

Barlow, J. (1988) The politics of land into the 1990s. Landowners, developers and farmers in lowland Britain. *Policy and Politics* 16, 111–21.

Barnes, B. (1988) *The Nature of Power*. Polity Press, Oxford.

Barnett, E., Slee, D. and Townley, R. (eds) (1989) *Caring for the Countryside*. County Planning Officers Society, Stafford.

Baumol, W. J. and Oates, W. E. (1988) *The Theory of Environmental Policy*. Cambridge University Press, Cambridge.

Bell, M. (1987) The impacts of CAP change: Putting the pieces together. *International Yearbook of Rural Planning* 1, 33–43.

Bell, M. and Bunce, R. G. H. (eds) (1987) *Agriculture and Conservation in the Hills and Uplands*. Merlewood, Institute of Terrestrial Ecology, Grange-over-Sands.

Bell, P. and Cloke, P. (1989) The changing relationship between the private and public sectors. Privatisation and rural Britain. *Journal of Rural Studies* 5, 1–15.

Benson, J. F. and Willis, K. G. (1988) Conservation costs, agricultural intensification and the Wildlife and Countryside Act. *Biological Conservation* 44, 157–78.

Bentham, G. (1986) Public satisfaction, Socio-economic and environmental conditions in the counties of England. *Transactions of the Institute of British Geographers, New Series* 11, 27–36.

Bibby, P. R. and Shepherd, J. W. (1991) *Rates of Urbanization in England 1981–2001.* HMSO, London.

Black, J. B. (1987) *Reducing Isolation: Telecommunications and Rural Development.* Arkleton Trust, Oxford.

Blincoe, B. (1987) Why development plans need to take account of market demand. *The Planner* 73, 37–9.

Blowers, A. (1980) *The Limits of Power: The Politics of Local Planning Policy.* Pergamon Press, Oxford.

——(1987) Transition or transformation? Environmental policy under Thatcher. *Public Administration* 65, 277–94.

——(1990) The environment – a political problem with no solution? *Town and Country Planning* 59, 132–3.

Blunden, J. and Curry, N. (1988) *A Future for the Countryside.* Basil Blackwell, Oxford.

Blunden, J. and Turner, G. (1985) *Critical Countryside.* BBC Publications, London.

Blunden, J., Curry, N. and Turner, A. (eds) (1985) *The Changing Countryside.* Croom Helm and the Open University, London.

Body, R. (1982) *Agriculture: The Triumph and the Shame.* Temple Smith, London.

——(1984) *Farming in the Clouds.* Temple Smith, Hounslow.

——(1987) *Red or Green for Farmers?* Broad Leys Publishing, Saffron Walden.

Bolton, N. and Chalkley, B. (1989) Counter–urbanisation, disposing of the myths. *Town and Country Planning* 58, 249–50.

——(1990) The rural population turnaround: a case study of North Devon. *Journal of Rural Studies* 6, 29–43.

Bonnieux, F. and Rainelli, P. (1988) Agricultural policy and the environment in developed countries. *European Review of Agricultural Economics* 15, 263–80.

Bovaird, T. Tricker, M. and Stoakes, R. (1984) *Recreation Management and Pricing.* Gower, Aldershot.

Bowers, J. (1990) *The Conservationist's Response to the Pearce Report.* British Association of Nature Conservationists, Telford.

Bowers, J. K. and Cheshire, P. C. (1983) *Agriculture, the Countryside and Land Use.* Methuen, London.

Bowler, I. R. (1979) *Government and Agriculture.* Longman, London.

——(1986) Direct supply control in agriculture: experience in Western Europe and North America. *Journal of Rural Studies* 2, 19–30.

Bowman, J. C. and Doyle, C. J. (1978) UK agricultural productivity and the land budget: a comment. *Journal of Agricultural Economics* 29, 329–30.

Bowman, J. C., Doyle, C. and Tranter, R. (1978) Why we need a coordinated land use policy. *Town and Country Planning* 46, 405–8.

Boyle, D. (1988) Could planning be privatised? *Town and Country Planning* 57, 259–60.

Bracewell-Milnes, B. (1988) *Caring for the Countryside: Public Dependence on Private Interest*. Social Affairs Unit, London.

Bradbury, J. K., Charlesworth, A. and Collins, C. A. (1990) Cereal supply policy instruments: An attitudinal survey among farmers in England. *Journal of Agricultural Economics* 41, 207–14.

Brennan, A. (1988) *Thinking about Nature. An Investigation of Nature, Value and Ecology*. Routledge, London.

Bressers, H. and Klok, P. J. (1988) Fundamentals for a theory of policy instruments. *International Journal of Social Economics* 15, 22–41.

British Association for Shooting and Conservation, and Scottish Development Agency (1990) *The Economic Impact of Sporting Shooting in Scotland*. The Association, Dunkeld.

British Organic Farmers, Organic Farmers Association and Soil Association (1989) *20% of Britain Organic by the Year 2000*. Soil Association, Bristol.

British Property Federation (1986) *The Planning System – A Fresh Approach*. The Foundation, London.

Brotherton, I. (1984) A better future for upland rural landscapes. *Planning Outlook* 27, 92–7.

——(1985) Farming in the Parks: Advancing the case for advance notification. *Ecos* 6, 31–5.

——(1986a) Party political approaches to rural conservation in Britain. *Environment and Planning A* 18, 151–60.

——(1986b) Agricultural and afforestation controls – conservation and ideology. *Land Use Policy* 3, 21–30.

——(1987a) Labour was not pushed: it leapt. *Environment and Planning A* 19, 415–18.

——(1987b) The case for consultation. *Ecos* 8, 18–23.

——(1988) Grant aided agricultural activity in National Parks. *Journal of Agricultural Economics* 39, 376–81.

——(1989a) Farmer participation in voluntary land diversion schemes: some observations from theory. *Journal of Rural Studies* 5, 299–304.

——(1989b) Arrangements for prior notification of agricultural operations in National Parks. *Town Planning Review* 60, 71–87.

——(1989c) What voluntary approach? *Ecos* 10, 36–40.

Brotherton, I. and Devall, N. (1987) More forestry: problem of opportunities, *Landscape Design* 169, 49–50.

——(1988) Forestry conflicts in National Parks. *Journal of Environmental Management* 26, 229–38.

Brotherton, I. and Lowe, P. (1984) Statutory bodies and rural conservation: agency or instrument. *Land Use Policy* 1, 147–53.

Brown, C. R. (1988) *The Changing World Food Prospect. The Nineties and Beyond*. Worldwatch Institute, Washington, DC.

Brown, D. A. H. and Taylor, K. (1988) The future of Britain's rural land. *Geographical Journal* 154, 406–11.

Bruce-Gardyne, J. and Lawson, N. (1976) *The Power Game – an Examination of Decision Making in Government*. Macmillan, London.

Bruton, M. J. and Nicholson, D. (1987a) Planners alter role to manage change. *Town and Country Planning* 56, 22–3.

——(1987b) A future for development plans. *Journal of Planning and Environmental Law* October, 687–703.

Buckwell, A. E., (1986) What is a set aside policy? *Ecos* 7, 6–11.

——(1989) Economic signals, farmer's responses and environmental change. *Journal of Rural Studies* 5, 149–60.

Burnham, P. (1985) What is countryside management? *Ecos* 6, 24–7.

——(1989) Returning set aside land to nature. *Ecos* 10, 13–17.

Burnham, P., Green, B. and Potter, C. (1986) *A Set Aside Policy for the United Kingdom*. Wye College, Ashford.

——(1988) *Set Aside as an Environmental and Agricultural Policy Instrument*. Wye College, London.

Burnham, P., Green, B., Potter, C. and Shinn, A. (1987) *Targetting for Conservation Set Aside*. Wye College, Ashford.

Burrell, A., (1987) EC agricultural surpluses and budgetary control. *Journal of Agricultural Economics* 38, 1–14.

Burton, T. (1990) Sea change in planning policy. *Ecos* 11, 52–3.

Business Strategies Limited (1989) *The Costs of the Green Belt*. ARC Properties, Bath.

Cambridge Econometrics and the Northern Ireland Economic Research Centre (1988) *Regional Economic Prospects. Analysis and Forecasts to the Year 2000*. Cambridge Econometrics, Cambridge.

Cameron, G. (1985) UK regional economic planning: the end of the line. *Planning Outlook* 28, 8–13.

Carlisle, K. (1984) *Conserving the Countryside*. Conservative Political Centre, London.

Central Office of Information (1984) *The British Parliament*. HMSO, London.

Centre for Agricultural Strategy (1976) *Land for Agriculture*. The Centre, Reading.

——(1980) *Strategy for the UK Forest Industry*. The Centre, Reading.

——(1986) *Countryside Implications for England and Wales of Possible Changes in the CAP*. The Centre, Reading.

Champion, A. G. (1987) Recent changes in the pace of population deconcentration in Britain. *Geoforum* 18, 379–401.

——(1989) Counterurbanisation in Britain. *Geographical Journal* 155, 52–9.

Cherry, G. E. (1982) *The Politics of Town Planning*. Longmans, London.

——(1988) British town planning in chains or in change? *Journal of the Hong Kong Institute of Planners* 4, 42–8.

Cheshire, P. and Sheppard, S. (1989) British planning policy and access to housing: some empirical estimates. *Urban Studies* 26, 469–85.

Chiddick, D. and Dobson, M. (1986) Land for housing. Circular Arguments. *The Planner* 72, 10–13.

Clark, D. (1988) *Affordable Homes in the Countryside*. ACRE, Cirencester.

——(1990) *Affordable Rural Houses: The Builders Guide*. BEC Publications, Birmingham.

Clark, D. and Dunmore, K. (1990) *Involving the Private Sector in Rural Housing*, Action with Communities in Rural England, Cirencester.

Clark, D. and Woollett, S. (1990) *English Village Services in the 1980s*. Rural Development Commission and ACRE, London, Cirencester.

Cloke, P. J. (ed.) (1987)*Rural Planning Policy into Action*. Harper & Row, London.

Cloke, P. J. and Little, J. (1986a) Implementation and county structure plan policies for rural areas in Britain. *Planning Perspectives* 1, 257–77.

——(1986b) The implementation of rural policies: a survey of county planning authorities. *Town Planning Review* 57, 265–84.

——(1987a) Rural policies in the Gloucestershire Structure Plan: 1) A study of motives and mechanisms; 2) Implementation and the county–district relationship. *Environment and Planning A* 19, 958–81; 1027–50.

——(1987b) Class distribution and locality in rural areas. *Geoforum* 18, 403–13.

——(1987c) Policy planning and the state in rural localities. *Journal of Rural Studies* 3, 343–52.

——(1988) Public sector agency influence in rural policy-making: examples from Gloucestershire. *Tijdschrift voor Economische en Sociale Geografie* 79, 278–89.

——(1990) *The Rural State? Limits to Planning in Rural Society.* Oxford University Press, Oxford.

Cloke, P. and McLaughlin, B. (1989) Politics of the alternative land use and rural economy (ALURE) proposals in the UK: crossroads or blind alley? *Land Use Policy* 6, 235–48.

Cloke, P. and Thrift, N. (1987) Intra-class conflict in rural areas. *Journal of Rural Studies* 3, 321–34.

Cochrane, A. and Anderson, J. (eds) (1989) *Politics in Transition.* Sage and the Open University, London.

Coleman, A. (1980) The place of forestry in a viable land use strategy. *Quarterly Journal of Forestry* 74, 20–9.

Coles, D. B. (1986) Rural transport needs. *Social Policy and Administration* 20, 58–73.

Collins, N., Bradbury, I. K. and Charlesworth, A. (1990) Formulation of the European Community Price Review: models of change. *Journal of Rural Studies* 6, 163–73.

Colman, D. (1989) Economic issues from the Broads Grazing Marshes Conservation Scheme. *Journal of Agricultural Economics* 40, 336–44.

Command 9397 (1984) *Acid Rain.* HMSO, London.

Command 43, (1986) *Planning Appeals, Call-in and Major Public Inquiries.* HMSO, London.

Commission of the European Communities (1989a) *Intensive Farming and the Impact on the Environment and the Rural Economy of Restrictions on the Use of Chemical and Mineral Fertilisers.* The Commission, Luxembourg.

——(1989b) *The Impact of Biotechnology on Agriculture in the European Community to the year 2005.* The Commission, Luxembourg.

Committee of Public Accounts of the House of Commons (1986) *CAP Achievements and Problems.* HMSO, London, H.C. 71 (85–86).

Comptroller and Auditor General (1985) *Achievements and Costs of the Common Agricultural Policy: Agricultural Policy in the United Kingdom.* HMSO, London, H.C. 578 (84–85).

Conservative Party (1989) *The First 10 Years: a Perspective on the Conservative Era that Began in 1979.* The Party, London.

Cooke, P. (1987) Britain's new spatial paradigm: technology, locality and society in transition. *Environment and Planning A* 19, 1289–301.

Coon, A. (1988) Local plan provision – the record to date and the prospects for the future. *The Planner* 74, 17–20.

Cotgrove, S. and Duff, A. (1980) Environmentalism, middle class radicalism and politics. *Sociological Review* 28, 333–51.

——(1981) Environmentalism, values and social change. *British Journal of Sociology* 32, 92–110.

Cottrell, R. (1987) *The Sacred Cow.* Grafton Books, London.

Coulson, A. (1990) *Devolving Power – The Case for Regional Government.* Fabian Society, London.

Council for the Protection of Rural England (1988a) *Less Intensive Farming Proposals.* The Council, London.

——(1988b) *Concrete Objections the Ministry of Agriculture's Response to Applications for Development of Rural Land.* The Council, London.

——(1989a) *Paradise Protection.* The Council, London.

——(1989b) *Welcome Houses – Housing Supply from Unallocated Land.* The Council, London.

——(1989c) *Land Use and Forestry.* The Council, London.

——(1990a) *From White Paper to Green Future?* The Council, London.

——(1990b) *Agenda 2000.* The Council, London.

——(1990c) *Paradise Destruction.* The Council, London.

——(1990d) *Our Finest Landscapes.* The Council, London.

Country Landowners Association (1983) *Planning and the Countryside.* The Association, London.

——(1989) *Enterprise in the Rural Environment.* The Association, London.

Countryside Commission (1984a) *Agricultural Landscapes: a Policy Statement CCP 173.* The Commission, Cheltenham.

——(1984b) *A Better Future for the Uplands CCP 162.* The Commission, Cheltenham.

——(1987a) *Shaping a New Countryside CCP 243.* The Commission, Cheltenham.

——(1987b) *Forestry in the Countryside CCP 245.* The Commission, Cheltenham.

——(1987c) *National Parks: Our Manifesto for the Next Five Years CCP 237.* The Commission, Cheltenham.

——(1987d) *Declarations of Commitment to the National Parks CCP 247.* The Commission, Cheltenham.

——(1987e) *Enjoying the Countryside: A Consultation Paper on Future Policies CCP 225.* The Commission, Cheltenham.

——(1987f) *Recreation 2000. Policies for Enjoying the Countryside (CCP 234)* and *Priorities for Action (CCP 235).* The Commission, Cheltenham.

——(1988a) *Planning for Change: Development in a Green Countryside CCD 24.* The Commission, Cheltenham.

——(1988b) *Changing the Rights of Way Network: A Discussion Paper CCP 254.* The Commission, Cheltenham.

——(1988c) *Paths, Routes and Trails: A Consultation Paper CCP 253.* The Commission, Cheltenham.

——(1989a) *Planning for a Greener Countryside CCP 264.* The Commission, Cheltenham.

——(1989b) *Incentives for a New Direction for Farming CCP 262.* The Commission, Cheltenham.

——(1989c) *National Parks Review: A Discussion Document CCD 56.* The Commission, Cheltenham.

——(1989d) *Managing Rights of Way: An Agenda for Action CCP 273*. The Commission, Cheltenham.

——(1989e) *Rights of Way: A Challenge for the 1990s CCD 48*. The Commission, Cheltenham.

——(1989f) *Paths, Routes and Trails: Policies and Priorities CCP 266*. The Commission, Cheltenham.

——(1989g) *A Countryside for Everyone CCP 265*. The Commission, Cheltenham.

——(1990a) *Ten Critical Years: An Agenda for the 1990s*. The Commission, Cheltenham.

——(1990b) *A New National Forest in the Midlands CCP 278*. The Commission, Cheltenham.

——(1990c) *Sustainable Development: A Challenge and Opportunity for the National Parks of England and Wales CCP 286*. The Commission, Cheltenham.

——(1991) *An Agenda for the Countryside CCP 336*. The Commission, Cheltenham.

Countryside Commission and Forestry Commission (1989) *Forests for the Community, CCP 270* and *The Community Forest CCP 271*, written by M. Johnston. The Commission, Cheltenham.

Countryside Commission for Scotland (1982) *A Park System and Scenic Conservation in Scotland*. The Commission, Perth.

Countryside Policy Review Panel (1987) *New Opportunities for the Countryside CCP 224*. Countryside Commission, Cheltenham.

County Planning Officers Society (1985) *Improving the Development Plan System: Some Ideas for Discussion*. The Society, Norfolk.

——(1987) *Agriculture and the Countryside*. Association of County Councils, London.

——(1990) *Regional Guidance and Regional Planning Conferences*. The Society, Aylesbury.

Cox, G. (1988) Reading nature: Reflections on ideological persistence and the politics of the countryside. *Landscape Research* 13, 24–34.

Cox, G. and Lowe, P. (1983) Countryside politics: Goodbye to good will. *Political Quarterly* 54, 268–82.

Cox, G., Lowe, P. and Winter, M. (1985) Changing directions in agricultural policy: Corporatist arguments in production and conservation policies. *Sociologia Ruralis* XXXV, 130–53.

——(1988) Private rights and public responsibilities: The prospects for agricultural and environmental controls. *Journal of Rural Studies* 4, 323–37.

Cox, G., Lowe, P. and Winter, M. (eds) (1986) *Agriculture: Policies and People*. Allen and Unwin, London.

Crabtree, J. R. and Macmillan, D. C. (1989) UK fiscal changes and new forestry planting. *Journal of Agricultural Economics* 40, 314–22.

Crewe, I. (1988) Voting patterns since 1959. *Contemporary Record* 2, 2–6.

Crewe, I. and Searing, D. (1988) Thatcherism: it's origins, electoral impact and implications for Down's theory of party strategy. *Essex Papers in Politics and Government* 37.

Crofts, T. (1987) *The Return of the Wild*. The Friendly Press, Stonesfield, Oxon.

Curry, N. (1985) Countryside recreation sites policy. A review. *Town Planning Review* 56, 70–89.

——(1988) Capital conspiracy in the countryside. *Town and Country Planning* 57, 22–3.

Curry, N. *et al.* (1987) *Recreation 2000: Perspectives on the Future Recreation Policies of The Countryside Commission.* Countryside Commission, Cheltenham.

Dean, N. (1988) Transport in rural areas. *The Planner* 74, 14–17.

De Gorte, H. and Meilke, K. D. (1989) Efficiency of alternative policies for the EC's Common Agricultural Policy. *American Journal of Agricultural Economics* 71, 592–603.

Denne, T., Bown, M. J. D. and Abel, J. A. (1986) *Forestry: Britain's Growing Resource.* UK Centre for Economic and Environmental Development, London.

Denton-Thompson, M. (1984) Proposal for a countryside register. *Landscape Design* 147, 37–8.

——(1986) Landscape conservation orders. *Landscape Design* 162, 9–10.

Development Board for Rural Wales (1989) *Strategy for the 1990's.* The Board, Newtown.

deWitt, C. T. (1988) Environmental impact of the CAP. *European Review of Agricultural Economics* 15, 283–96.

Dryzek, J. S. (1987) *Rational Ecology, Environmental and Political Economy.* Basil Blackwell, Oxford.

Duncan, S. and Goodwin, G. (1988) *The Local State and Uneven Development.* Polity Press, Cambridge.

Dunn, R., Forest, R. and Murie, A. (1987) The geography of council sales in England 1979–85. *Urban Studies* 24, 47–59.

Economist Intelligence Unit (1989) *The Future of European Agriculture: Trade, Technology and the Environment.* The Unit, London.

Edwards, A. (1986) *An Agricultural Land Budget for the United Kingdom.* Wye College, Ashford.

——(1987) *A Balance Sheet for Crops.* Wye College, Ashford.

Edwards, A. M. and Wibberley, G. P. (1971) *An Agricultural Land Budget for Britain 1965–2000.* Wye College, Ashford.

Ehrman, R. (1988) *Planning Planning: Clearer Strategies and Environmental Controls.* Centre for Policy Studies, London.

Elkington, J. and Burke, T. (1987) *The Green Capitalists: Industry's Search for Environmental Excellence.* Victor Gollancz, London.

Elson, M. J. (1986) *Green Belts: Conflict Mediation in the Urban Fringe.* Heinemann, London.

English Tourist Board (1988) *Visitors in the Countryside. Rural Tourism: A Development Strategy.* The Board, London.

Environment, Department of (1986a) *Conservation and Development: The British Approach.* The Department, London.

——(1986b) *The Future of Development Plans.* The Department, London.

——(1986c) *Protecting the Countryside – The Government's Consultation Proposals for Landscape Conservation Orders.* The Department, London.

——(1987 and 1988) *Land Use Change in England – Statistical Bulletins. 87(7) and 88(5).* The Department, London.

——(1988a) *Possible Impacts of Climate Change on the Natural Environment in the United Kingdom.* The Department, London.

——(1988b) *Our Common Future: A Perspective by the United Kingdom on the Report of the World Commission on Environment and Development*. The Department, London.

——(1988c) *Planning Policy Guidance Notes, 1: General Policy and Principles: 3: Land for Housing; 7: Rural Enterprise and Development; and 12: Local Plans*. HMSO, London.

——(1988d) *Household Projections 1985–2001*. The Department, London.

——(1988e) *Planning Policy Guidance Note 2, Green Belts*. HMSO, London.

——(1988f) *Green Belts*. HMSO, London.

——(1988g) *Housing in Rural Areas: Village Housing and New Villages: A Discussion Paper*. The Department, London.

——(1990a) *This Common Inheritance (Command 1200)*. HMSO, London.

——(1990b) *Regional Planning Guidance, Structure Plans and the Content of Development Plans*. HMSO, London.

——(1990c) *Draft Planning Policy Guidance, Sport and Recreation*. The Department, London.

——(1990d) *Land for Housing, Progress Report 1989*. The Department, London.

Environment Committee of the House of Commons (1986) *Planning: Appeals Call-in and Major Public Inquiries*. HMSO, London. H.C. 181-I and -II (85–86).

——(1987) *Pollution of Rivers and Estuaries*. HMSO, London. H.C. 183 (86–87).

Ermisch, J. (1990) *Fewer Babies, Longer Lives*. Joseph Rowntree Foundation, York.

Errington, A. (1988) Disguised unemployment in British agriculture. *Journal of Rural Studies* 4, 1–7.

Ervin, D. E. (1988a) Cropland diversion (set aside) in the US and the UK. *Journal of Agricultural Economics* 39, 183–95.

——(1988b) Set aside programmes. Using US experience to evaluate UK proposals. *Journal of Rural Studies* 4, 181–91.

Ervin, D. E. and Dicks, M. R. (1988) Cropland diversion for conservation and environmental improvement: an economic welfare analysis. *Land Economics* 64, 256–68.

European Communities (1988) *Forestry Strategy and Action [COM (88/255)]*. HMSO, London.

European Communities Commission (1989) *The Future of Rural Society* [COM (88) 371 final] and [COM (88) 501], HMSO, London.

Evans, A. (1988) *No Room No Room: The Costs of the British Town and Country Planning System*. Institute of Economic Affairs, London.

Fairgreive, R. (1979) *A Policy for Forestry*. Conservative Political Centre, London.

Fallows, S. J. and Wheelock, J. V. (1982) Self sufficiency and United Kingdom food policy. *Agricultural Administration* 11, 107–25.

Faludi, A. (1987) *A Decision Centred View of Environmental Planning*. Pergamon, Oxford.

Fearne, A. (1989) A 'satisficing' model of CAP decision making. *Journal of Agricultural Economics* 40, 71.

Femia, J. V. (1981) *Gramsci's Political Thought, Hegemony, Consciousness and the Revolutionary Process*. Clarendon Press, Oxford.

Flyn, A. and Lowe, P. (1987) The problems of analysing party politics: Labour and Conservative approaches to rural conservation. *Environment and Planning A* 19, 409–14, 415–18.

Forestry Commission (1978) *The Wood Production Outlook in Britain.* HMSO, London.

Frankel, B. (1987) *The Post Industrial Utopians.* Polity Press, Cambridge.

Friend, J. and Hickling, A. (1987) *Planning Under Pressure.* Pergamon, Oxford.

Friends of the Earth (1986a) *Towards the Demise of Part II of the 1981 Wildlife and Countryside Act.* The Friends, London.

——(1986b) *Countryside Controls: A National Poll of Chief Planning Officers.* The Friends, London.

Garner, R. (1989) National Parks in Scotland? The Designations Debate. *Ecos* 10, 13–16.

Gasson, R. (1986) *Farm Families with Other Gainful Activities.* Wye College, Ashford.

——(1988) Farm diversification and rural development. *Journal of Agricultural Economics* 39, 175–82.

Gasson, R. and Potter, C. (1988) Conservation through land diversion: a survey of farmer's attitudes. *Journal of Agricultural Economics* 39, 340–51.

Gibson, D. K. (1987) 'Set-aside' and the environmental use of agricultural resources. *Environmental Education and Information* 6, 279–89.

Giddens, A. (1984) *The Constitution of Society: Outline of the Theory of Structuration.* Polity Press, London.

Gilfoyle, I. (1989) Setting the planning agenda for the 1990s: strategic planning. *Town Planning Review* 60, iii–vi.

Gilg, A. W. (1978a) *Countryside Planning.* David and Charles, Newton Abbot.

——(1978b) Policy forum: Needed a new 'Scott' inquiry. *Town Planning Review* 49, 353–71.

——(1985a) Environmental policies in the United Kingdom. In: Park, C. (ed.), *Environmental Policies – An International Review.* Croom Helm, London.

——(1985b) *An Introduction to Rural Geography.* Edward Arnold, London.

——(1985c) Land Use Planning in Switzerland. *Town Planning Review* 56, 315–38.

——(1991) Planning for agriculture: the growing case for a conservation component. *Geoforum* 22, 75–9.

Girling, R. (1990) Why life will never be the same again. *Sunday Times Magazine* 13 May, 34–51.

Goldsmith, E. (1988a) *The Great U-turn: De-industrialising Society.* Green Books, Launceston.

Goldsmith, E. (ed.) (1988b) Rethinking man and nature – towards an ecological world view. *Ecologist* 18, 118–85.

Goldsmith, E. and Hildyard, N. (eds) (1986) *Green Britain or Industrial Wasteland?* Polity Press, Oxford.

Goodman, D. and Redclift, M. (1985) Capitalism, petty commodity production and the farm enterprise. *Sociologia Ruralis* 25, 231–47.

Gorz, A. (1976) *Paths to Paradise: on the Liberation from Work.* (Translated from the French.) Pluto Press, London.

Grainger, A. and Hildyard, N. (1981) Reforesting Britain. *Ecologist* 11, 54–81.

Green, B. (1988) Conservation and countryside management. *International Yearbook of Rural Planning* 2, 35–8.

——(1989) Agricultural impacts on the rural environment. *Journal of Applied Ecology* 26, 793–802.

Green, C. (1986) Rural development areas. Progress and problems. *The Planner* 72, 18–19.

Green, R., Curry, N., Roberts, P., Ekins, P., Lee-Steere, G., Bate, R., Dean, N., Clark, M., Shoard, M. and Hall, D. (1989a) A way forward for the countryside. *Town and Country Planning* 58, 230–45.

Green, R., Holliday, J. and Arden-Clarke, C. (1989b) *The Future Planning of the Countryside*. Town and Country Planning Association, London.

Green Party (1986) *Green Politics: Fact and Fiction*. The Party, London.

Greenwood, J. L. (1989) *Planning for Low Cost Rural Housing*. School of Planning, Oxford Polytechnic, Oxford.

Gresch, P. and Smith, B. (1985) Managing spatial change. The planning system in Switzerland. *Progress in Planning* 23, 157–251.

Griffiths, A. (1989) *Change in the Countryside: The Cornish Perspective*. Rural Development Commission, Truro.

Gwilliam, M. (1989) The future of regional and strategic planning. *Town and Country Planning* 58, 274–5.

Gyford, J., Leach, S. and Game, C. (1989) *The Changing Politics of Local Government*. Unwin Hyman, London.

Hague, C. (1985) *The Development of Planning Thought*. Hutchinson, London.

Haigh, N. (1987) Environmental assessment – the EC directive. *Journal of Planning and Environmental Law* January, 4–20.

Hall, D. (1989) The case for new settlements. *Town and Country Planning* 58, 111–14.

Hall, P. (1988a) The industrial revolution in reverse. *The Planner* 74, 15–20.

——(1988b) The coming revival of town and country planning. *Town and Country Planning* 57, 40–5.

——(1989) Planning for a golden age. *The Planner* 75, 20–4.

Hardy, D., Lock, D., Stranz, W. *et al.* (1990) Into the environmental decade. *Town and Country Planning* 59, 1–31.

Harper, S. (1987) The rural–urban interface: population and settlement. *Transactions of the Institute of British Geographers, New Series* 12, 284–302.

Harrison, A. and Tranter, R. B. (1989) *The Changing Financial Structure of Farming*. Centre for Agricultural Strategy, Reading.

Harvey, D. R. (1987) Extensification schemes and agricultural economics: who will take them up? In: Jenkins, N. R. and Bell, M. (eds), *Farm Extensification. Implications of EC Regulation 1760/87*. Institute of Terrestrial Ecology, Merlewood pp. 1–19.

Harvey, J. and Wilson, R. (1990) Green grows the groups but the union shrinks. *Farmers Weekly* 16 March, 26–7.

Hatfield, G. R. (ed.) (1988) *Farming and Forestry, Conference Proceedings, September 1986*. Forestry Commission, Edinburgh.

Haynes, J. (1987) *National Parks: The Next Thirty Years*. South West Branch. Royal Town Planning Institute, Dulverton.

Hays, S. (1984) The British conservation scene: A view from the United States. *Ecos* 5, 20–7.

Hayton, K. (1989) *The Future of Local Economic Development*. Centre for Planning. University of Strathclyde, Glasgow.

Healey, M. and Ilbery, B. (eds) (1986) *The Industrialisation of the Countryside*. Geo Books, Norwich.

Healey, P. (1988) *Planning for the 1990s*. Department of Town and Country Planning, University of Newcastle upon Tyne, Newcastle upon Tyne.

——(1989) Directions for change in the British planning system. *Town Planning Review* 60, 125–49.

——(1990) Democracy in the planning system. *The Planner* 76, 14–15.

Healey, P., McNamara, P. F., Elson, M. J. and Doak, A. J. (1988) *Land Use Planning and the Mediation of Urban Change*. Cambridge University Press, Cambridge.

Hearn, K. (1988) The National Trust and nature conservation. Problems for the next decade. *Ecos* 9, 11–16.

Heath, A. (1991) *Understanding Political Change. The British Vote 1964–87*. Pergamon Press, Oxford.

Held, D. (1984) Power and legitimacy in contemporary Britain. In: G. McLennan, D. Held and S. Hall (eds), *State and Society in Contemporary Britain*. Polity Press, Oxford, pp. 299–369.

Hill, B. (1989) *Farm Incomes, Wealth and Agricultural Policy*. Avebury, Aldershot.

Hill, B., Young, N. and Brookes, G. (1989) *Alternative Support Systems for Rural Areas*. Wye College, Ashford.

Hodge, I. (1988) Property institutions and environmental improvement. *Journal of Agricultural Economics* 39, 369–75.

——(1989) Compensation for nature conservation. *Environment and Planning A* 21, 1027–36.

Holliday, J. C. (1986) *Land at the Centre: Choices in a Fast Changing World*. Shepheard–Walwyn, London.

Hooper, A., Pinch, P. and Rogers, S. (1988) Housing land availability: circular advice, circular arguments and circular methods. *Journal of Planning and Environmental Law* April, 225–39.

House Builders Federation (1989a) *More Homes and a Better Environment*. The Federation, London.

——(1989b) *Meeting Community Housing Needs – The New Challenge*. The Federation, London.

House of Lords (1982) *Scientific Aspects of Forestry*. HMSO, London, H.L. 83 (81–82).

——(1983) *Guidelines on Land Use*. HMSO, London, H.L. II (83–84).

House of Lords Select Committee on the European Communities (1979) *Policies for Rural Areas in the European Community*. HMSO London, H.L. 129 (79–80).

——(1980) *The Common Agricultural Policy*. HMSO, London, H.L. 156 (79–80).

——(1983) *Supply Controls*. HMSO, London, H.L. 55 (83–84).

House of Lords Select Committee on Science and Technology (1980) *Scientific Aspects of Forestry*. HMSO, London, H.L. 381-I and -II (79–80).

——(1985) *Agricultural and Environmental Research: Government Response*. London, H.L. 233 (84–85).

Howarth, R. (1985) *Farming for Farmers?* Institute of Economic Affairs, London.

Ilbery, B. W. (1988) Agricultural change on the West Midlands urban fringe. *Tijdschrift Voor Economische en Sociale Geografie* 79, 108–21.

Institute of Fiscal Studies (1990) *Options for 1990: The Green Budget*. Institute for Fiscal Studies, London.

Irvine, S. and Ponton, A. (1988) *A Green Manifesto: Policies for a Green Future*. Macdonald Optima, London.

Jeffers, J. (1988). Decision thinking about land use. *Land Use Policy* 5, 75–8.

Jenkins, T. N. (1990) *Future Harvests: The Economics of Farming and the Environment*. Council for the Protection of Rural England and the World Wide Fund for Nature (UK), London.

John, B., Robertson, J. H. and Randall, S. (1987) *Towards a New Agriculture*. The Labour Party, London.

Johnson, J. A. and Price, C. (1987) Afforestation, employment and depopulation in Snowdonia. *Journal of Rural Studies* 3, 195–205.

Johnston, R. J. (1987) The rural milieu and voting in Britain. *Journal of Rural Studies* 3, 95–103.

Johnston, R. J., Pattie, C. and Allsop, G. (1988) *A Nation Dividing? The Electoral Map of Great Britain 1979–81*. Longmans, London.

Johnstone, D., Nicholson, C., Stone, M. and Taylor, R. (1990) *Countrywork*. ACRE, Cirencester.

Jones, R. (1982) *Town and Country Chaos*. Adam Smith Institute, London.

Joseph, S. (1990) Roads to where? *Ecos* 11, 17–20.

Kavanagh, D. (1988) Thatcher's third term. *Parliamentary Affairs* 41, 1–12.

Kay, G. (1989) Routes for recreational walking. *Town and Country Planning* 58, 78–81.

Keynes, J. M. (1930) Economic possibilities for our grandchildren. In: *The Collected Writings of J. M. Keynes*, Volume IX: Essays in persuasion. Macmillan, London, pp. 321–32.

King, D. (1987) Grasping the nettle in the numbers game. *Planning* 4 December, 10–11.

Kleinman, M. and Whitehead, C. (1989) Demand for new housebuilding 1986–2001. *Development and Planning* 1, 71–7.

Klosterman, R. E. (1985) Arguments for and against planning. *Town Planning Review* 56, 5–20.

Koester, U. (1989) Financial implications of the EC Set Aside programme. *Journal of Agricultural Economics* 40, 240–8.

Korbey, A. (ed.) (1984). *Investing in Rural Harmony*. Centre for Agricultural Strategy, Reading.

Kropotkin, P. A. (1912) *Fields, Factories and Workshops Tomorrow*. Nelson, London.

Kula, E. (1986) The developing framework for the economic evaluation of forestry in the United Kingdom. *Journal of Agricultural Economics* 37, 365–76.

——(1988) *The Economics of Forestry: Modern Theory and Practice*. Croom Helm, London.

Labour Party (1979) *Rural Areas: An Interim Statement*. The Party, London.

——(1981) *Out of Town Out of Mind: A Programme for Rural Renewal*. The Party, London.

——(1985) *Labour's Charter for the Environment*. The Party, London.

——(1986a) *Charter for Rural Areas*. The Party, London.

——(1986b) *The Environment in 'Statement to the Annual Conference'*. The Party, London, pp. 15–23.

——(1989) *Meet the Challenge, Make the Change*. The Party, London.

——(1990a) *Framework for the Future – Labour's New Approach to Planning*. The Party, London.

——(1990b) *Looking to the Future*. The Party, London.

——(1990c) *Out in the Countryside.* The Party, London.

Labour Party., Shepley, C., Hall, P. and Soley, C. (1988) Labour and the environment. *The Planner* 74, 11–20.

Laurence Gould Consultants (1986) *Wildlife and Countryside Act 1981: Financial Guidelines for Management Agreements.* The Consultants.

——(1989) *Conserving the Countryside – Costing it Out.* Council for the Protection of Rural England, London.

Lefcoe, G. (1987) The voices of landtronics. *Land Use Policy* 4, 243–56.

Leonard, P. (1982a) A public role for landscape conservation. *The Planner* 68, 19–25.

——(1982b) Management agreements: a tool for conservation. *Journal of Agricultural Economics* 33, 351–60.

——(1985) National Parks: Why do we need them? *Landscape Research* 10, 25–8.

Liberal Democrats (1991) *Shaping Tomorrow, Starting Today.* The Democrats, Dorchester.

Liberal Party (1984a) *Liberal Country: A Manifesto for Rural Britain.* The Party, London.

——(1984b) *Planning, People and the Environment.* The Party, London.

Lloyd, M. G. (1989) Land development and the free market lobby. *Scottish Planning Law and Practice* 26, 8–10.

Lobley, M. (1989) A role for ESAs? *Ecos* 10, 27–9.

Lock, D. (1989) *Riding the Tiger – Planning the South of England.* Town and Country Planning Association, London.

London and South East Regional Planning Conference (1988) *The Countryside in the South East.* The Conference, London.

——(1990) *Shaping the South East Planning Strategy: Consultation Paper.* The Conference, London.

Lovelock, J. (1979) *Gaia: A New Look at Life on Earth.* Oxford University Press, Oxford.

——(1988) *The Ages of Gaia: a Biography of our Living Earth.* Oxford University Press, Oxford.

Lowe, P. and Morrison, D. (1984) Bad news or good news: environmental politics and the mass media. *Sociological Review* 32, 75–90.

Lowe, P. and Rudwig, W. (1986) Politics, ecology and the social sciences – The State of the Art. *British Journal of Political Science* 16, 513–50.

Lowe, P., Bradley, M. and Wright, A. (eds) (1986) *Deprivation and Welfare in Rural Areas.* Geo Books, Norwich.

Lowe, P., Cox, G., MacEwan, M., O'Riordan, T. and Winter, M. (1986) *Countryside Conflicts of Farming, Forestry and Conservation.* Gower, Aldershot.

MacEwan, M. and MacEwan, A. (1982) The Wildlife and Countryside Act 1981: An unprincipled Act? *The Planner* 68, 69–71.

MacEwan, M. and Sinclair, G. (1983) *New Life for the Hills.* Council for National Parks, London.

MacGregor, B. D. and Robertson, D. S. (1987) An agenda for policy and research for rural housing in Scotland. In: MacGregor, B. D., Robertson, D. S. and Shucksmith, M. (eds) *Rural Housing in Scotland.* Aberdeen University Press, Aberdeen, pp. 185–93.

Mackay, G. A. and Farrington, J. H. (1988). *Bus Deregulation – Monitoring Study Second Report.* Scottish Consumer Council, Glasgow.

Maillet, P. (1987) A Common Agricultural Policy for tomorrow: A European economists view. *Journal of Regional Policy* 7, 359–73.

Marsden, T., Whatmore, S., Munton, R. and Little, J. (1986a) The restructuring process and economic centrality in capitalist agriculture. *Journal of Rural Studies* 2, 271–80.

——(1986b) Towards a political economy of capitalist agriculture: A British perspective. *International Journal of Urban and Regional Research* 10, 498–521.

Marsh, I. (1988) Interest groups and policy making – a new role for select committees. *Parliamentary Affairs* 41, 469–89.

Martin, W. H. and Mason, S. (1982) *Leisure and Work – the Choices for 1991 and 2001*. Leisure Consultants, Sudbury.

Mather, A. S. (1988) New private forests in Scotland: characteristics and contrasts. *Area* 20, 135–43.

Mather, A. S. and Murray, N. C. (1986) Disposal of Forestry Commission land in Scotland. *Area* 18, 109–16.

——(1988) The dynamics of rural land use change: the case of private sector afforestation. *Land Use Policy* 5, 103–20.

Mather, G. (1988) *Pricing for Planning*. Institute of Economic Affairs, London.

Maxwell, T. J., Sibbald, A. R. and Eadie, J. (1979) Integration of forestry and agriculture: a model. *Agricultural Systems* 4, 161–88.

McAuslan, P. (1989) Agricultural development and the law. *Town and Country Planning* 58, 246–7.

McCallum, J. D. and Adams, J. G. L. (1980) Charging for countryside recreation. *Transactions of the Institute of British Geographers, New Series* 5, 350–68.

McCluskey, J. (1986) Shroud for the Scottish Landscape. *Landscape Design* 164, 48–51.

McDonald, G. J. (1989) Rural land use planning decisions by bargaining. *Journal of Rural Studies* 5, 325–35.

McInerney, J. (1986) Agricultural policy at the crossroads. *Countryside Planning Yearbook*, 7, 44–75.

McInerney, J. (1988) *Milk Production Before and After Quotas*. HMSO, London.

McInerney, J., Turner, M. and Hollingham, M. (1989) *Diversification in the Use of Farm Resources*. Agricultural Economics Unit, Exeter.

McLaughlin, B. (1986) Rural policy in the 1980s: the revival of the rural idyll. *Journal of Rural Studies* 2, 81–90.

——(1987) Rural policy into the 1990s – self help or self deception. *Journal of Rural Studies* 3, 361–4.

Merrett, S. (1984) Villages which have an appetite for land. *Town and Country Planning* 53, 140–2.

Micklewright, S. (ed.) (1988) *Sites for Science or for Heritage: Problems with the SSSI Designation and Possible Solutions*. Ecology and Conservation Unit, London.

Midwinter, A, Mair, C. and Moxen, J. (1988) *Rural Deprivation in Scotland – An Investigation into the Case for a Rural Aid Fund*. Strathclyde University, Glasgow.

Miller, R. (1981) *State Forestry and the Axe*. Institute of Economic Affairs, London.

Miliband, R. (1982) *Capitalist Democracy in Britain*. Oxford University Press, Oxford.

Mishler, W., Hoskin, M. and Fitzgerald, R. (1989) British parties in the balance: a time series analysis of long term trends in Labour and Conservative support. *British Journal of Political Science* 19, 211–36.

Montgomery, J. and Thornley, A. (1988) Phoenix ascending. Radical planning initiatives for the 1990s. *Planning Practice and Research* 4, 3–6.

Moore, L. (1988) Agricultural protection in Britain and its economy-wide effects. *World Economy* 11, 249–65.

MORI (1988) *The Conservation and Development Programme for the UK. Results of a MORI Poll on Public Attitudes to Resource Use.* MORI, London.

Mount, F. (1987) The new song of the land. *The Spectator* 258, 10 January, 9–13.

Mowle, A. (1986) *Nature Conservation in Rural Development: The Need for New Thinking about Rural Sector Policies.* Nature Conservancy Council, Peterborough.

Moyes, A. (1989) *The Need for Public Transport in Mid-Wales: Normative Approaches and Their Implications.* Rural Surveys Research Unit, University College Wales, Aberystwyth.

Naisbitt, J. and Aburdene, P. (1990) *Megatrends.* Sidgwick and Jackson, London.

National Association of Local Councils (1980) *Rural Life, Change or Decay.* The Association, London.

National Agricultural Centre Trust (1987) *Village Homes for Village People.* The Trust, Stoneleigh.

National Audit Office (1986) *Review of the Forestry Commission: Objectives and Achievements.* HMSO, London, H.C. 75 (86–87).

National Council for Voluntary Organisations (1982) *Rural Housing Policies for the 80s.* The Council, London.

National Economic Development Council (1987) *Directions for Change: Land Use in the 1990s.* The Council, London.

National Economic Development Office: Economic Development Committee (1987) *Directions for Change. Land Use in the 1990s, Conference Proceedings.* The Office, London.

National Economic Development Office (1989) *Work in the Countryside. Agricultural and Rural Employment in the 1990s.* The Office, London.

National Farmers Union (1986) *Farming Trees: the Case for Government Support for Woodland on Farms.* The Union, London.

——(1988a) *Farm Support Policies: The Reasons Why.* The Union, London.

——(1988b) *The Reform of the CAP.* The Union, London.

——(1988c) *The Image of British Farmers in 1988.* The Union, London.

——(1990) *Land Use Policy Review: Final Report.* The Union, London.

National Federation of Housing Associations (1986) *Housing – a Countryside Problem.* The Federation, London.

National Parks Review Panel (1991) *Fit for the Future, CCP 334*, Countryside Commission, Cheltenham.

Nature Conservancy Council (1984) *Nature Conservation in Great Britain: Summary of Objectives and Strategy.* The Council, Peterborough.

——(1986) *Nature Conservation and Afforestation.* The Council, Peterborough.

——(1987) *Corporate Plan 1987–88.* The Council, Peterborough.

——(1990) *The Cost of Habitat Restoration and Management to Conserve Britain's Rare Species.* The Council, Peterborough.

——(1991) *Nature Conservation and Agricultural Change*. The Council, Peterborough.

Newby, H. (1985) *Rural Communities and New Technology*. Arkleton Trust, Oxford.

——(1988) *The Countryside in Question*. Unwin Hyman, London.

Nicholls, P. H. (1985) New prospects for increasing forest productivity in Britain. *Transactions of the Institute of British Geographers, New Series* 10, 191–204.

Nijkamp, P. and Soetman, F. (1988) Ecologically sustainable economic development: key issues for strategic environmental management. *International Journal of Social Economics* 15, 88–102.

Nisbet, T. R. (1990) *Forests and Surface Water Acidification*. HMSO, London.

North, J. (1989) How much land will be available for development in 2015? *Development and Planning* 1, 29–34.

Northfield, Lord (1989) Private sector development of new country towns. *Town and Country Planning* 58, 14–15.

Norton-Taylor, R. (1982) *Whose Land is it Anyway?* Turnstone Press, Wellingborough.

Nuffield Foundation (1986) *Town and Country Planning*. The Foundation, London.

Nutley, S. D. (1988) 'Unconventional modes' of transport in Rural Britain: Progress to 1985. *Journal of Rural Studies* 4, 73–86.

O'Riordan, T. (1977) Environmental ideologies. *Environmental and Planning A* 9, 3–14.

——(1981) Environmental issues. *Progress in Human Geography* 5, 393–407.

——(1982) *Putting Trust in the Countryside: A Conservation and Development Programme for the UK*. Nature Conservancy Council, Peterborough.

——(1985a) Future directions for environment policy. *Environment and Planning A* 17, 1431–46.

——(1985b) *Competing Uses of Land*. Arkleton Trust, Oxford.

——(1988) The politics of environmental regulation in Great Britain. *Environment* 30, 4–9, 39–44.

——(1989) Anticipatory environmental policy implements and opportunities. *Environmental Monitoring and Assessment* 12, 115–25.

Office of Population Censuses and Surveys (1988) *Population Projections, Area, 1985–2001, PP3 No. 7*. HMSO, London.

Organisation for Economic Cooperation and Development (1989) *Agricultural and Environmental Policies: Opportunities for Integration*. HMSO, London.

Owens, S. (1986) Environmental politics in Britain: new paradigm or placebo? *Area* 18, 195–201.

——(1989) Agricultural land surplus and concern for the countryside. *Development and Planning* 1, 35–8.

Pacione, M. (1990) Private profit and public interest in the residential development process: a case study of conflict in the urban fringe. *Journal of Rural Studies* 6, 103–16.

Paris, C. (ed.) (1982) *Critical Readings in Planning Theory*. Pergamon, Oxford.

Parker, K. (1986) A tale of two villages. *Landscape Design* 159, 14–16.

Parry, M. and Porter, J. (1990) Countdown to a new climate. *Countryside Commission News* 41, 3.

Paterson, J. (1984) *Conservation and the Conservatives*. Bow Publications, London.

Paterson, T. (1989) *The Green Conservative – A Manifesto for the Environment.* Bow Publications, London.

Pearce, D., Markandya, A. and Barbier, E. B. (1989) *Blueprint for a Green Economy.* Earthscan, London.

Perring, F. H., Harvey, H. J., Rothschild, M. *et al.* (1987) Changing attitudes to nature conservation in the UK. *Biological Journal – Linnean Society* 32, 147–236.

Peterken, G. F. and Allison, H. (1989) *Woods, Trees and Hedges: A Review of Changes in the British Countryside.* Nature Conservancy Council, Peterborough.

Petit, M., de Benedictus, M., Britton, M., de Groot, M., Henrichsmeyer, W. and Lechi, F. (1987) *Agricultural Policy Formulation in the European Community.* Elsevier, Amsterdam.

Phillips, A. (1985) Conservation at the crossroads. The countryside. *Geographical Journal* 151, 237–45.

Phillips, A. and Ashcroft, P. (1987) The impact of research on countryside recreation policy development. *Leisure Studies* 6, 315–28.

Phillips, H., Porter, R., Denyer-Green, B., *et al.* (1985) Six commentaries on the Wildlife and Countryside Act 1981. *Ecos* 6, 2–23.

Planning, Economic and Development Consultants (1986) *Forestry in Great Britain: An Economic Assessment for the National Audit Office.* HMSO, London.

——(1987) *Budgeting for Forestry. Recommendations for Reform of Forestry Taxation Policy.* Council for the Protection of Rural England, London.

Porritt, J. (1987) *Seeing Green.* Basil Blackwell, Oxford.

——(1990) Extensification. In: *Farming: Options for the 1990s.* National Farmers Union, London.

Porritt, J. and Winner, D. (1988) *The Coming of the Greens.* Fontana, London.

Potter, C. (1983) *Investing in Rural Harmony. An Alternative Package of Agricultural Subsidies and Incentives for England and Wales.* World Wildlife Fund, London.

——(1986a) The environmental implications of CAP reform. *Countryside Planning Yearbook* 7, 76–88.

——(1986b) Processes of countryside change in lowland England. *Journal of Rural Studies* 2, 187–95.

——(1987) Set-aside: friend or foe? *Ecos* 8, 36–8.

——(1988) Environmentally sensitive areas in England and Wales: an experiment in countryside management. *Land Use Policy* 5, 301–13.

——(1990) Conservation under a European farm survival policy. *Journal of Rural Studies* 6, 1–7.

Potter, C. and Adams, B. (eds) (1989) Thatcher's countryside. *Ecos* 10, 1–29.

Potter, C. and Gasson, R. (1987) *Set Aside and Land Diversion: The View from the Farm.* Wye College, Ashford.

——(1988) Farmer participation in voluntary land diversion schemes: some predictions from a survey. *Journal of Rural Studies* 4, 365–75.

Potter, S. (1986) New towns in the real world. *Town and Country Planning* 55, 304–9.

Price, C. (1987) The economics of forestry – any change? *Ecos* 8, 31–5.

——(1989) *The Theory and Application of Forest Economics.* Basil Blackwell, Oxford.

Price, C. and Dale, I. (1982) Price predictions and economically afforestable area. *Journal of Agricultural Economics* 33, 13–23.

Price, C. and Kula, E. (1987) The developing framework for the economic evaluation of forestry in the United Kingdom. A comment and reply by E. Kula. *Journal of Agricultural Economics* 38, 497–503.

Pye-Smith, C. and Hall, C. (eds) (1987) *The Countryside We Want*. Green Books, Bideford.

Pye-Smith, C. and North, R. (1984) *Working the Land: a New Plan for a Healthy Agriculture*. Maurice Temple Smith, London.

Pye-Smith, C. and Rose, C. (1984) *Crisis and Conservation*. Penguin, London.

Ramblers Association (1980) *The Case Against Afforestation*. The Association, London.

——(1983) *Make for the Hills*. The Association, London.

Ratcliffe, D. A. (1981) The purpose of nature conservation. *Ecos* 2, 8–13.

Raymond, W. F. (1985a) Options for reducing inputs to agriculture: A non-economist's view. *Journal of Agricultural Economics* 36, 345–54.

——(1985b) *Lower Inputs and Alternatives in Agriculture*. Arkleton Trust, Oxford.

Reade, E. (1987) *British Town and Country Planning*. Open University Press, Milton Keynes.

Redclift, M. (1984) *Development and the Environmental Crisis: Red or Green Alternatives*. Methuen, London.

Redhead, B. (1988) *The National Parks of England and Wales: Not Ours but Ours to Look After*. Oxford Illustrated Press, Yeovil.

Rees, W. E. (1988) A role for environmental assessment in achieving sustainable development. *Environmental Impact Assessment Review* 8, 273–91.

Regional Studies Association (1990) *Beyond Green Belts: Managing Urban Growth in the 21st Century*, Written by J. Herrington. Jessica Kingsley Publishers for the Association, London.

Richards, P. G. (1988) *Mackintosh's The Government and Politics of Britain*. Hutchinson, London.

Robinson, G. (1990) *Conflict and Change in the Countryside*. Bellhaven, London.

Robson, N., Gasson, R. and Hill, B. (1987) Part-time farming – implications for farm family income. *Journal of Agricultural Economics* 38, 167–91.

Roche, F. L. (1986) New communities for a new generation: The case for consortium development's new country towns. *Town and Country Planning* 55, 312–13.

Rogers, A. (1985) Local claims on rural housing. *Town Planning Review* 56, 367–80.

——(1987) Voluntarism, self help and rural community development. *Journal of Rural Studies* 3, 353–60.

Rogers, A., Blunden, J. and Curry, N. (eds) (1985) *The Countryside Handbook*. Croom Helm, London.

Roome, N. J. (1984) A better future for the uplands. *Planning Outlook* 27, 12–17.

——(1986) New directions for rural policy. *Town Planning Review* 57, 253–63.

Rose, C. (1984) The case for a National Heritage Bill. *Ecos* 5, 42–8.

Rose, C. and Secrett, C. (1982) *Cash or Crisis*. Friends of the Earth, London.

Rose, R. and McAllister, I. (1990) *The Loyalties of Voters: A Lifetime Learning Model*. Sage, London.

Royal Institution of Chartered Surveyors (1986) *Strategy for Planning*. The Institution, London.

——(1990) *A Place to Live. Housing in the Rural Community*. The Institution, London.

Royal Society for the Protection of Birds (1987) *Forestry in the Flows of Caithness and Sutherland*. The Society, Sandy.

——(1988) *The Reform of the Common Agricultural Policy: New Opportunities for Wildlife and the Environment*. The Society, Sandy.

——(1990) *Agriculture and the Environment: Towards Integration*. The Society, Sandy.

Royal Town Planning Institute (1977) *Planning and the Future*. The Institute, London.

——(1988) Improving the planning system for the 1990s. *The Planner* 74, 24–5.

Rural Development Commission (1991) *Rural Housing Supply – 1990 Survey of Affordable Homes*. ACRE, Cirencester.

Rural Voice (1981) *A Rural Strategy 1981*. Rural Voice, London.

——(1987) *A Rural Strategy*. Action for Communities in Rural Areas, Fairford.

——(1990) *Employment on the Land*. Action with Communities in Rural Areas, Cirencester.

——(1991) *Manifesto for Rural England in the 90s*. Voice, Cirencester.

Russell, N. P. and Power, A. P. (1989) UK Government expenditure – implications of changes in agricultural output under the Common Agricultural Policy. *Journal of Agricultural Economics* 40, 32–9.

Rydin, Y. (1985) Residential development and the planning system. *Progress in Planning* 24, 1–69.

——(1988) Joint housing studies: housebuilders, planners and the availability of land. *Local Government Studies* 14, 69–80.

Ryle, G. (1988) *Ecology and Socialism*. Radius Century Hutchinson, London.

Sagoff, M. (1988) *The Economy of the Earth: Philosophy, Law and the Environment*. Cambridge University Press, Cambridge.

Sandbach, F. (1980) *Environment Ideology and Practice*. Basil Blackwell, Oxford.

Scottish Affairs Committee of the House of Commons (1985) *Highlands and Islands Development Board*. HMSO, London, H.C. 22-I (84–85).

Scottish Development Department (1974 onwards) *National Planning Guidelines*. The Department, Edinburgh.

Scottish Homes (1990) *The Rural Housing Challenge*. Scottish Homes, Edinburgh.

Scrambler, A. (1989) Farmer's attitudes towards forestry. *Scottish Geographical Magazine* 105, 47–9.

Scrase, A. (1988) Agriculture – 1980s industry and 1947 definition. *Journal of Planning and Environmental Law* July, 447–60.

Selman, P. H. (1988a) Rural land use planning – resolving the British paradox. *Journal of Rural Studies* 4, 277–94.

——(1988b) Potential planning implications of changing agricultural priorities. *Scottish Planning Law and Practice* 23, 8–9.

——(1989) Conservation, development and land use planning: Scotland leads the way. *Scottish Geographical Magazine* 105, 142–8.

Selman, P. H. and Barker, A. J. (1989) Rural land use policy at the local level: mechanisms for collaboration. *Land Use Policy* 6, 281–94.

Selman, P. H. and Blackburn, S. P. (1986) Landscape improvement in central Scotland. *Arboricultural Journal* 10, 211–20.

SERPLAN. See London and South East Regional Planning Conference.

Sewel, J. (1987) Reorganised Scottish Local Government: a review. *Scottish Geographical Magazine* 103, 5–11.

Shaw, M. (1989) Development plans and local discretion. *Development and Planning* 1, 39–43.

Shoard, M. (1980) *The Theft of the Countryside.* Maurice Temple Smith, London.

——(1987) *This Land is Our Land: The Struggle for Britain's Countryside.* Paladin, London.

Short, J. R., Fleming, S. and Witt, S. (1986) *Housebuilding, Planning and Community Action.* Routledge and Kegan Paul, London.

Short, J. R., Witt, S. and Fleming, S. (1987) Conflict and compromise in the built environment. Housebuilding in central Berkshire. *Transactions of the Institute of British Geographers, New Series* 12, 29–42.

Shucksmith, D. M., Bryden, J., Rosenthal, P., Short, C. and Winter, M. (1989) Pluriactivity, farm structures and rural change. *Journal of Agricultural Economics* 40, 345–50.

Sillince, J. (1986) *A Theory of Planning.* Gower, Aldershot.

Sinclair, D. (1990) *Shades of Green: Myth and Model in the Countryside.* Grafton Books, London.

Sinclair, G. (1985) *How to Help Farmers and Keep England Beautiful.* Council for the Protection of Rural England, London.

——(1988) Over the top and down to the root. *Ecos* 9, 7–10.

Sinclair, J. and Heppel, B. (1986) *A Feeling for the Land.* BB Communications, London.

Smart, G. and Wright, S. (1983) *Decision Making for Rural Areas: A Research Report.* Bartlett School of Architecture and Planning, London.

Smith, B. C. (1976) *Policy Making in British Government.* Martin Robertson, London.

Smith, C. (1978) *National Parks.* Fabian Society, London.

Social and Liberal Democrats (1988) *Policy Declaration.* The Democrats, London.

——(1989a) *Shadow Environmental Bill.* The Democrats, London.

——(1989b) *England's Green and Pleasant Land?* The Democrats, London.

——(1989c) *White Paper on Housing.* The Democrats, London.

Society of Local Authority Chief Executives (1986) *Local Government – the Future.* The Society, London.

Sorenson, A. D. and Auster, M. L. (1989) Fatal remedies: the sources of ineffectiveness in planning. *Town Planning Review* 60, 29–44.

Spilsbury, M. J. and Crockford, K. J. (1989) Woodland economics and the 1988 budget. *Quarterly Journal of Forestry* 83, 25–32.

Sports Council, (1990) *Towards a Policy for Sport and Recreation in the Countryside.* The Council, London.

Stanley, P. A. and Farrington, J. H. (1981) The need for rural public transport. *Tijdschrift voor Economische en Sociale Geografie* 72, 62–80.

Statham, D. (1986) Issues in countryside planning. Upland land uses. *The Planner* 72, 19–21.

Steen, A. (1988) *PLUMS: Public Land Utilisation Management Scheme.* Conservative Political Centre, London.

Stevens, T., More, T. and Allen, P. G. (1989) Pricing policies for public day use of outdoor recreation facilities. *Journal of Environmental Management* 28, 43–52.

Stewart, P. (1985) British forestry policy: time for change? *Land Use Policy* 2, 16–29.

Stirrat, R. (1989) Legacy and the Scottish landscape. *Ecos* 10, 28–33.

Streiber, W. and Kunetka, J. (1986) *Nature's End*. Warner Books, New York.

Sullivan, A. (1985) *Greening the Tories, New Policies on the Environment*. Centre for Policy Studies, London.

Swanwick, C. (ed.) (1983) What future for upland scenery. Seminar response. *Landscape Research* 8, 20-2.

Thornley, A. (1988) Planning in a cool climate. The effects of Thatcherism. *The Planner* 74, 17–19.

Tibbalds, F. (1988) The future of town and country planning. *The Planner* 74, 21-3.

Tompkins, S. (1986) *The Theft of the Hills*. Ramblers Association, London.

——(1989a) *Forestry in Crisis – the Battle for the Hills*. Christopher Helm, Bromley.

——(1989b) Forestry in crisis. *Town and Country Planning* 58, 276–7.

Town and Country Planning Association (1984) *A New Prospectus*. The Association, London.

——(1989) *Bridging the North–South Divide*. The Association, London.

Towse, R. J. (1988) Industrial location and site provision in an area of planning restraint: part of south west London's metropolitian green belt. *Area* 20, 323–32.

Tracy, M. (1989) *Government and Agriculture in Western Europe 1880–1988*. Harvester Wheatsheaf, Hemel Hempstead.

Transport and Road Research Laboratory (1980) *Transport and Road Research 1979*. The Laboratory, Crowthorne.

——(1988) *Bus Deregulation in Great Britain: A Review of the First Year*. The Laboratory, Crowthorne.

Turner, K. (ed.) (1988a) Pluralism in environmental economics – a survey of the sustainable economic development debate. *Journal of Agricultural Economics* 39, 352–9.

——(1988b) *Sustainable Environmental Management: Principles and Practice*. Belhaven Press, London.

Underwood, D. A. and King, P. G. (1989) On the ideological foundation of environmental policy. *Ecological Economics* 1, 315–34.

Veal, A. J. (1987) *Leisure and the Future*. Allen & Unwin, London.

Waite, A. J. (1988) Public law, private laws and conservation in England and Wales. *Environmental Policy and Law* 18, 159–72.

Waldegrave, W., Byng, J., Paterson, T. and Pye, G. (1986) *Distant Views of William Waldegrave's Oxford Speech*. Centre for Policy Studies, London.

Wannop, U. (1988) Do we need regional local government and is the Scottish experience relevant? *Regional Studies* 22, 439–46.

Wathern, P., Young, S. N., Brown, I. W. and Roberts, D. A. (1987) Assessing the impacts of policy: a framework and an application. *Landscape and Urban Planning* 14, 321–30.

Watkins, C. (1984) The use of grant aid to encourage woodland planting in Great Britain. *Quarterly Journal of Forestry* 74, 213–24.

Weekley, I. (1988) Rural development and counterurbanisation: a paradox. *Area* 20, 127–34.

Whatmore, S., Munton, R., Marsden, T. and Little, J. (1987a) Towards a typology of farm businesses in contemporary British agriculture. *Sociologia Ruralis* 27, 21–37.

——(1987b) Interpreting a regional typology of farm businesses in southern England. *Sociologia Ruralis* 27, 103–22.

Whelan, R. (1989) *Mounting Greenery*. Institute of Economic Affairs, Warlingham.

Whitby, M. (1989) The social implications for rural populations of new forestry planting. In: Adamson, K. (ed.), *Cumbrian Woodlands, Past, Present and Future*. HMSO, London, pp. 31–5.

Whitby, M. C. and Thompson, K. J. (1979) Against coordination. *Town and Country Planning* 48, 51–2.

White, P. (1986) *Public Transport: It's Planning Management and Operation*. Hutchinson, London.

White, S. K. (1988) *The Recent Work of Jurgen Habermas. Reason, Justice and Modernity*. Cambridge University Press, Cambridge.

Wibberley, G. P. (1982) Public pressures on farming: The conflict between national agricultural and conservation policies. *Farm Management* 4, 373–9.

——(1985) The famous Scott report. A text for all time? *The Planner* 71, 13–20.

Willis, K. G. (1989) Option, value and non-user benefits of wildlife conservation. *Journal of Rural Studies* 5, 245–56.

Willis, K. G. and Benson, J. F. (1988) Financial and social costs of management agreements for wildlife conservation in Britain. *Journal of Environmental Management* 26, 43–63.

Willis, K. G., Benson, J. F. and Saunders, C. M. (1988) The impact of agricultural policy on the costs of nature conservation. *Land Economics* 64, 147–57.

Willis, K. G. and Whitby, M. C. (1985) The value of green belt land. *Journal of Rural Studies* 1, 147–62.

Willis, K. G., Mitchell, L. A. R. and Benson, J. F. (1987) Valuing wildlife: a review of methods. *Planning Outlook* 30, 57–63.

Wilson, R. (1987) The political power of the forestry lobby. *Ecos* 8, 11–17.

Winter, J. (1989) Is local plan review underway? *The Planner* 75, 22–7.

Winter, M. (1985) County Agricultural Committees: A good idea for conservation? *Journal of Rural Studies* 1, 205–9.

Winter, M. and Rogers, A. (eds) (1988) *Who Can Afford to Live in the Countryside?* Centre for Rural Studies and ACRE, Cirencester.

Wise, W. S. and Fell, E. (1978) UK agricultural productivity and the land budget. *Journal of Agricultural Economics* 29, 1–8 and 331.

Wood, C. and Lee, N. (1988) The European directive and environmental impact assessment: implementation at last? *Environmentalist* 8, 177–86.

Wood, W. and McDonic, G. (1989) Environmental assessment: challenge and opportunity. *The Planner* 75, 12–18.

World Commission on Environment and Development (1987) *Our Common Future* (Brundtland report). Oxford University Press, Oxford.

Young, H. (1989) *One of Us: a Biography of Margaret Thatcher*. Macmillan, London.

Young, K. (1987) Interim report: The Countryside. In: Jowell, R., Witherspoon, S. and Brook, L. (eds), *British Social Attitudes, 1987 Report*. Gower, Aldershot, pp. 153–69.

Young, T. and Allen, P. G. (1986) Methods for valuing countryside amenity: an overview. *Journal of Agricultural Economics* 37, 349–64.

Index